Revolutionary Politics
in Massachusetts

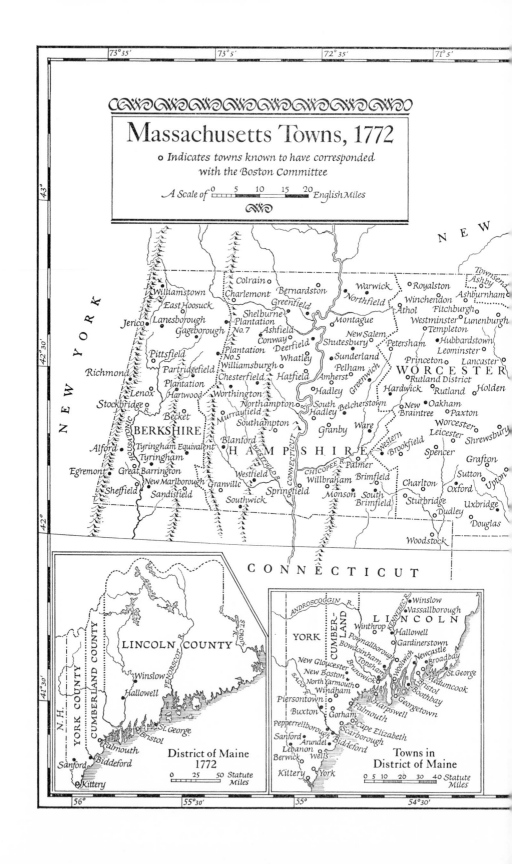

Massachusetts Towns, 1772

o *Indicates towns known to have corresponded with the Boston Committee*

A Scale of 0 5 10 15 20 *English Miles*

Revolutionary Politics
in Massachusetts

*The Boston Committee of Correspondence
and the Towns, 1772-1774*

Richard D. Brown

Harvard University Press
Cambridge, Massachusetts
1970

Preface

More than a century and a half ago John Adams urged that historians study the interaction between the Boston Committee of Correspondence and the committees of other towns. "There is," he said, "another large tract of inquiry to be travelled in the correspondence of the committees of the town of Boston with the other towns and States, commonly called the committees of correspondence." "What an engine!" he exclaimed: they had set a revolutionary pattern not merely for America, but for the world. Adams maintained that until this bulky correspondence had been explored, "the history of the United States never can be written."[1]

But in the first half of the nineteenth century no one chose to follow Adams' advice. The history of the Revolution and of the United States was written and rewritten with only the briefest mention of committees of correspondence. George Bancroft was the first historian to consider the committees seriously, yet when he did, at last, study the records, they made no significant impact upon his interpretation. From his standpoint, the activities of the committees of correspondence merely served as a mine of examples of the heroic and democratic spirit which, his contemporaries knew, swelled in the bosoms of their Revolutionary ancestors.[2]

1. John Adams to Jedidiah Morse, Quincy, Dec. 22, 1815, in John Adams, *The Works of John Adams, Second President of the United States*, ed. Charles Francis Adams (Boston, 1850–1856), X, 196–197.
2. George Bancroft, *History of the United States*, Centenary ed. (Boston, 1876), IV, 241–251.

vii

In the century since Bancroft, however, committees of correspondence have received more notice. At the turn of the century, historians who were interested in formal political institutions gave the committees some attention, and by the middle third of the twentieth century they had become a major element in the modern revisionist interpretation of the American Revolution. They were seen as vital sources of radical agitation; they were, in the words of one scholar, "revolutionary cells."[3] Yet the committees of correspondence were never made the subject of monographic research, and the most important of them, the Boston Committee of Correspondence, was discussed largely as an adjunct to the career of its most famous member, Samuel Adams.[4] Although committees of correspondence were recognized as central institutions in the Revolutionary movement, they had not been subjected to intensive, systematic study.

This work began, therefore, as an examination of committees of correspondence in the American Revolution. Like most other students, I was unaware that subsumed under a common name, "committee of correspondence," lay a considerable variety of organizations which possessed no common symmetry. The provincial committees, for example, were largely perfunctory bodies which wrote and received correspondence on behalf of provincial legislatures. They never displayed independence or initiative, and their records (where they survive) show little of significance. The Virginia assembly has usually been credited with founding this type in March 1773, although occasionally in the past several of the colonies had used such committees to administer their correspondence. The Continental Congress from 1774 onward urged the creation of committees of correspondence at the local level in towns and counties, and hundreds were established. Their functions were diverse and their life-spans ranged from several months to several years. At the same time some state legislatures maintained committees of correspondence for varying purposes and periods of time. Consequently, whatever my initial intentions, there was clearly no logic in treating committees of correspondence as a single genus.

Yet there was one committee, the Boston Committee of Correspondence, which had not only initiated the revolutionary use of local committees of correspondence, but which had gone on to develop a large

3. Crane Brinton, *Anatomy of Revolution* (New York, 1956), 42; first published in 1938.
4. John C. Miller, *Sam Adams: Pioneer in Propaganda* (Boston, 1936).

political role. Moreover the Boston committee was unique in that it left behind a substantial record of its activity — including nearly a thousand pages of letters and an equally voluminous set of minutes covering a two-year period. Modern scholars had used these records, notably John C. Miller for his biography of Samuel Adams and Philip Davidson for a general study of propaganda in the Revolution, but they used them only in passing and they drew from them highly simplified views of the role and functions of the Boston Committee of Correspondence. As they saw it, Samuel Adams ran the Boston committee and the committee ran the Massachusetts countryside by the adroit use of propaganda.[5] The dynamics of provincial politics were that simple.

But this view of Massachusetts politics was undermined in the 1950's by the writings of Robert E. Brown, Robert J. Taylor, and Lee N. Newcomer, who together demonstrated the limits of Boston's influence and the importance of local affairs.[6] Furthermore, the rudimentary conceptions of propaganda which Miller and Davidson shared had been based on the theories of political scientists working in the 1920's and 1930's, theories which were now obsolete. The simple process of domination and manipulation of provincial politics which they had described became incredible.

As a result the field lay open for a specialized study, and my work came to center on the Boston Committee of Correspondence and the relations between Boston and the other Massachusetts towns. Quickly it became apparent that the dynamics of provincial politics, of influence and leadership, would be substantially illuminated by the correspondence which passed between the capital and the countryside. Moreover at a time when scholars were rediscovering the importance of ideology in the American Revolution, it was clear that a study of the Boston committee and the towns could provide some basis for judging the extent to which Revolutionary ideas penetrated the countryside, and whether these ideas exercised any impact on actual behavior. Exploring these questions became the purpose of this study.

Obviously these issues are connected to previous historical scholarship, but they are also closely related to the work of political scientists

5. *Ibid.*, 256–275, and Philip Davidson, *Propaganda and the American Revolution, 1763–1783* (Chapel Hill, N.C., 1941), 56–60.
6. Robert E. Brown, *Middle-Class Democracy and the Revolution in Massachusetts, 1691–1780* (Ithaca, 1955); Robert J. Taylor, *Western Massachusetts in the Revolution* (Providence, 1954); Lee N. Newcomer, *The Embattled Farmers: A Massachusetts Countryside in the American Revolution* (New York, 1953).

examining political development and modernization in the emerging nations of the twentieth century. Early modern Massachusetts, with its agricultural village society, shared many of the characteristics of transitional societies which are today moving away from their traditional orientation toward modernity. In this context the story of the Boston Committee of Correspondence and the towns of Massachusetts may be seen as an example of the process of political integration among a colonial people engaged in an independence movement and emerging into nationhood. The parallels with some twentieth-century phenomena are striking — whether one is considering the role of bureaucracy (local and metropolitan), elites (local and cosmopolitan, indigenous and metropolitan), geography, ideology and identity, communication, tradition, or any of the other analytic categories favored by students of political development. From such a viewpoint, this account of Revolutionary politics in Massachusetts provides a kind of case study of political development in a transplanted western European society some two hundred years ago. For those seeking comparisons across time as well as culture, this study should be useful.

But it is not a case study in any formal sense, nor have I attempted to employ the scientific and quasi-scientific methods common to the behavioral sciences. Because of the broad series of questions raised in this study, conventional historical methodology seemed most appropriate. Data has been quantified in some cases, especially the data on local behavior; and I did use a sampling technique to draw inferences. But nothing more sophisticated than grade-school arithmetic was employed. Elaborate quantitative analysis was hazardous owing to the irregularity and incompleteness of much of the data. For similar reasons no effort has been made to perform a content analysis of local rhetoric. Technically this was feasible, but owing to the influence of conventional phraseology any analysis based on word-counting would blur distinctions. In addition the specific character of any given document was a function of so many variables, both known and unknown, that the conclusions based on such a procedure would be no more scientific, or persuasive, than those available through impression, intuition, and "good judgment."

John Adams believed that an understanding of the communications of the Boston Committee of Correspondence would reveal the underlying impetus of the Revolutionary movement. It is the contention of this study that, for Massachusetts at least, they do precisely that. The

Boston committee was only a fraction of the entire working political structure, but it was a crucial fraction because it was led by experts in both local and provincial politics and it was located at a vital intersection of Massachusetts public life. The career of the Boston committee, emerging as it did at a critical point in time, exposed the attitudes and assumptions of Massachusetts inhabitants regarding imperial issues as well as the larger question of active participation in politics beyond the local level. The committee's activities and the behavior of the towns show the ways in which communication and leadership operated, and they illustrate the interaction between political behavior and ideology. The examination of these attitudes and relationships in their variety and complexity reveals the dynamics of opposition, resistance, and revolution in Massachusetts.

I am grateful to a number of people, libraries, and foundations for their help with this study. Professor Bernard Bailyn of Harvard University read this work closely and critically at an early stage, providing suggestions and encouragement when they were most needed. The fact that he was willing to spend hours reading and discussing my draft while he was on sabbatical is a measure of both his generosity and his devotion to professional training. Insofar as I have acquired and developed the skills of a historian, I am most indebted to Professor Bailyn. In addition the following scholars read all or part of the manuscript at various stages, contributing their advice: Geoffrey T. Blodgett, Irene Quenzler Brown, Richard V. Buel, Jr., John D. Cushing, Stanley N. Katz, Kenneth A. Lockridge, Pauline R. Maier, and Barry McGill. Daniel Horowitz, friend and scholar, helped in many ways. My debts to the published and unpublished writings of other historians are too numerous to list individually, but they are, I trust, all cited in the footnotes.

A major part of the research was done at the Massachusetts Historical Society, whose staff (especially Winifred V. Collins and the now retired Warren Gage Wheeler) was most hospitable and obliging, day after day. The Society and its library stand as an exemplar for the way in which a private institution can fulfill a public trust with grace and efficiency. I am also grateful to Harvard College Library and Houghton, and the New York Public Library for the use of their rich collections. The law requires town clerks to make town records available to the public on request, and I thank the many who did so cheerfully.

Financial support for this study came from a Harvard Teaching Fellowship, a Woodrow Wilson Dissertation Fellowship, and grants from Oberlin College and the Carnegie Corporation of New York. The views expressed in this work are my own and so are the errors.

R.D.B.

Oberlin, Ohio
January 1970

Contents

Illustrations

Revolutionary Politics
in Massachusetts

The other Day being at the North End I fell into Conversation with an honest Ship Carpenter:

"Very dull Times Mr. R———."

'Yes Sir very dull. The last Vessel which was upon the Stocks in this Part of the Town was launch'd this Week, & there is not like to be another set up, for the Admiral will not let them sail, after they are launched.'

"This is very discouraging, pray don't you think it almost Time for us to submit, pay for the Tea & get the Harbour opened?"

'Submit! (reply'd the indignant Mechanic) NO — it never can become Time to become Slaves. I have yet got some Pork & Meal, & when they are gone I will eat Clams. And after we have dug up all the Clam Banks, if the Congress will not let us fight, I will retreat to the Woods. I am always sure of ACORNS.'

What a Roman! By Heavens the glory in being this Man's fellow Citizen. When I meet with such Sentiments from such a Person, I easily anticipate the Period when Bostonian shall equal Spartan Virtue, and the American Colonies rival in Patriotism & Heroism the most celebrated of the Grecian Republics.

—William Tudor to John Adams,
Boston, Sept. 26, 1774

Quotations from the Adams Papers are from the microfilm edition, by permission of the Massachusetts Historical Society.

I

Massachusetts Politics in
the Mid-Eighteenth Century

For at least a generation preceding the revolutionary turmoil of the
1760's and 1770's, Massachusetts enjoyed an era in which the fundamental character of provincial politics was relatively stable. There was
conflict, to be sure, and the wheel of political fortune turned to favor
first one and then another set of politicians, but the manner and motives
for gaining and using political power remained very nearly constant.
Massachusetts possessed the kind of political stability which J. H.
Plumb had defined as "the acceptance by society of its political institutions, and of those classes of men or officials who control them." [1]

The most significant exception to this pattern of "acceptance by
society of its political institutions" was the perennial conflict between
the governor and the House of Representatives over their precise relationship. From 1728 onward this conflict was dramatized by every
governor's unsuccessful annual demand for a permanent salary from
the House. Yet even in this tension over the limits of the prerogative
power there was a stability, an equilibrium produced by the refusal of
either party to yield. During the administration of Governor William
Shirley (1741–1756) the structural stability of Massachusetts politics
was even overlaid by a lull in controversy and infighting. As a result,
though the basic elements of provincial politics remained much as they

---

1. J. H. Plumb, *The Origins of Political Stability in England, 1675–1725* (Boston,
1967), xvi.

I

had under Governor Jonathan Belcher (1730–1741) and as far back as Lieutenant Governor Jeremiah Dummer (1723–1728), Shirley, by "his system of political alliances brought an era of relative good feeling." [2]

In some ways this stability was more brittle than it appears. Certainly there were strains inherent in provincial political life, and in a political theory which, while grounded on the right of the people to overthrow an unjust government, at the same time demanded their loyal obedience to rulers even when rulers erred. Moreover the explosive events of the 1760's were not entirely without precedent. But tracing precedents is hazardous because imperial policy and the wars with France enabled the adroit Shirley to mold a provincial unity that curbed the unsettling, polarizing tendencies which had emerged in the land bank struggle of 1739–1741, when the province had divided over whether to issue notes backed by silver or notes backed by land in order to expand the currency. Later on, in the 1760's when the royal government attempted to reform imperial decadence, Governor Francis Bernard discovered that the harmony of Shirley's day was fragile and that political stability was evanescent.

I

The formal structure of Massachusetts political institutions was laid out in part by the royal charter of 1692 and partly by the accretion of executive, legislative, and local practices. The charter, which the people of Massachusetts generally believed possessed the constitutional status of a contract between the inhabitants of Massachusetts and the Crown rather than being a mere corporate grant, established a provincial government analogous to the government of England. At its head stood the governor, representing the King. As commander in chief he directed the military and appointed its officers. His legislative role included the power to veto acts of the assembly, and as the principal executive officer he appointed all judicial officials from the justices of the peace to the chief justice of the Superior Court of Judicature. In contrast to the other elements in the provincial structure, the office of the governor formed a direct link between the internal government of the colony and the control exercised by the British government.

2. John A. Schutz, *William Shirley, King's Governor of Massachusetts* (Chapel Hill, N.C., 1961), v.

The legislature, known as the General Court, consisted of two chambers, a House of Representatives elected by the towns, and a Governor's Council elected by the representatives and the outgoing councillors with the governor's consent. The competence of this legislature was nowhere precisely stipulated, but certain limits were prescribed by the Charter, which provided both the governor and the Crown with veto power and required all laws to be consistent with those of England. The authority of royal instructions to the governor, while originally intended to bind the legislature, had declined by the mid-eighteenth century and so the General Court had come to play a major role in establishing its own broad sphere of responsibility.[3]

In some ways the model for the legislature was Parliament. Thus the Council, as the upper house, was the counterpart of the House of Lords, advising the governor, consenting to judicial appointments, joining in legislation, and performing judicial functions on an irregular basis. The House of Representatives was the Commons, possessing exclusive power to originate money bills, and sharing more than equally in other legislation. But although representatives self-consciously patterned their chamber on the House of Commons, the Masssachusetts House in fact performed many administrative functions, enforcing the collection of its taxes and compliance with its own independent resolves. Its dozens of committees, and the House as a whole, actually spent more time in administrative and judicial activity than in legislation. Indeed, the House of Representatives, more than the justices of the peace, furnished the administrative ties between provincial and local government.[4]

The sphere of local government in the towns and districts was defined in part by province law, partly from patterns gradually evolving through House resolves, as well as through habit. In every way except representation in the legislature, town and district government were identical. Districts could not send their own representatives to the House, but they were administered by general meetings of the inhabitants and their elected selectmen, and like the towns they were responsible for raising local taxes and regulating local behavior. Much as the provincial gov-

3. Leonard Woods Labaree, *Royal Government in America: A Study of the British Colonial System Before 1783* (New Haven, 1930), 30–36.
4. Robert M. Zemsky, "The Massachusetts Assembly, 1730–1755," Ph.D. diss., Yale University, 1967, chs. 1 and 2; Michael W. Zuckerman, "The Massachusetts Town in the Eighteenth Century," Ph.D. diss., Harvard University, 1967, pp. 46, 47, 58, and ch. 1 passim.

ernment was largely autonomous in relation to Britain, so the local governments were substantially autonomous within the confines of provincial law. From the standpoint of structure, authority was described within concentric circles of local, provincial, and ultimately imperial government. And for the vast majority of Massachusetts inhabitants, the smallest circle exercised the most immediate control, involving their most immediate interests, and demanding the most active participation.

Actually, the effective authority of Massachusetts government resided in the towns. Justices of the peace and county courts played an important part in law enforcement, but order was maintained by the towns. Enforcement of provincial law rested far more on the towns' voluntary compliance than on any coercive mechanism of government. Moreover the core of the provincial government, the General Court, was dominated by the House of Representatives, the branch whose membership embodied the collective existence of local corporations. Towns, after all, were not merely the creations of the General Court but also covenanted communities. As a result, even though many towns expressed only passive interest in provincial affairs, the operation of provincial politics was founded on local political behavior.[5]

The nature of local politics, whether democratic or elitist, has been a matter of controversy among historians for nearly two decades, and substantial evidence has been adduced in support of both views. As a result, in recent years scholars have begun to question whether either concept is wholly adequate in describing local politics.[6] In some towns,

5. See Clifford K. Shipton, "The Locus of Authority in Colonial Massachusetts," in George A. Billias, ed., *Law and Authority in Colonial America* (Barre, Mass., 1965), 136–148; Zuckerman, "The Massachusetts Town in the Eighteenth Century," ch. 1; Page Smith, *As a City Upon a Hill: The Town in American History* (New York, 1966), 3–16.

6. For evidence of the more-or-less "democratic" character of local politics see: Robert E. Brown, *Middle-Class Democracy and the Revolution in Massachusetts, 1691–1780* (Ithaca, 1955); Zuckerman, "The Massachusetts Town in the Eighteenth Century," ch. 4, and his "The Social Context of Democracy in Massachusetts," *William and Mary Quarterly*, 3d Ser., XXV (1968), 523–544; Kenneth A. Lockridge and Alan Kreider, "The Evolution of Massachusetts Town Government, 1640 to 1740," *William and Mary Quarterly*, 3d Ser., XXIII (1966), 549–574; Charles S. Grant, *Democracy in the Connecticut Frontier Town of Kent* (New York, 1961). Evidence supporting the contrary view is contained in James A. Henretta, "Economic Development and Social Structure in Colonial Boston," *William and Mary Quarterly*, 3d Ser., XXII (1965), 75–92; Benjamin W. Labaree, *Patriots and Partisans: The Merchants of Newburyport, 1764–1815* (Cambridge, Mass., 1962), 12–15. The applicability of the concept of democracy to eighteenth-century political institutions is discussed in Jack R. Pole, "Historians and the Problem of Early American Democracy," *American Historical Review*, LXVII (April 1962), 626–646; and Richard Buel, Jr., "Democracy and the American Revolution: A Frame of Reference," *William and Mary Quarterly*, 3d Ser., XXI (1964), 165–190.

clearly, the pattern was more elitist than in others, and variations were contingent on factors like the age and size of a community and the occupations and wealth of its inhabitants. In a port town possessing not only a highly educated, well-to-do class of people with leisure but also a landless artisan and marine population, the possibility of elite dominance was always real. In contrast, out-of-the-way farming communities where property was distributed within a narrow range among men of equal leisure and education could hardly fail to maintain an egalitarian character. Yet no town, however narrow its range of social and economic status, was entirely free of social stratification. The idea of a stratified community was as fundamental to the mid-eighteenth-century Massachusetts mind as a total egalitarianism was foreign; and if striking differences of wealth or education did not exist, then differences of character, piety, and family could function in the same manner. Normally status derived from some compound of material and personal characteristics, so that even in towns of small farmers, social and political roles could be stratified in relation to some conception of hierarchy however informal and fluid. Yet at the same time, even in a town like Newburyport where an elite politics could flourish, the elite was always responsible to a broadly-based town meeting which never relinquished primary authority.[7]

According to the charter, the provincial franchise was limited to forty-shilling freeholders, but given the broad diffusion of freehold tenure, this was rarely very restrictive, and even this limitation was often ignored. Moreover voting in the selection of town officers was even less restricted, so the vast majority of men could and did participate to some degree in political affairs. As a result, nonparticipation in town politics or in the choice of a representative was frequently the consequence of political apathy rather than political exclusion. Still there was an effective barrier to equal participation in the holding of certain offices, particularly those of selectman and representative. For town offices, it was agreed, should not be a source of profit and they were mostly unpaid. As a result those offices that required the most time were in fact limited to men of some means and leisure. In a sense, officeholding was a form of taxation based on wealth, and men of small means were content to divide these lesser burdens of lower offices among themselves, designating those of greater wealth and higher status to carry the larger public load.

7. Labaree, *Patriots and Partisans*, 12–15.

The social and economic qualifications that limited access to the higher offices did not, however, normally create local oligarchies. Instead, some rotation of the burdens of office was typical, with selectmen and representatives usually serving only a few years and seldom holding either office for as much as a decade in the course of a lifetime. There were, of course, exceptions, where a handful of men occupied the major offices continuously for a generation. But this was nowhere typical. In most towns the concept of oligarchy is difficult to apply. Excepting a few ports, the towns were highly integrated as social and political units, with ties of kinship and religion as well as economic interest binding the layers of society into one community. As contemporaries often put it, they were all "embark'd in one bottom." [8]

Although these conditions prevailed generally, the character of local politics and society in mid-eighteenth-century Massachusetts was not entirely stable. Though much remains unknown, a few recent studies point to several dynamic tendencies based largely on the evolution and ecology of community life. In the first half of the century at least, it appears that in some towns the powers of selectmen were being eroded by increasingly active town meetings, suggesting a democratizing process. At the same time there is evidence that the range of social stratification was increasing, and by the second half of the century eastern Massachusetts was experiencing a population pressure which led to a decline in farming opportunities. Thus it is certainly possible that some mid-eighteenth-century towns were moving toward an elite-dominated politics, while others were moving in the contrary direction. [9]

The impact of such changing local conditions on provincial politics has yet to be carefully examined and so remains largely unknown. It is significant, however, that the House of Representatives, the branch of provincial government most directly connected to local affairs, did experience distinct changes in its pattern of membership. Between 1720 and 1760 annual turnover among representatives showed a definite although irregular decline. It fell from a high of 61 percent at the beginning of the period to a low of 28 percent in 1760, and in the next decade it dropped further. [10] This change may have resulted from a

8. Zuckerman, "The Massachusetts Town in the Eighteenth Century," 231–253.
9. Lockridge and Kreider, "The Evolution of Massachusetts Town Government"; Kenneth A. Lockridge, "Land, Population and the Evolution of New England Society, 1630–1790," Past & Present, no. 39 (April 1968), 62–80.
10. Susan L. Grigg, "The Office of Representative in Eighteenth-Century Massachusetts," seminar paper, Oberlin College, 1968, table II, "Per Cent Turnover in the

shift in local attitudes toward the office of representative, or it may also have been the consequence of a maturation process in the towns, through which an increasingly stable leadership class was emerging at the local level. Both possibilities are plausible and they may be complementary. In any case, the consequence was an increasingly experienced, self-conscious body of representatives.

The precise meaning of representation for Massachusetts townsmen has never been adequately explained, and it apparently varied depending on local habit as well as a town's location and size. Sending representatives was viewed as a right, a duty, and by some as an onerous expense. Representatives often acted as town agents with regard to some particular local business, but they were rarely instructed.[11] Provincial political questions seldom entered into town meeting consideration although it was known to happen, and representatives could be voted in or out of office on the basis of a provincial political issue, as was the case with the land bank in 1741. It was this turmoil of 1739–1742 which popularized the terms "court" and "country" party to describe provincial division, terms which were to remain in use, haphazardly, for at least a generation until they were replaced by "Tory" and "Whig." Yet the phenomena which gave rise to the use of these terms in provincial politics were aberrations. Turnover in the House of Representatives had often fluctuated quite sharply and would continue to do so, often without connection to any province-wide political issue. Moreover the normal pattern of internal leadership within the House placed the representatives from Boston, the eastern counties, and a few Connecticut Valley towns at the head of the entire body — so "court" and "country" were usually united.[12] Party politics as we understand them were no more characteristic of the General Court than the towns.

In fact the operation of provincial politics in the General Court

House of Representatives, 1704–1774," follows p. 28. Grigg's percentages were compiled from counting new and returning delegates.

11. See Kenneth Colegrove, "New England Town Mandates: Instructions to the Deputies in Colonial Legislatures," Publications of the Colonial Society of Massachusetts, *Transactions*, XXI (1919), 411–449.

12. George Athan Billias, *The Massachusetts Land Bankers of 1740*, University of Maine Studies, 2d Ser., no. 74 (Orono, Me., 1959), 32–33, 37–40; Schutz, *William Shirley*, 40; for the application of various party names see Thomas Hutchinson, *The History of the Colony and Province of Massachusetts-Bay*, ed. Lawrence S. Mayo, (Cambridge, Mass., 1936), II, 280, 284, 297, 307; Grigg, "The Office of Representative," graph II, "Per Cent Turnover in the House of Representatives, 1704–1774," follows p. 28, and 16–17. Robert M. Zemsky has used roll-call analysis to demonstrate the nonexistence of parties, and he has also delineated the role of the provincial political elite in "The Massachusetts Assembly," chs. 3, 4, 7.

appears to have taken its character from town politics as well as from the structure and functions of the assembly. Town politics, which produced rotation of representatives who were normally chosen to perform their governing duty and not on the basis of colony-wide issues or ideology, determined the nature of the body. Forming a party, or even a durable faction was difficult in this context although not entirely unknown. The governor, through the prestige and patronage of his office, could win friends and create a following, but while he could lead, he could not dictate, and the circumstance of conflicting interests always limited his capabilities. A small group of experienced representatives drawn mostly from seaboard towns, provided such House leadership as it possessed, but this elite like its followers seldom remained constant for more than a few years. Moreover the members of the House, broken up into scores of committees, occupied themselves primarily with the disposition of individual disputes, hardship cases, complaints, and the like. In this mélange of administrative and judicial activity, the possibilities for issue-oriented politics were limited. The result was that provincial politics were not normally polarized and partisan appeals to either the representatives or to the public, while not unknown, were unusual and ephemeral. Instead the excitement and conflict which were a regular part of Massachusetts politics were limited to a small, shifting number of interested persons such as major officeholders jockeying for position, merchants and land operators, and a handful of attorneys.[13] This was a distinctly "traditional" politics of personal advantage, seldom interrupted by more general political questions and broad public involvement.

II

Generally speaking, Massachusetts inhabitants were satisfied with the character of their polity both at the local and provincial levels. Efforts to reform politics were scarcely considered and never attempted because the existing system of government inspired pride. Nevertheless people recognized that the political state of the province was imperfect and they yearned to realize an ideal which continually escaped their grasp. Statements of this political ideal, delivered annually to the legislature by pastors elected for the purpose alternately by the House and

13. Zemsky, "The Massachusetts Assembly," chs. 2, 3, 4, and his "Power, Influence, and Status: Leadership Patterns in the Massachusetts Assembly, 1740–1755," *William and Mary Quarterly*, 3d Ser., XXVI (1969), 502–520; Grigg, "The Office of Representative," 16–17; Zuckerman, "The Massachusetts Town in the Eighteenth Century," 238–241.

Council, revealed the ways in which people believed Massachusetts fell short and the anxieties these deficiencies generated.[14]

These sermons, offered by a different clergyman every year, were given in the assembled presence of the three branches of government on the occasion of the election of the new Council. Normally they began with an exposition of the biblical foundation of government and then proceeded to a lesson in morality, concluding with an application of the lesson to the governor, councillors, representatives, and, on occasion, the people in general. Although the sermons varied from year to year, depending on the personal opinions of the minister and political circumstances, in most respects they represented a ritual incantation of the ideal toward which the province strove.

This political ideal, an amalgam of Puritan political doctrine and old-fashioned Whiggery, was founded on a conception of natural and social inequality. "The Notion of *Levelism*," William Cooper declared in 1740, "has as little Foundation in Nature as in Scripture. If we look up to the *Heavens, there is one Glory of the Sun, and another Glory of the Moon, and another Glory of the Stars*; neither are these of the same Magnitude and Lustre, but *one Star differeth from another Star in Glory.*" Cooper went on to explain that the heavenly order had its counterparts here below:

If we look round the Earth, we see it is not cast into a Level; it has Mountains and Plains, Hills and Vallies. Even so in the *political* World, there are the Distinctions of Superiours and Inferiours, Rulers and Ruled, publick and private Orders of Men: Some sit on the Throne of Majesty, some at the Council Table, and some on the Bench of Justice; and some hold subordinate Places of Power; while others serve their Generation only in a private Capacity.[15]

That Cooper found it useful to elaborate on this theme suggests that some tendencies toward levelism may have been operating in Massachusetts politics, especially in the midst of the conflict over the land bank. Normally, however, the idea was treated more casually, as when Charles Chauncy remarked that "a superiority in some, and inferiority in others, is perfectly adjusted to the present state of mankind." The

14. Alice M. Baldwin, *The New England Clergy and the American Revolution* (Durham, N.C., 1928), 5–9, discusses the general character of the election sermons.

15. William Cooper, *The Honours of Christ demanded of the magistrate. A sermon preach'd in the audience of his excellency the governour, the honourable the council and representatives of the Province of the Massachusetts-Bay, in New-England, May 28, 1740* . . . (Boston, 1740), 6–7. Hereafter in all citations to election sermons the titles will be shortened, omitting the references to the governor, Council, and representatives.

idea was congruent with the general view of man, a creature who "could not live, either comfortably or safely" without such inequality.[16]

This divinely ordained social arrangement of superiors and inferiors translated directly into politics, where all rulers were properly endowed with power over their inferiors, private citizens. This power was carefully circumscribed by law, but the essential idea was hierarchical and expected inferiors to defer to persons of higher rank. Rulers were "Heads," serving as "Guides to the Body to lead it in right ways." [17] As a result the personal attributes of rulers were seen as crucial to the good of the commonwealth.[18] Indeed, judging from the election sermons of the middle decades of the eighteenth century, wisdom and moral stamina were more critical attributes of magistrates than of the people, who, it was believed, would follow paths of virtue or of vice depending on the example and wise governance of their superiors in authority.

The ideal ruler, whether a King, a governor, a representative, or a selectman, was a Moses, a "wise and tender" patriarch whose personal piety equipped him for the just and humane direction of his people.[19] Repeatedly the officers of government were described as "fathers," expected to guide, nourish, and protect their people.[20] Like good fathers, good rulers must not be arbitrary and severe, but should be gentle and concerned, earning the respect of their people, rather than compelling their cringing submission.[21] The responsibility of rulers extended beyond the mere defense of the commonwealth and the rights of its people, to include their advancement, both moral and material.[22]

The ministers, in addressing the members of the House of Repre-

16. Charles Chauncy, Civil magistrates must be just, ruling in the fear of God. A sermon preached . . . May 27, 1747 . . . (Boston, 1747), 9. Richard Buel, Jr., provides a perceptive general analysis of the relationship between rulers and ruled in his "Democracy and the American Revolution" cited in note 6 above.

17. William Williams, God the strength of rulers and people, and making them to be so, to each other mutually. A sermon preach'd . . . May 27th, 1741 . . . (Boston, 1741), 25.

18. E.g., Nathaniel Appleton, The Great blessing of good rulers, depends upon God's giving his judgements and his righteousness to them. A sermon preached . . . May 26, 1742 . . . (Boston, 1742), 1.

19. Samuel Cooper, A Sermon preached . . . May 26th, 1756 . . . (Boston, 1756), 9–24.

20. E.g., William Welsteed, The Dignity and duty of the civil magistrate. A sermon. Preached . . . May 29th, 1751 . . . (Boston, 1751), 26–27; Daniel Lewis, Good rulers the fathers of their people, and the marks of honour due to them. A sermon preach'd . . . May 25, 1748 . . . (Boston, 1748), 12; Williams, God the strength of rulers and people, 34.

21. Lewis, Good rulers, 21.

22. John Barnard, The Presence of the great God in the assembly of political rulers. A sermon preached . . . May 28th, 1746 . . . (Boston, 1746), 10.

sentatives, urged them to apply these standards immediately in choosing councillors. Certainly, they agreed, it was desirable that councillors "be Gentlemen of good Extract, and of large Interests," but their family name and economic interests were less important than their personal character.[23] Councillors, they said:

must be Men of Capacity, wise and understanding, i.e. who know the World, Men and Things; the Constitution, the civil and religious Interests of their Country; of a Genius for Government, of real, exemplary Vertue and Religion; of inflexible Integrity, who dare to be honest in all Times; act vote and advise, agreeable to the inward Sentiments of their Souls, in every Case; undaunted by Frowns on the one Hand, and Clamours on the other; not of a mean and sordid, selfish and worldly Spirit, but of a truly generous and public Spirit: In a Word, Men who are known to be such, tried Men, and generally approved of.[24]

They should be independent servants of the common good, judging according to their "inward Sentiments" and not in response to the political desires of either the few or the many. The ideal was a kind of detached leader, a Moses consulting privately with God and coming back to deliver judgment.

With this image as the standard, it was obvious that good rulers could never be officeseekers. The ambitious man who eagerly sought "Places of Honour and Authority" was actually the least fit for office. Such men were unlikely to be faithful public servants because they were unwilling to "patiently stay 'till God calls them." Actually the best rulers were those whose attitude toward officeholding was precisely the opposite; for it was "they who seek their own Promotion least, [who] give the most convincing Evidence of real Worth."[25] A posture of detachment, the disinterested stance, these were positive qualities according to the ideal. Therefore the people should not expect an intimate relationship with their magistrates. Indeed they should be suspicious of any who attempted a deliberate appeal to their affections. Such men were probably seeking private ends under the guise of popular liberty.[26]

23. Samuel Phillips, *Political rulers authorized and influenc'd by God our Saviour, to decree and execute justice: a sermon preached . . . May 30th, 1750 . . .* (Boston, 1750), 39.

24. Welsteed, *The Dignity and Duty of the Civil Magistrate,* 48–49; the same views may be found in Jonathan Mayhew, *A sermon preach'd . . . May 29th, 1754 . . .* (Boston, 1754), 27.

25. Ebenezer Gay, *The Character and work of a good ruler, and the duty of an obliged people . . . A sermon preach'd . . . May 29th, 1745 . . .* (Boston, 1745), 23.

26. Chauncy, *Civil magistrates,* 34.

The people did not, it was recognized, always enjoy leadership which exactly matched the ideal, but their role as obedient followers was nevertheless constant. Government was one of God's institutions, to be reverenced, and magistrates, however they might err, remained "Christ's ministers." [27] Rulers were temporal fathers and should be obeyed according to the Fifth Commandment as children obeyed parents.[28] Yet as Jonathan Mayhew pointed out, this regular obedience was not unlimited. Obedience was an essential duty but it did not extend beyond the bounds of law.[29] None of the election sermons treated the right of resistance as fully as Mayhew did in his famous 1750 *Discourse Concerning Unlimited Submission*, but allusions to the Glorious Revolution and the limits on rulers were common.

The stress, however, ran in the other direction. Unruliness was apparently a more perceptible danger in Massachusetts than excessive reverence for officials and slavish submission. As a result the proper limits of criticizing rulers were repeatedly stated. Criticism of rulers should be limited to those who were well informed of the facts, and their criticism should be "manag'd with Decency, and temper'd with Charity." [30] The people at large, therefore, should not be critics, because "most Men indeed, (as one observes) by their Condition in Life, are set at too great a Distance from the Springs of Government to be rightly instructed in Facts and Circumstances, and much less to enter into the Reason and Foundation of public Councils." Even people of wealth and education living close to Boston were warned against judging their rulers, since persons outside of government were not likely to be fully informed.[31] Yet as with the question of obedience, restraints on criticism were not to be understood as absolute. Though individuals varied in their emphasis, Nathaniel Appleton, a Cambridge pastor, summed up the common understanding in 1742:

> I acknowledge indeed that the common People are not always able to judge what is just and righteous in a public Administration, and are very often carried away with popular Cries of Injustice and Oppression, when their [sic] is the strictest Justice, and the greatest Tenderness to the Publick. And there are *Arcana Imperii, Secrets of State*, that none but such as are

27. Cooper, *A Sermon preached*, 45.
28. James Allen, *Magistracy an institution of Christ upon the throne. A sermon preached . . . on the day of election of councillors for said Province . . .* (Boston, 1744), 39–40.
29. Mayhew, *A sermon preach'd*, 20.
30. Cooper, *A Sermon preached*, 10.
31. Gay, *The Character and work of a good ruler*, 30–31.

concerned in them are supposed capable, fully to judge about: But yet in general, Justice and Righteousness is a Self-evident Thing, and every One can feel when he is oppressed and injured, or done justly by. And therefore altho' the *Ignorance of People* should make them very cautious so much as of entertaining hard Thoughts of their Rulers, much more of speaking Evil of them; yet after all, it is by the Manner of their Administration that they must regulate their Thoughts of them.[32]

Appleton's appreciation of the necessity of hesitating before criticizing rulers was generally shared. Lacking any theoretical justification for regular political opposition to men in authority, criticism was suspect. For whatever its foundation, it was likely to generate contention and, it was observed, "the natural consequence of contention, in all societies, is common ruin."[33] Since experience and the gospel both taught that houses divided against themselves could not stand, the ideal politics made little allowance for conflict and criticism.[34] Normally they were regarded as signs of disease in the body politic, and explained as consequences of immorality. As Jonathan Mayhew concluded in his remarks to the representatives in 1754, "it is, usually at least, the pursuit of separate, distinct interests, and a want of public spirit, that is the source of party and contentions in any state." Its opposite was the source of public well-being; for, he said, "a public spirit, is a spirit of union; and union is the source of public happiness."[35]

Such observations were commonplaces, repeated in one way or another in every sermon. And it is these observations which reveal the essential elements of the value structure that lay beneath the political ideal. For in this pre-Adam Smith generation, "public spirit," the disinterested pursuit of the common good, was again and again contrasted to its antithesis, the selfish pursuit of private ends, as if the two were mutually exclusive. People expected that individual gains might conflict with the public good, and their measure of virtuous citizenship was the willingness and ability to forego private temptations in favor of the community. Union and harmony carried an immense moral sanction, and in order to achieve their fulfillment every member of society owed a duty to perform his proper political role.

From the perspective of contemporaries, the disparity between the

32. Appleton, *The Great Blessing*, 34–35.
33. Samuel Checkley, *A Day of Darkness. — A sermon preach'd . . . May 28th, 1755 . . .* (Boston, 1755), 21.
34. Zuckerman, "The Massachusetts Town in the Eighteenth Century," chs. 2, 3, 4, and his "The Social Context of Democracy in Massachusetts," 523–544.
35. Mayhew, *A sermon preach'd*, 44.

real and the ideal was not so great as to be alarming. There were no jeremiads delivered to the provincial officials who gathered for the election sermons. Yet the sermons do reveal significant anxieties growing out of Massachusetts politics. The character of rulers, upon whom so much depended — whether they would act independently in the public interest or fall prey to selfish ambitions — was a continuous worry. The behavior of the people, too, was a standing danger, because they might be led into contention and disobedience by factious men. In the 1740's and 1750's these political anxieties never burst out of control. The traditional politics maintained an equilibrium which permitted rulers and ruled to perform their appointed roles. Conflict broke out sporadically and friction was never eliminated, but the system withstood these apparently natural, random challenges.

III

The stability of the working political structure may be best illustrated by examining the conflicts which tested its durability. For in the fifteen years from 1739 to 1754 there were no fewer than four major episodes of political turmoil — relating to banking, impressment, currency, and taxation — all issues of immediate material importance.[36] Passions were inflamed in all of these struggles, and in a number of cases unpopular politicians were turned out of office. Yet the system itself remained unchallenged and, excepting the anti-impressment riots of 1747 in Boston, there was no resort to extra-legal or extra-institutional politics.

The struggle over banking, which lasted from 1739 until 1742, gave the system its severest test. Before it was over much of the province had become polarized around two alternative banking schemes, one based on land and the other on silver, and both intended to ease the chronic currency shortage. The climax came in May 1741 when dozens of towns elected representatives who were committed to the land bank cause, an example of general public involvement in a provincial political issue which was unmatched until the furor over the Stamp Act in 1765. This involvement, however, proved short-lived, and though the polarization it engendered would echo through Massachusetts politics

36. For a recent estimate of the broad social impact of impressment see Jesse Lemisch, "Jack Tar in the Streets: Merchant Seamen in the Politics of Revolutionary America," *William and Mary Quarterly*, 3d Ser., XXV (1968), 371–407, especially 383–391. In her article "Popular Uprisings and Civil Authority in Eighteenth-Century America," *William and Mary Quarterly*, 3d Ser., XXVII (1970), 3–35, Pauline Maier argues that disorders such as impressment riots were regarded as normal, periodic occurrences which could be quite consistent with a stable social and political structure.

for a generation, the system remained unchanged. In 1742 the House restored the councillors it had ousted the previous year, and politics returned to normal. Moreover when the British government proscribed any Massachusetts banking plan, land or silver, the province quietly accepted the decision. As Thomas Hutchinson later recalled, "the authority of parliament to controul all public and private persons and proceedings in the colonies was, in that day, questioned by no body." [37] In spite of the continuing currency shortage and in spite of the popularity of a paper system backed by land, the issue was closed. There were no attempts to alter or circumvent the customary political process.

Though certainly less moderate and less disciplined, the resistance to impressment in 1747 also demonstrated the general acceptance of the established political system. The targets of the resistance, royal officials engaged in impressing sailors for the navy, were extraneous to Massachusetts politics, and their authority to impress was not recognized by provincial custom. In the Boston riot of 1747, when a mob threatened the governor in its attempt to stop impressments, it subsequently dispersed when faced by armed legislators gathered at the governor's house. Angry as they were, people in the mob declined to attack members of the legislature. Their target was impressment, not the structure of authority in Massachusetts. Indeed in an informal way such riots appear to have been part of the authority structure, an accepted if unwelcome element in eighteenth-century Anglo-American politics.[38] Certainly the impressment disturbances, whose impact was limited to a few port towns, did not alter politics under Governor Shirley. There was a ripple in the House in 1747 when a councillor who had played a role in impressment was denied election to the Council, and in the following year the representatives of several coastal towns took up the issue, but no action was taken and basically nothing changed.[39]

In 1749 the perennial problem of the currency was once more considered, and once more there was conflict, although its range and intensity did not compare to the land bank excitement. The issue was settled when the House acceded to the governor's instructions and passed a bill terminating paper currency. As a result several coastal towns turned their representatives out of office at the May election, but

37. Billias, *Massachusetts Land Bankers*, 37–40; Schutz, *William Shirley*, 40–41; Hutchinson, *History of Massachusetts-Bay*, II, 301.
38. Schutz, *William Shirley*, 127–129; Pauline R. Maier, "From Resistance to Revolution: American Radicals and the Development of Intercolonial Opposition to Britain, 1765–1776," Ph.D. diss., Harvard University, 1968, ch. 1.
39. Schutz, *William Shirley*, 111, 142.

the province in general made no such protest and the politics of the province continued in their old paths.[40]

The final challenge to the internal tranquillity of Governor Shirley's administration occurred in 1754, in response to a liquor excise tax which had been enacted the previous year. Here the rum-producers launched a campaign to abolish the tax, attempting to arouse the province through a series of pamphlets. Their arguments, lifted from the English excise controversy of the 1730's, appealed primarily to economic interest, not morality or the British constitution. The result was a pamphlet war which, though it may have stirred its participants, did not stir the province. The issue had been settled by the legislature in 1753, and in the absence of any widespread dissatisfaction there was no need to reconsider; thereafter the excise was not even debated in the House.[41]

Yet this self-conscious effort to engage public opinion through pamphleteering was a departure from the conventions of traditional politics. The fact of its utter failure seemed to be a testimony to the vitality of the old ways, even though the failure most likely resulted from the nature of the issue and the arguments surrounding it, and not from any conscious rejection of the idea of appealing to public opinion. Either way the consequences were the same, since the character of Massachusetts politics remained unchanged. Local affairs continued to be the primary focus of political activity, and involvement in provincial politics remained an occasional, sporadic phenomenon. Only a small group of politicians were continuously engaged in public life at the provincial level, and within their sphere these leaders possessed the respect and deference of the inhabitants. The stability of the election sermons' traditional ideal was substantially reflected in practice, and the people of Massachusetts sought no revision of their system. Institutions, both formal and informal, enjoyed wide acceptance.[42] Massachusetts had apparently achieved political stability.

40. Alden Bradford, *History of Massachusetts for Two Hundred Years: From the Year 1620 to 1820* (Boston, 1835), 112–113; Schutz, *William Shirley*, 146. Schutz claims that forty-five representatives were not returned owing to the currency issue, but offers no evidence to connect their nonreturn to that issue. Actually the 1749 turnover was relatively low (36 percent), so it seems very unlikely that the currency issue exercised much influence in local elections.

41. Paul S. Boyer, "Borrowed Rhetoric: The Massachusetts Excise Controversy of 1754," *William and Mary Quarterly*, 3d Ser., XXI (1964), 328–351, especially 349–350.

42. Zemsky, "The Massachusetts Assembly, 1730–1755," draws similar conclusions.

2

The Beginning of the
Revolution in Massachusetts

This stability in provincial politics, which lasted through the brief tenure of Governor Thomas Pownall (1757–1760) and into the early years of Francis Bernard's administration, led many to expect it would endure. After all, the religious turmoil of the 1740's had receded, and the controversial political issues of banking and currency had been laid to rest. Military victory had finally ended the French threat, and Massachusetts had survived the disruptions of war without serious dislocations in its social or political life. Beneath the surface, long-term shifts in social and economic structure that could erode political stability may have been occurring, but contemporaries saw nothing to suggest that the character of politics was on the eve of any radical transformation.[1] Nor is there much reason to suppose that political life would have changed rapidly without the appearance of the imperial revenue and reform programs of the 1760's. The new British measures, not indigenous forces, stimulated the polarization of Massachusetts politics along substantially ideological lines.

1. Kenneth Lockridge argues that just such a long-term shift was occurring and that population pressure and economic stratification were increasing, leading to tensions within the political structure. See his "Land, Population and the Evolution of New England Society, 1630–1790," *Past & Present*, no. 39 (April 1968), 62–80.

I

The movement away from traditional politics began in a series of commonplace incidents soon after the arrival of Governor Francis Bernard in 1760. Bernard, a career administrator who had been promoted to the governorship of Massachusetts as a reward for his quiet rule in New Jersey, hoped to repeat this success when he arrived in Boston. But one of his early judicial appointments quickly drew him into a typical, old-fashioned patronage wrangle. Bernard had chosen his lieutenant governor, Thomas Hutchinson, to head the Superior Court of Judicature although Colonel James Otis, a Barnstable County figure of some note, claimed to have been promised the appointment by Bernard's predecessors, William Shirley and Thomas Pownall. The opposition that was raised to Hutchinson's appointment would hardly warrant consideration had it not been for the character and subsequent career of its leader, James Otis, the thirty-five-year-old son of the disappointed candidate.

Otis, a Boston lawyer and representative, was one of the brilliant orators and legal minds of his generation and, like his father, ambitious for public recognition. Personally, he could be abrasive with his quick temper, caustic wit, and apparent readiness to contrast his own excellence with the defects he perceived in others. His political maneuvers sometimes lent substance to the charge that he was a trimmer, if not actually an opportunist. Nonetheless he was to exercise a major influence in Massachusetts politics in the 1760's, and though he was periodically insane in the years after 1769, he remained an important participant until late 1774 when his mental disorder became semipermanent. As a result, though the opposition he led against Hutchinson's appointment was neither numerous, successful, nor radical, some contemporaries would later trace the origins of Massachusetts' political polarization to the Otis-Hutchinson feud.[2]

The reason they followed the polarization back to the dispute over

---

2. This sketch of Otis is primarily based on that of Clifford K. Shipton, "James Otis," *Sibley's Harvard Graduates* (Boston, 1873 ——), XI, 247–286. Shipton's hostility to Otis and sympathy for Hutchinson colors his highly informed analysis, but it is reliable. John J. Waters, Jr., offers a more sympathetic view of Otis in *The Otis Family in Provincial and Revolutionary Massachusetts* (Chapel Hill, N.C., 1968), chs. 7, 8. The context of the Otis-Hutchinson feud is provided in John J. Waters and John A. Schutz, "Patterns of Colonial Politics: The Writs of Assistance and the Rivalry between the Otis and Hutchinson Families," *William and Mary Quarterly*, 3d Ser., XXIV (1967), 543–567.

the judgeship was that Otis, although at first an almost isolated figure, would in the course of successive battles emerge as one of the leaders of a more or less continuous opposition to the governor and imperial policy. This opposition, centered in the Boston town meeting and the House of Representatives, became known variously as the "faction," the "radicals," the "plebian party," and the "Whigs."

Though the term "party" was and is often used to describe the opposition as well as those who supported the administration, it is misleading because there were no party organizations and political alignments were fluid. There was a recognizable group of politicians who repeatedly led opposition to administration policy, among them Samuel Adams, Thomas Cushing, John Hancock, Joseph Hawley, and James Warren.[3] Yet Otis himself drifted in and out of this opposition grouping during the course of the 1760's, and judging from the fluctuation in the votes of the House so did many others. At various times hundreds, even thousands, of individuals all over Massachusetts, both in and out of public office, were part of the opposition, depending on their political beliefs and the position they held on particular issues. Such coherence as this opposition grouping enjoyed was not based on any common program, electioneering union, or political patronage, the normal ad-

3. More names might be mentioned, but from the standpoint of longevity in opposition and prominence these are the most important. Samuel Adams (1722–1803), son of a prominent land-banker, had been active in Boston politics since the 1740's and was first elected to the House of Representatives in 1765. In the 1760's he was on the eve of a brilliant political career which is traced in William V. Wells, *The Life and Public Services of Samuel Adams*, 3 vols. (Boston, 1865), and in John C. Miller, *Sam Adams: Pioneer in Propaganda* (Boston, 1936). Thomas Cushing (1725–1788), who came from a prominent political family, was a merchant who had served as a Boston selectman from 1753 through 1764 and as representative since 1761. Between 1766 and 1774 he was to serve almost continuously as speaker of the House. His character and career are treated by Shipton in *Sibley's Harvard Graduates*, XI, 377–395. John Hancock (1737–1793), a wealthy merchant was new to politics in the 1760's, but after his election to the House in 1766 he rapidly became an important leader. His life has been examined in Herbert S. Allan, *John Hancock, Patriot in Purple* (New York, 1948), William T. Baxter, *The House of Hancock: Business in Boston, 1724–1775* (Cambridge, Mass., 1945), and most recently by Shipton, *Sibley's Harvard Graduates*, XIII, 416–446. Joseph Hawley (1723–1788), a respected Northampton lawyer, was a leader in the House after his election in 1766. His opposition to the administration was somewhat less constant than that of Adams or Hancock and he suffered from periodic psychological depressions which limited his active participation from time to time. Ernest Francis Brown has written his biography, *Joseph Hawley, Colonial Radical* (New York, 1931). James Warren (1726–1808) of Plymouth was first elected to the House of Representatives in 1766. In 1769 and 1770 he served as speaker. Warren was a close associate of Samuel Adams and the brother-in-law of James Otis. His life is sketched in Shipton, *Sibley's Harvard Graduates*, XI, 584–606.

hesives of political parties. Instead the opposition formed around an ideology which articulated their joint hostility to the innovations in imperial policy that threatened the economic and political status quo. Consequently, although some of the Boston leaders might be called radicals, the term Whig is probably the most nearly descriptive of the opposition.[4]

In English usage everyone who supported the Glorious Revolution and the Hanoverian succession was a Whig, but in Massachusetts it meant something more, an amalgamation of the Puritan political tradition represented in the election sermons with the Radical Whiggism of the eighteenth-century "commonwealthsman." There was, obviously, no precise proportion of Radical Whig ideology and Puritan tradition in the minds of those who participated in opposition, and probably many shared more in the attitudes and prejudices than in the theoretical particulars. Though some had read the tracts of English Radical Whigs like John Trenchard and Thomas Gordon in addition to the annual election sermons, many more had absorbed their assumptions casually, over the years, largely through the Boston newspapers, the political doctrine of the clergy, and their own experience in town and province affairs.[5] For such people, whether country representatives,

4. Historians like Arthur M. Schlesinger, Sr., and John C. Miller who emphasized the revolutionary character of the opposition have often used "radical" to describe Samuel Adams and the others. For them "radical" represents the degree of opposition to British measures and the readiness to resist. It does not mean that radicals were egalitarian democrats. Pauline R. Maier, "From Resistance to Revolution: American Radicals and the Development of Intercolonial Opposition to Britain, 1765–1776," Ph.D. diss., Harvard University, 1968, employs the same term in another sense, the contemporary sense of eighteenth-century English politics. She accurately connects people like Samuel Adams to the Radical Whig ideology of the Thomas Hollis, Catherine Macaulay set. I have chosen "Whig" for the reasons given above and because it was the most commonly used term in the 1760's and 1770's in Massachusetts and in that setting, at least, is relatively unambiguous.

5. These impressions are based on a reading of the press, public statements by the legislature and various localities, and the private correspondence of a number of important political leaders. The *Boston Gazette* was vigorously Whig and Radical Whig, and according to Thomas Hutchinson it was the most popular newspaper in Massachusetts, commanding seven-eighths of the reading population (Hutchinson to Francis Bernard, Boston, Aug. 12, 1770, Thomas Hutchinson Letter Books, Massachusetts Archives, XXVI, 534–535). The other Boston papers, whatever their allegiance, sometimes contained essays and reports treating English political events from a Radical Whig perspective. The role of the clergy in laying the ideological foundations for the Revolution may not have been quite what Alice M. Baldwin argued (*The New England Clergy and the American Revolution*, Durham, N.C., 1928), but the election sermons which were distributed to every representative and every parish in the province enjoyed an influential platform and a wide audience. These ideas, emanating from press and pulpit, could be readily applied to actual experience with representative government based on consent. Bernard Bailyn treats the emergence of

local selectmen, or simply private individuals, the governor's insistence on obedience to the Stamp Act in 1765–1766 was unacceptable and it was on this issue that the Whig opposition coalesced.

These Massachusetts Whigs were prepared to accept the conventional English expression that Parliament was supreme, but at the same time they were absolutely certain that Parliament could trangress the constitution. In contrast to Governor Bernard and his allies, who saw the constitution as a framework for the exercise of sovereign power, they pictured the constitution as a complicated system of old, inviolable safeguards — rights — which protected the citizen from both his fellows and the state. Their respect for the state and the vehicles of sovereign power within it were limited. These institutions were man-made expedients, accidents. The essence was individual rights and the practical devices which protected them. They believed that the fundamental greatness of the English constitution was Magna Carta together with the subsequent defensive, procedural guarantees which generations of freemen had built into the structure of government. Here was the focus of their loyalty, not Parliament. Thus, by opposition standards, resistance to any unconstitutional measure was not only permissible, it was a necessary duty. Moreover they regarded both the decision to resist as well as active resistance itself as primarily the duty of the people and their representatives, since the private and political interests of appointed officials were likely to blind them to constitutional violations and attach them to the offending measures.

These opposing views came into direct conflict, not only as abstract arguments, but as actual programs for Massachusetts political conduct at the time of the Stamp Act. The issue was obedience or resistance. As a result both the techniques and goals of the traditional politics of personal advantage were swept aside. Instead public opinion, the opinion of those who elected officials and who obeyed or disobeyed laws and rulers, dominated provincial politics. The governor and his supporters were forced to answer their adversaries and to expound the administration position to the public; for the first time in the history of the province its rulers were directly and overtly campaigning for public support on a broad scale.

The administration, using the forums provided by the General Court, meetings of the grand juries, and the press, argued the necessity of

this form of Whig ideology in America in the first four chapters of his *The Ideological Origins of the American Revolution* (Cambridge, Mass., 1967).

obedience to the Stamp Act, however onerous its burdens. The wisest course, they advised, would be a humble and loyal petition to Parliament explaining the inconveniences of the law and begging relief. Certainly, they admitted, resistance to unconstitutional measures might in some cases be justified—but that was irrelevant here, since the acts of the supreme, sovereign power, Parliament, were constitutional by definition. To resist the Stamp Act was to rebel.[6]

The opposition, which was led by Boston representatives, traditionally leaders in the House, flatly rejected this policy. Parliamentary taxation of Massachusetts inhabitants was no mere inconvenience, but a violation of the British constitution. Rather than humbly begging relief, they urged that Massachusetts defend its rights by resisting unconstitutional violations. As a consequence inhabitants of the province ultimately turned to extra-legal measures beyond the bounds of established political institutions and the stability of the old political structure was shattered.

From the administration perspective, extra-legal resistance to an act of Parliament was more than illegal, it was rebellion. Consequently the governor and his adherents became convinced that the men who led the opposition were treasonous. When Governor Bernard saw the tumultuous disorders which convulsed Boston in 1765 he connected them to the attitude of resistance displayed by the House of Representatives and recently visible in many of the towns. He concluded that this was all part of a seditious plot. The governor and his friends could neither recognize nor respect the distinctions which Whigs drew between the popular demonstration of August 14, 1765, which destroyed Peter Oliver's property and forced his resignation as stamp master, and the even more destructive attack on Lieutenant Governor Hutchinson's house on August 26.[7]

Yet these distinctions were critical from the viewpoint of those in

6. These arguments were reiterated in the governor's addresses, articles in the press, and in the private letters of both Bernard and Hutchinson. On the political use of addresses to grand juries see John D. Cushing, "The Judiciary and Public Opinion in Revolutionary Massachusetts," in George A. Billias, ed., *Law and Authority in Colonial America* (Barre, Mass., 1965), 168–186.

7. Thomas Hutchinson saw both as mob sedition, but he did recognize a distinction between constitutional and unconstitutional mobs. See Thomas Hutchinson to John or Robert Grant, Boston, July 27, 1768, Thomas Hutchinson Letter Books, Massachusetts Archives, XXVI, 317. For a full examination of ideas describing the limits of justifiable resistance see, Maier, "From Resistance to Revolution," 88–91, 94–95. Edmund S. and Helen M. Morgan describe events in Boston in *The Stamp Act Crisis: Prologue to Revolution*, rev. ed. (New York, 1963), 163–168.

opposition, since their whole justification for active popular resistance was contingent on them. Organized popular demonstrations of resistance, where an assembly of citizens joined in expressing their views and in the collective exertion of their influence in defense of the constitution, were among the only means possible to avoid a suicidal submission. For submission as recommended by the governor's party meant self-destruction, according to the opposition. It would, they said, encourage not discourage further encroachments on constitutional rights. Boston Sons of Liberty and their friends celebrated the demonstration of August 14 which had culminated in the stamp master's resignation. Ignoring the physical destructiveness which accompanied the demonstration, they chose to regard it as an example of properly expressed popular power, whereas they denied responsibility for the assault on Hutchinson's house, condemning it as a riotous, violent, mass destruction of property.[8]

Among Englishmen such a differentiation seemed ridiculous to all but the most radical Whigs. Any organized, popular resistance to acts of government was the boldest, most blatant sedition conceivable. The town of Boston, which not only permitted but seemed to justify such behavior, was widely regarded as seditious in England. But reactions within the province were more sympathetic. To the governor's dismay, the people of Massachusetts not only refused to condemn Boston, they shared its spirit of opposition.

II

Massachusetts' attitude, as it emerged, was similar to Boston's; the entire province was tinged with Radical Whiggery. Though tumults and disorders were generally wrong, it did not follow that public resistance to tyranny was wrong. The right of resistance had long been accepted, and although there was some uncertainty over exactly which forms of resistance were lawful, there was near unanimity in the belief that public remonstrances at least were acceptable. Remonstrances by the General Court, as well as local remonstrances in the form of town instructions to representatives were an old, lawful practice.

In May 1764 Boston had set an example by instructing its representatives to oppose the Sugar Act, but other towns had remained silent. Even though Boston radicals had mounted a vigorous effort in the press to arouse sentiment against the Sugar Act, the towns had

8. Maier, "From Resistance to Revolution," 88–91, 94–95.

expressed no opinion. It was only after the inhabitants of Boston had actively resisted the Stamp Act that an attitude of vocal resistance spread. Consequently in September and October 1765, the old vocabulary of defending the constitution and resisting tyranny, already expressed in Boston, was articulated all over the province by several dozen towns instructing their representatives in time for the autumn session of the assembly.

Town instructions had always been recognized as legitimate expressions of local opinion, but they were uncommon and in the past they had typically provided concrete directions to the town representative who was acting as town agent on some issue of local concern. Except in the land bank controversy, they had never been important in provincial politics. Yet now, suddenly, in 1765 this traditional form emerged as a vehicle for local expression of Whig views. Moreover the instructions of one town, Braintree, became a general manifesto which was rapidly adopted by more than forty other towns.[9] Somehow the language and substance of the Braintree Resolves stimulated enthusiastic approval and local action where previously there had been silence. Clearly the character of local politics was changing.

The author of the resolves, John Adams, was an obscure young barrister, educated at Harvard, Worcester, and Boston.[10] He had never been farther west than Worcester, farther north and east than Boston, or farther south than Cape Cod. In experience, training, and outlook he was a native, provincial product — both intimately acquainted with and sharing the ideas and attitudes of his Massachusetts countrymen. The instructions, when compared with any of those adopted by Boston, are conspicuous for their stumbling, repetitive prose and their awkward organization. Yet they spoke more accurately for the province at large than the "correct, genteel and artful" compositions of Boston-bred Samuel Adams which John Adams so much admired.[11]

The Braintree instructions opened with professions of loyalty to the King, veneration for the houses of Parliament, and friendship for all

9. John Adams, *Diary and Autobiography of John Adams*, ed. Lyman H. Butterfield (Cambridge, Mass., 1961), III, 282.

10. Although the report of instructions was signed by Samuel Niles, Norton Quincy, James Penniman, and John Hayward as well as John Adams, in his autobiography Adams named himself as the sole author and initiator of the instructions (*Diary and Autobiography*, III, 282). The text that appears in Samuel A. Bates, ed. *Records of the Town of Braintree, 1640 to 1793* (Randolph, Mass., 1886), 404–406, is fuller than that printed by Charles Francis Adams in *The Works of John Adams*, and it is the Braintree version that is used below.

11. *Diary and Autobiography of John Adams*, I, 271.

fellow Britons, but went on to explain that the townspeople felt an "unkindness" in recent measures of the ministry and Parliament. The "unconstitutional" Stamp Act was particularly offensive because it combined economic and constitutional threats. "In this infant, sparcely settled Country," the instructions explained, "considering the present scarcity of money, the execution of that act for a short space of time would dreign the Country of Cash, strip multitudes of the poorer people of all their property and Reduce them to absolute beggary." "So sudden a shock and such a convulsive change in the whole course of our business & Subsistence," would threaten "the peace of the Province." Furthermore, the Stamp Act was contrary to Magna Carta: "We have always understood it to be a grand & fundamental principal of the British Constitution that no Freeman should be subjected to any Tax to which he has not given his own consent in person or by proxy." The act ran counter to every maxim of the law, "because we are not Represented in that assembly [Parliament] in any sense unless it be by a Fiction of Law as insensible in Theory as it would be Injurious in Fact if so heavy a Taxation should be grounded on it."

Yet in spite of these economic and constitutional evils, by itself the Stamp Act formed only part of the problem:

The most Grevious of all is the allarming extension of the Powers of the Court of Admiralty. In the Courts one Judge presides alone, no Juries have any concern there, the Law and the Fact are to be decided by the same single Judge whose commission is only during pleasure and with whom as we are told the most mischievous of all customs has become established that of taking commissions on all Condemnations, so that he is under a pecuniary temptation always against the subject.

Impartial justice, a keystone in the complex structure of English procedures which protected the individual from the awesome power of the state, would be demolished. Had not the mother country "thought the Independence of the Judges so essential to an impartial Administration of Justice as to render them Independent of any power on Earth, Independent of the King the Lords the Commons & the People"? If weak or wicked men should become judges, then colonists would become "the most sordid & forlorn of Slaves. We mean the slaves of a slave of the Servant of a Minister of State." This was the path down which the late acts of Parliament and ministry led. All the old supports would tumble together, the right to property, jury trial, impartial justice. Braintree grieved that "such a distinction . . . such a difference be-

25

tween Great Brittain & America" could be established by the Parliament
which was supposed to be "the Guardian of Liberty in both." Braintree
and the other towns found the necessity for resisting "by all Lawfull
means" self-evident.[12]

Unlike speeches or polemic, the Braintree instructions were not designed to persuade or vanquish. There was no clearly defined adversary, not King, not Parliament, not ministry, and not even the Stamp
Act itself was attacked systematically. Instead, attention focused on
direct expression of the sensations provoked by recent English policy.
Indeed, the lack of precise definition among the grievances was the
salient characteristic of the whole performance. For it revealed the partly
explicit belief that the grievances were not distinct or finite; constitutional and economic dangers were interwoven and possessed an infinitely
destructive potential. For that reason Braintree dwelt on the shocking,
terrible consequences, which seemed not merely possible but almost
inevitable. The dike of procedural rights, once breached, could hardly
be restored. As to the character and location of sovereignty, the question of Parliament's authority, it was not considered. Sovereignty seemed
to be a theoretical abstraction, extraneous to the issues at hand. Such
expressions of resistance, which began in Boston and were now embraced by Braintree and many other towns, demonstrated that the opposition arguments were acceptable in Massachusetts, while the doctrine
of obedience was rejected.

The commitment of Massachusetts to the principles of resistance
was ratified during the following year by both the House of Representatives and the electors of the province. The House, by censuring
Timothy Ruggles, the Massachusetts representative to the Stamp Act
Congress who had condemned its proceedings, declared that in Massachusetts public resistance to unconstitutional acts of Parliament was
orthodox, and that contrary opinions were heretical. Their constituents,
the people of the province, underscored this declaration when, in the
annual elections, they responded to the call of Boston Whigs and
"purged" seventeen of the thirty-two representatives listed in the *Boston
Gazette* as friends of the Stamp Act and advocates of submission. Soon
after, when the General Court reconvened, the commitment to resistance was confirmed by the election of a Council sympathetic to the
popular, opposition view.[13]

12. The preceding quotations are all taken from Bates, ed., *Records of the Town
of Braintree*, 404–406.
13. *Boston Gazette*, March 31, 1766, 3:3. Robert E. Brown reports that twenty

With these public declarations coming from both the legislature and the provincial electorate, Boston Whigs scored significant gains in making their own cause the cause of Massachusetts. Otis and the Boston representative Thomas Cushing, who was elected speaker of the House, had led the censure movement in the House, while others of the same group had inserted the list of Stamp Act friends in the newspaper a month before the House election, and followed it up with articles urging retribution at the polls. Yet the administration was mistaken in judging these reversals as merely the victories of a skillful opposition faction. For the three events, two in the assembly and one in the towns themselves, showed that the province was ready to embrace the idea of defending constitutional rights, even when it meant resisting Parliament. Further, the electoral purge, like the outburst of town instructions, demonstrated that many townspeople recognized a responsibility to act on their belief in resistance, even though it might run contrary to the wishes of prominent local leaders like their representatives. People had made it clear that resistance "by all lawfull means" meant not only remonstrating as towns, but also voting as individuals. Elections could be used to maintain government by consent, not merely on local matters, but on questions of unlimited constitutional significance.

Next to the resistance to the Stamp Act itself, this dramatic shift in provincial behavior of 1765–1766 was scarcely noticed at the time. Instead, contemporaries viewed the active resistance to the Stamp Act itself as remarkable because of its intensity and its intercolonial character. Ruggles' censure and the electoral purge in the House and Council seemed more ordinary, having occurred within regular political channels. Moreover within Massachusetts, mature men remembered that the land bank controversy had inflamed the countryside a generation earlier. Competitive politics, like the conflicts between the governor and the assembly, were not entirely new. Contemporaries recognized that a polarization had occurred around the "friends of government" on one side and the Boston Whigs at the head of the people in opposition, but they did not yet see that the polarization of political leader-

---

were purged, since twenty of the names do not appear on the legislative list for 1766–1767, *Middle-Class Democracy in Massachusetts, 1691–1780* (Ithaca, 1955), 228. However in three of these cases the town sent no representative at all in 1766, so one can hardly infer a purge. The actual extent of the purge should not be exaggerated, since normal turnover would have eliminated perhaps six to ten of the listed representatives. On the Council see Francis G. Walett, "The Massachusetts Council, 1766–1774: The Transformation of a Conservative Institution," *William and Mary Quarterly*, 3d Ser., VI (1949), 605–627.

ship along ideological lines, coupled with the engagement of the public, had fundamentally altered the structure of Massachusetts politics.

Gradually though, this division came to be regarded as semipermanent as the battle was joined and rejoined again and again. Governor Bernard, Lieutenant Governor Hutchinson, and their friends persisted, still using official speeches, the press, and the power of appointment in pursuit of provincial support and tranquillity. Their opposition, now a majority in both the House and the Council, continued to use the press, assembly addresses, correspondence, and, in Boston, town instructions. But the Boston Whigs also went on to make significant departures, introducing new forms of resistance which extended and intensified the level of popular participation. The most important innovations were the nonimportation and boycott covenants directed against the Townshend Acts and the convention of towns which was called in 1768. Both of these initiatives were grounded on the attitudes that had been revealed by the provincial response to the Braintree resolves, the censure of Timothy Ruggles, and the electoral purge. In each case they confirmed the experience of the Stamp Act resistance and stimulated a wider comprehension that it was the responsibility of individuals acting in concert as towns to stand up in defense of the constitution.

The political covenants that the Boston Whigs introduced in 1768 were not entirely new. Merchants had used them to enforce nonimportation agreements; but Whigs, seeking more effective resistance, extended their use to all citizens on an undifferentiated basis. Believing that the defense of the constitution, and hence resistance to parliamentary taxes, was the duty of every citizen, boycott covenants were passed from hand to hand in Boston and several other towns in 1768 and 1769. The individuals who signed the covenants affirmed their responsibility to uphold the rights of all by refusing to submit to violations of those rights.

In early 1770 these boycott covenants assumed greater importance when a growing number of towns in the eastern half of Massachusetts followed Boston's example and adopted covenants in town meeting. Frequently they focused on duties tea, and some towns created inspection committees to enforce the boycott, threatening offenders with sanctions ranging from the town's official displeasure to social and commercial boycotts. Short-cutting the task of soliciting each individual, town meetings assumed the moral responsibility to boycott on behalf of their constituents. It was apparently assumed that members of the town meeting were as competent to contract for the constitutional resistance of their community as they were to contract for the payment of provincial taxes.[14]

These covenants proved ephemeral. By late 1770 they began to break down because their immediate political utility seemed doubtful. Nevertheless the principle of resistance was fixed. People might question the tactical value of covenants, or object to their capacity to divide communities, but few doubted that both the covenants and the responsibility to resist were proper. Ironically, even though the administration regarded the covenants as seditious combinations, its actions confirmed the popular belief, since it never attempted to prosecute offenders for fear that Massachusetts juries would acquit them.

The convention of Massachusetts towns, called in September 1768, was an equally significant innovation. Conventions of clergy had been in existence for a generation or more, but a convention of towns was new, and the circumstances in which it was created were complex. Earlier that summer the House and the governor had come into conflict over the famous circular letter of February 1768 in which the Massachusetts House invited other assemblies to unite in expressing opposition to the Townshend Acts. Bernard, acting on the instructions of Secretary of State Hillsborough, directed the House to rescind this letter, but to the satisfaction of Boston Whigs the House had dramatically refused by a vote of 92 to 17. Therefore Bernard chastened the House by dissolving it. Soon after, word arrived that the Crown intended to station two regiments of soldiers in Boston. It was in this context that Samuel Adams and Thomas Cushing apparently originated the idea of a convention of towns as a way to peacefully protest the dissolution of the House of Representatives and the introduction of troops at Boston.

The convention was hastily called together by Boston after the governor refused the town's request to call a meeting of the assembly to consider the crisis. Its promoters never elaborated on its specific purposes, so observers then and later have been prompted to speculate. Some have claimed that this was an abortive attempt to arouse forcible

14. Boycott covenants in Massachusetts are treated in some detail in Alden Bradford, *History of Massachusetts* (Boston, 1822–1829), I, 119–146, 165–172. Of the ninety-six towns whose records I have examined (see Chapter 5 and the Appendix below), eleven voted some form of boycott and four established committees of inspection. The eleven are here listed, with those that created inspection committees in italics: Falmouth (Cumberland County), Holliston, Ipswich, *Lynn, Marblehead, Plymouth, Roxbury*, Sandwich, Topsfield, Upton, Watertown.

resistance to the landing of troops, though it was more likely just another attempt to cultivate provincial opposition to the royal administration and assert Massachusetts' rights.[15] The convention met for a week and was attended by representatives of more than 100 of the 250 towns and districts in the province. The turnout was comparable to a typical meeting of the House, but towns that opposed the convention did not participate, nor did the governor's allies, and none of the seventeen representatives who had voted to rescind the circular letter attended, so the convention was even more Whiggish than the House. The convention elected Speaker of the House Thomas Cushing as chairman, and went on to adopt a petition to the King and an address to the governor. Then they ordered the publication of their proceedings, and went home. There were no tumults; the troops landed without incident.[16] As the lieutenant governor described it: "They met and spent a week and made themselves ridiculous and then dissolved themselves." He found their publication both "illnaturd and impotent." Boston radicals, he believed, had suffered a set-back.[17]

Yet in spite of Hutchinson's scorn for the convention, it was reported that "the people have, at present, great confidence in them [the delegates to the convention]." Fearful of the presence of troops and anxious to preserve Massachusetts liberty, scores of towns from all over the province displayed a willingness to go beyond the limits of established institutions. Even though the administration called the whole proceeding illegal, and the governor refused to hear its address, the towns behaved as if sovereignty was theirs. Without any discussion of the fundamental structure of the constitution, many towns assumed that their powers to meet, discuss, and send representatives to confer with others were unlimited. The administration argument that only the governor could call an assembly, and that it was criminal to convene without the sanction of formal authority, caused some hesitation; but

15. John C. Miller, basing his argument on administration sources, takes the first view in "The Massachusetts Convention of 1768," *New England Quarterly*, VII (1934), 445–474. I argue the second view in "The Massachusetts Convention of Towns, 1768," *William and Mary Quarterly*, 3d Ser., XXVI (1969), 94–104. Robert E. Brown presents a third view in *Middle-Class Democracy*, 253–254.

16. See Miller, "The Massachusetts Convention of 1768," 445–474; Brown, "The Massachusetts Convention of Towns, 1768," 94–104; Hutchinson to Lord ?, Boston, Dec. 8, 1768, Hutchinson Letter Books, Mass. Arch., XXVI, 333; Alden Bradford, *History of Massachusetts for Two Hundred Years: From the Year 1620 to 1820* (Boston, 1835), 195.

17. Hutchinson to Thomas Whately, Boston, Oct. 5, 1768, Hutchinson Letter Books, Mass. Arch., XXV, 281–282.

it could not prevent towns from assuming what they regarded as their fundamental responsibility to defend their rights. As Hutchinson himself observed: "We have had a mock Assembly, called by the Town of Boston who have made a ridiculous figure but not so in the eyes of the body of the people."[18] Hutchinson, viewing provincial politics from the traditional perspective of a ruler vested with authority, saw nothing to redeem this demonstration of local activism which had by-passed regular political channels. His orthodox outlook would dominate the royal administration in the province during the crucial years ahead, for in mid-1769 Thomas Hutchinson became acting governor.

III

Hutchinson, now sixty years old, had served the public in many capacities during his entire adult life. In the 1730's he had represented Boston in the House of Representatives and in the 1740's he had been elected speaker. More recently he had worked in the Council and in various appointive offices. During the turbulent 1760's he had distinguished himself as a mainstay of British rule.[19] No one was more experienced in the operation of politics at the provincial level than Thomas Hutchinson and there were few who could match his keen political understanding. As governor, his views both influenced the royal government and epitomized its highest level of insight. Therefore Hutchinson's understanding of events — his perceptions and blind spots — demand particular attention if one is to understand the context of Massachusetts politics in the early 1770's.

Hutchinson's elevation to the governorship satisfied a private ambition. He assumed office believing that he could restore peace and good government to Massachusetts if anyone could.[20] He knew he faced an immense, complicated task in which provincial politics were directly connected to the measures of Parliament and ministry. The relationship, he saw, was reciprocal, the acts of one conditioned the behavior

18. Andrew Eliot to Thomas Hollis, Boston, Sept. 27, 1768, Massachusetts Historical Society, *Collections*, 4th Ser., IV (1858), 428–429; Hutchinson to Richard Jackson, Boston, Oct. 5, 1768, Hutchinson Letter Books, Mass. Arch., XXV, 282.

19. For the period prior to 1760 these remarks rest on Malcolm Freiberg, "Thomas Hutchinson: The First Fifty Years (1711–1761)," *William and Mary Quarterly*, 3d Ser., XV (1958), 35–55.

20. Hutchinson to Nathaniel Rogers, Milton, May 31, 1768, Hutchinson Letter Books, Mass. Arch., XXV, 259.

of the other. The crisis had arisen, he believed, as a result of parliamentary policy. In 1766 Hutchinson had written:

Had our confusions proceeded from any interior cause we have good men enough in the country towns to have united in restoring peace and order and would have put an end to the influence of the plebian party in the Town of Boston over the rest of the province. But as our misfortunes are attributable to a cause without us, many of those persons, who in the other case would have been friends to government are now too apt to approve of measures inconsistent with government and unite with those whom they would otherwise abhor under a notion of opposing by a common interest a power which we have no voice in creating and which they say has a distinct and separate interest from us.

This circumstance, he thought, provided a fertile soil in which the delusion of independence from Parliament could grow. To argue the truth as he saw it, that there must be one supreme authority, in this case Parliament, and that colonies could not expect exactly the same rights as Englishmen living in the mother country, was "singing to the deaf." By 1768 he had found people were "more inclined to independence than they have been, . . . it is a principle which spreads every day and before long will be universal." Leading people had come to believe that Parliament had no power to bind the province, and Hutchinson thought that they might as well deny Crown authority too, "although I do not think a man of them at present has it in his thoughts." The "delusion," as Hutchinson called it, had touched nearly everybody: "It is the lowest part of the vulgar only who have not yet been taught that if they are to be governed by Laws made by any persons but themselves or their representatives they are Slaves." The worst part was that "it is infused into the minds of the people that these Duties are a prelude to many more and much heavier and that a Standing Army is to enforce Obedience and the Legislative power of the Colonies to be taken away." [21]

By itself Hutchinson found the delusion pernicious in its impact on provincial affairs, but it had the additional effect of provoking Parliament. Hutchinson himself had never favored parliamentary taxation. He had opposed as impolitic the Sugar, Stamp, and Townshend Acts, as well as the extension of the vice-admiralty jurisdiction and a pro-

21. Hutchinson to Richard Jackson, Boston, April 21, 1766, to Thomas Pownall, n.p., March 26, 1768, to Duke of ? , n.p., March 27, 1768, to Richard Jackson, Boston, Oct. 20, 1767, Hutchinson Letter Books, Mass. Arch., XXVI, 227–228, 297, 298, XXV, 206.

posed alteration of the Massachusetts Council. He had phrased his opposition mildly, stressing the inexpediency of these measures, always recognizing the competence of Parliament within Massachusetts. He was sure that this attitude, soothing to Parliament, was the only way to restore the relationship which had existed prior to 1763. But by late 1769 when Hutchinson assumed power, he found the delusion so entrenched and enjoying so many platforms and sanctuaries, that for the moment he thought the best course was to quiet the province while continuing to press the ministry to establish a firm policy, so as to settle the question of dependence permanently.

The way to fix the principle of parliamentary supremacy, he argued, was not by assaulting the colonies with direct taxes. Parliament should act as a gentle parent, establishing mild, general laws useful to the colonies, covering matters like currency, wills, and court procedures; this would induce subordination.[22] Further, the governor should receive more immediate official support from home, otherwise "they will be ready enough to infer that all they have advanced is right and will persevere in it." Finally, Parliament should fix a line of authority and then enforce it firmly, without ambiguity or hesitation. Otherwise the constitutional uncertainty would lead the people to outright independence. Repeatedly Hutchinson's pleas and warnings made the same point:

> Repeal as many of the Laws now in force as you please but what remain take some effectual method to carry them into execution. It is difficult to do I confess. But it must be done first or last or you lose the Colonies. The longer you delay the more difficult it will be.[23]

Within the province the Parliament should seek ways to prevent the multitude of illegal assemblies and combinations that were fostered by the spirit of "absolute Democracy" which frequently prevailed in towns. They rendered the royal government impotent, since they "very often meet with the approbation of the body of the people and in such case there is no internal power which can be exerted to suppress them." As a remedy, Hutchinson proposed that those persons participating in

22. Hutchinson to Richard Jackson, Boston, Oct. 20, 1767, to Richard Jackson, Boston, July 14, 1768, Hutchinson Letter Books, Mass. Arch., XXV, 206–208, XXVI, 313–314.

23. Hutchinson to Lord Hillsborough, Boston, May 13, 1770, to Francis Bernard, Boston, Feb. 18, 1770, to Richard Jackson [?], Boston, Aug. 18, 1769, Hutchinson Letter Books, Mass. Arch., XXVI, 482, 442–444, 365–366. See also Hutchinson to Thomas Whately, Boston, Aug. 24, 1769, *ibid.*, 367–368.

such affairs be permanently disqualified from holding all offices by act of Parliament. Some strong, inclusive measure was needed since "every man in the Government being a Legislator in his town thinks it hard to be obliged to submit to Laws which he does not like." Unless this tendency was suppressed by a vigorous Parliament, "the government of this province will be split into innumerable divisions and every particular club or connexion will meet and vote and carry their votes into execution just as they please." [24]

After the ordeal of the Boston Massacre in 1770, Hutchinson's tone hardened. The fray had left five civilians dead of bullet wounds; it had brought ten British soldiers to stand trial for murder and manslaughter; and it had inflamed the province to a point where Hutchinson had been forced to withdraw the troops from Boston to Castle William in the harbor. Therefore Hutchinson believed that the seditious opposition must be totally suppressed. The combinations should not only be punished by a penal act, but by something stronger "which I dare not trust to a Letter." Moreover Boston must be isolated. The "faction" there had always been troublesome, but now Hutchinson believed it was intolerable and blocked the way for any reassertion of constitutional principles in the province. The furor surrounding the Massacre had both spread and strengthened the delusion, so that his friends "Williams of Hatfield [Hampshire County] and Ruggles [of Hardwick, Worcester County] tell me it spread to their Towns so remote and great part of their people would have been down to join Boston." Williams and Ruggles had even lost their influence at their town elections. At this point, several weeks after the Massacre, Hutchinson was convinced that only a large scale reformation of affairs in Massachusetts, enacted by Parliament and accompanied by the appointment of some great man as governor with broad powers, could provide a remedy. For his own part he was ready to resign, acknowledging that his capacity for further service was limited. [25]

But as the spring of 1770 wore on, his mood changed and his spirits

24. Hutchinson to Richard Jackson, Boston, Nov. 19, 1767, to Lord Hillsborough, Boston, Oct. 19, 1769, to John Pownall, Boston, Oct. 23, 1769, to Francis Bernard, Boston, Oct. 19, 1769, Hutchinson Letter Books, Mass. Arch., XXV, 226–227, XXVI, 391–392, 394, 391.

25. Hutchinson to Francis Bernard, Boston, April 19, 1770, Hutchinson Letter Books, Mass. Arch., XXVI, 473; also Hutchinson to Lord Hillsborough, Boston, June 26, 1770, to Francis Bernard, Boston, March 18, 1770, to John Pownall, Boston, March 21, 1770, to Francis Bernard, March 22, 1770, to Thomas Whately, Boston, April 30, 1770, ibid., XXVI, 473, 508, 456, 464, 459, XXV, 399–400.

lifted. Nonimportation, to him the most grievous of popular activities, disappeared as the merchants divided. The port of Boston began to resume its normal activities, and the remaining Townshend duty, that on tea, was collected by the customs officials. When the assembly met in April, Hutchinson reported that he "met with but little trouble." Recapturing the offensive, he decided that the new assembly should convene at Cambridge instead of Boston. He knew this would be "deemed a Grievance," but he had made up his mind that it was time to take a more rigid stand. He would adhere to his instructions strictly, for, he thought, "If I recede from my Instructions in one point, it will be like the Concessions made by Parliament, and cause them to be more restless until they have gained every other Point." [26]

To provide a means for the suppression of all "destructive" combinations, at least until Parliament acted, Hutchinson went on to initiate a regular correspondence with the governors of New York and Pennsylvania. As he explained to Governor John Penn, "A Correspondence kept up by the Servants of the Crown . . . may be made very useful," and he suggested that their correspondence be kept secret. Describing his innovation to Lord Hillsborough, he expressed the hope that the regular exchange of information would permit "every circumstance in either of the Governments favorable to the bringing to an end these most illegal and destructive combinations may be improved." Yet this attempt ended in frustration. Confiding in his old colleague Francis Bernard, he wrote the obituary for this governors' committee of correspondence:

> I wrote to Governor Penn and Lieutenant Governor Colden with a view to settle a Correspondence and convey reciprocally a more certain knowledge of facts and prevent the effects of the false representations . . . I send you Coldens Answer you see he excuses himself . . . I fancy Mr. Penn was not at home having received no answer from him.[27]

Nevertheless, in spite of his frustrations, he believed that politics were returning to the old equilibrium of the early 1760's. Hutchinson had not been able to prevent the summer session from adopting an

26. Hutchinson to Thomas Gage, Boston, April 29, 1770, Hutchinson Letter Books, Mass. Arch., XXV, 399. For a detailed analysis of Hutchinson's decision and the controversy it engendered see Donald C. Lord and Robert M. Calhoon, "The Removal of the Massachusetts General Court from Boston, 1769–1772," *Journal of American History*, LV (1969), 735–755.

27. Hutchinson to Gov. Penn, Boston, May 26, 1770, to Lord Hillsborough, Boston, May 27, 1770, to Francis Bernard, June 17, 1770, Hutchinson Letter Books, Mass. Arch., XXVI, 494, 495, 506.

address drawn by Samuel Adams which "breaths the seditious Spirit," but he had, he believed, made a successful rejoinder. He would have preferred not to argue, "but I found it absolutely necessary to remove the Prejudices which the Inhabitants were under . . . and it has certainly had a good Effect on many Towns." He had, he thought, begun to "undeceive the People." Nonimportation had crumbled and the trial of the Boston Massacre soldiers, which he had successfully delayed, ended quietly with only light penalties and several acquittals. The autumn session of the assembly gave the administration another victory when, as Hutchinson put it, "the real Interest of the Country struck the honest, which proved by far the major, Part of the House." Of the assembly he had so recently viewed as irrational, the governor now surmised: "They really only want a few good Conductors to keep them steady to the same Interest." Moreover the countryside was returning to sanity: "In almost every Town great part of the people say they have been deluded and abused." Boston and its leaders had, he thought, been tarnished by the Massacre affair. Miraculously, the isolation of Boston and peace in the province seemed to be occurring without the intervention of Parliament. Hutchinson began to look forward to the arrival of his official commission as governor.[28]

When the commission arrived in March 1771, his outlook was hopeful. His elevation to the governorship was popular. Yet Hutchinson was aware that the delusion still existed and that the dangers from it had not entirely passed. He believed "the Enemies of Government here who although every day decreasing yet are still very numerous." In an effort to enlighten them, he had earlier urged his friends in all parts of the province to fill the press with sound political writings. With his brother-in-law Peter Oliver he had even published his own paper, *The Censor,* for a year in Boston. But now, since "the people were opening their eyes," he thought it best "to be silent." "My ambition," he wrote, "is to be instrumental in quieting the minds of the people." Quiet in the province would conciliate Parliament to a mild rule which would reestablish the old amity between England and the colonies. If the province and Parliament could once begin to ascend this spiral ladder of harmony, the delusion of independence would waste itself, and Massa-

28. Hutchinson to Lord Hillsborough, Boston, Aug. 5, 1770, Hutchinson to Francis Bernard, Boston, Aug. 4, 1770, H. Y. Brown to Hutchinson, Portsmouth, Nov. 28, 1770, Hutchinson Letter Books, Mass. Arch., XXVI, 532, 530-531, XXV, 453-454. Hutchinson to Israel Williams, Dec. 10, 1770, Israel Williams Papers, II, 165, Massachusetts Historical Society.

chusetts politics might return to the familiar pattern he had known before the Stamp Act.[29]

Most of the inhabitants of Massachusetts shared the governor's aspiration to return to the stability and relative harmony of the years before 1765. Their ideal of a tranquil politics free of contention remained unchanged, but the popular resistance of the 1760's had shown that the administration idea of the terms on which harmony must rest — submission to Parliament — stood in direct opposition to the general view. Moreover the growing belief in the need for an active, interested public, participating in political determinations, at least when the constitution was threatened, had seriously undermined the traditional conception of a serene populace content to be directed by wise magistrates. At the same time recent events had given a special immediacy to the twin fears latent in the traditional political outlook, fears of untrustworthy rulers willing to betray the public interest for the sake of private gain and of a tumultuous, disobedient people led by a demagogic faction. For the time being, in 1771, the consequences of these developments were not obvious to contemporaries and no one knew the future direction of English policy. The administration had so far succeeded in riding out the storm of opposition and maintaining its authority at least on the surface. But whether the province would return to its old equilibrium with political disputes confined to politicians no one knew. After six years of activity it was also possible that local assertions of constitutional rights and an expanding political consciousness among the public might become a regular part of Massachusetts politics.

29. Boston Barristers to Hutchinson, Boston, March 21, 1771, Israel Williams to Hutchinson, Hatfield, March 28, 1771, Hutchinson Letter Books, Mass. Arch., XXV, 469, 473.

3

The Creation of the Boston
Committee of Correspondence

While Governor Hutchinson sought to promote the cause of constitutional government by quieting the province, the anxieties of the Boston Whigs mounted. They feared that if the governor achieved the order he was seeking, then the ruler's right to obedience would come to equal and surpass the popular right to justice. The constitution as they knew it would disappear, expiring with the rights of the people. As a result, they saw new hazards in this provincial administration policy, less obvious but no less dangerous than parliamentary taxation. Their responses to this, as they believed, new administration challenge led directly to the creation of the Boston Committee of Correspondence.

I

This challenge they saw had several sides. Most immediate, and most conventional, was the threat posed by the governor's admitted efforts to rally an administration party. His appointments, they believed, went only to faithful "friends of government," however ill-qualified.[1] Hutch-

1. "T.H.," *Boston Gazette*, July 27, 1772, 3:1; see also Thomas Hutchinson to Israel Williams, Jan. 1, 1772, Israel Williams Papers, II, 169, Massachusetts Historical Society. For a general examination of colonial disillusionment and gloom regarding imperial politics from 1768 to 1772, see Pauline R. Maier, "From Resistance to Revolution: American Radicals and the Development of Intercolonial Opposition to Britain, 1765–1776," Ph.D. diss., Harvard University, 1968, chs. 4, 5, 6.

inson himself privately admitted that "the Cause of Government . . . depends much upon the Servants of the Crown and the connexions they can form." He was not fond of such maneuvers, but he had found that "in this popular Constitution there is no making a party in favour of the Government in any other way [;] every branch of the Authority depend more or less upon the voice of the people." The governor recognized that he could not always appoint the best men since "the three professions Lawyers Physicians and Clergy [,] depending entirely on the people for their support [,] must comply with popular humours." Since Hutchinson felt he could entrust authority only to men who would not "comply with popular humours," these men alone were appointed both at the province and county levels.[2] Boston Whigs and their allies elsewhere in the province saw this policy as a self-conscious program of venality, invading every corner of Massachusetts. They feared that this "bought" party of administration "tools" might soon control the people and the province entirely.

The side effects of the army of "placemen and pensioners" were equally distressing to them. They feared that since these officials enjoyed the prestige of authority, their manners were setting a dangerous example for the people. Luxurious habits and licentious behavior seemed to emanate from Crown officials, corrupting the simple virtue of Massachusetts inhabitants. Boston Whigs feared for the spiritual and political health of the province. Vicious officeholders aroused contempt for their offices while they encouraged corrupt behavior.[3] Lowering the standards of both public and private morals, they loosened the discipline which maintained society and government, making the public vulnerable to all manner of evils.

None of these presumed threats had entirely originated with the new governor. During Governor Bernard's administration they had seen the same forces at work. Yet now they feared the effect would be greater, because of Hutchinson's popularity and his plausible tongue. Moreover the peace and quiet which had settled over the province was, they thought, giving Hutchinson and his accomplices an ideal climate for practising their seduction of public virtue. The people, lulled by the administration, seemed to them to be sinking into docile acquiescence in the invasion of their rights. Local concern for constitutional

2. Hutchinson to Lord Hillsborough, June 29, 1770, to Francis Bernard, Aug. 8, 1769, Thomas Hutchinson Letter Books, Massachusetts Archives, XXVI, 513, 362.
3. Israel Williams to Francis Bernard, Aug. 19, 1761, Israel Williams Papers, II, 119, Mass. Hist. Soc.

rights which had been so evident in 1766, had sharply declined in 1770. Surrounded by corruption, the people would soon recline in sloth, relaxing their grips on their rights; and then they would be helpless to defend themselves.

The governor and his friends believed all these ideas were nonsense, merely the demagogic fantasies of politicians out of office. Certainly, the governor believed, the people, returning as they were to good order, could not take these apprehensions seriously. Yet for the opposition, though their rhetoric was doubtless inflated for effect, these fears were evidently genuine, enmeshed as they were in their larger view of politics and society. At the same time it is certainly true that Whigs in Boston and elsewhere would have been far less anxious had they controlled administration in Massachusetts. But then from their viewpoint, this would have made the threat much less immediate; Massachusetts would then have been protected from English designs by its provincial administration in much the same way as Rhode Island and Connecticut.

Corruption and the movement for quiet excited their fears because they directly threatened the people's discipline, the only ultimate bulwark of liberty. Liberty, as they knew it, was not a powerful, irresistible force which could defend itself. Rather, they described it as a fragile virgin goddess, infinitely pure, infinitely sweet, but essentially passive and defenseless. Liberty could inspire her devotees to come to her aid, but that was the best she could manage. Her adversary, unlimited power, was in their view identical with tyranny. Power was masculine, aggressive, insatiable, and possessed the satanic capacity to exploit human depravity in its own behalf. History showed that man, in most times and most places had been made a slave of power by his own vices. The condition was universal: "all government tends to despotism, and like the human frame brings at its birth the latent seed which finally shall destroy the constitution."[4]

History taught them that only a handful of societies had been able for a time to enjoy liberty. These few, all essentially republics, included Athens, the Roman Republic, the Swiss Confederacy, the Dutch Republic, Sweden, pre-Norman England, and modern England after 1688. Their strength in every case rested on the patriotic virtue of their citizens. Past experience proved that public virtue, aroused and vigorous, was liberty's only defense against the ravening strides of power, and

---

4. Joseph Warren as "Hyperion," *Boston Gazette*, Sept. 28, 1767, 1:1-2. This general outlook is explored in Bernard Bailyn, *The Ideological Origins of the American Revolution* (Cambridge, Mass., 1967), ch. 3.

that the successful defense of liberty must be a continual process. Athens and Rome had relaxed, luxuriating in their wealth, and the public stamina of their citizenry had been destroyed. It had happened in Sweden, and was happening now in the Netherlands and England. Samuel Adams, Joseph Warren, and their friends believed it was even happening in Massachusetts.

They knew that the approaches which power made on liberty could be various. Direct assaults on property rights like the Stamp Act, or an attempt to awe the people into submission with a standing army, were only the most obvious means of gaining a foothold to annihilate liberty. Other alterations in government, less conspicuous because their immediate threat was less evident, might, they thought, be just as dangerous. No "illegal attempt" was "inconsiderable"; because "a smaller will ever pave the way to a greater, and that to a greater still."[5] Like a rising flood, tyranny could catch a people unawares and drown them before they could resist.[6] Historically, this had been repeated over and over: "it is not usual for a free People to lose all their Liberties at once. Liberty once Lost, how *hardly, hardly,* REGAINED."[7]

Silence in the face of this threat was criminal. To assert one's rights, they were convinced, was an important way to defend them. To keep "a timid and dastardly *silence*" was to "consent to our own slavery."[8] Yet the governor and his friends continually urged that Massachusetts only seek continuation of its privileges and keep silent on the question of rights, counseling towns and the assembly to put their trust in authority and not to agitate themselves or Britain with constitutional discussion. Whigs believed such a course meant tacit acknowledgment of the violability of all colonial rights. In their view, the duty of every town, of every man, was to assert their rights. This was the minimum defense which conscience could allow.

II

Before Governor Hutchinson entered office, many believed that the people had been generally successful in defending their rights. The Stamp Act had been repealed, the standing army withdrawn from the

5. Anonymous article, *Boston Gazette*, Sept. 23, 1765, 2:1–2, letter from New London, Conn.
6. Jonathan Mayhew, *A Discourse Concerning Unlimited Submission to the Higher Powers* (Boston, 1750), ii.
7. Anonymous article, *Boston Gazette*, Sept. 23, 1765, 2:1–2, letter from New London, Conn.
8. "Fervidus," *Boston Gazette*, March 16, 1772, 2:2–3.

metropolis, and of the Townshend duties, only one remained in force. But now Boston Whigs feared that the ministry's flanking assault on public virtue, led by the distinguished, reputedly virtuous governor, was disarming the people. In their view Parliament's seeming retreat was a maneuver, like the peace and order which the administration offered so as to make towns and individuals careless.[9] They worried because people failed to notice, and failed to take alarm at what seemed to be the entering wedge of despotism. Every day they saw the Hutchinson party grow stronger, while each collection of the duty on tea was confirming Parliament's unlimited power over the province.

The Boston Whigs saw this as a devious, unrelenting attack, the classic approach of power toward its fragile prey. To counter it, they would have to develop the fundamental defense of liberty, an aroused, informed public jealous of its rights.[10] The people had already risen to magnificent heights in 1765, when their jealous ardor had swept away complacency with dozens of towns speaking out in liberty's defense.[11] Surely the province could regain this virtuous spirit, despite Hutchinson's blandishments. Yet now they saw the problem was more difficult, since the people were not threatened with an innovation so gross as the Stamp Act. For the people to resist, they would have to be keener, more sensitive, better educated, and better informed.

Ignorance meant slavery. The Boston Whigs knew that Massachusetts owed its freedom, such as it was, entirely to the remarkable diffusion of learning in the province. The common schools, a prime legacy of their forbears, had given the province a population which could, they thought, be led by reason, not merely coerced by force.[12] But the schools did not provide education in government or popular rights to either children or adult freeholders. Only the press, kept free by their own untiring defense, could communicate with the people, keeping them informed of public affairs. By these means they had been nourishing the spirit of liberty. Nevertheless it seemed to weaken.

A free clergy, they knew, free of bishops, could also inform and

9. Thomas Cushing to Roger Sherman, Jan. 21, 1772, Massachusetts Historical Society, *Collections*, 4th Ser., IV (1858), 358–359.

10. Anonymous article from the New York press, *Boston Gazette*, Aug. 24, 1767, 2:2–3.

11. John Adams as "Clarendon," *Boston Gazette*, Jan. 20, 1766, 2:2.

12. See John Adams, "A Dissertation on the Canon and Feudal Law," *The Works of John Adams, Second President of the United States*, ed. Charles Francis Adams (Boston, 1850–1856), III, 445–464, especially 448–449; published originally in the *Boston Gazette* in Aug. 1765. Also Andrew Eliot to Thomas Hollis, Jan. 29, 1769, Mass. Hist. Soc., *Collections*, 4th Ser., IV, 436; Worcester Instructions of May 1767, *Boston Gazette*, June 1, 1767, 2:2.

instruct the people in their public duty. Yet the clergy, they felt, were also relaxing.[13] Only a handful preached on public affairs. Furthermore clerics usually regarded public afflictions as only the just retribution for a declining morality, and so counseled their congregations to look inward to their own hearts, not outward to the conduct of the administration. According to Samuel Adams, they too needed to be aroused and informed.

Boston leaders knew that the assembly had long been a prestigious and effective institution for public instruction. It alone could reach people all over the province with certainty. Representatives came from many towns and every county, and returned to their communities with newspaper copies of public discussion between the governor, the Council, and the House. Yet these addresses were not systematically presented to the towns, and the information and instruction which representatives could provide was irregular, haphazard, and informal. Moreover meetings of the assembly were only semiannual, and were convened at the governor's pleasure. Events of the 1760's had shown the Boston Whigs that the assembly was less effective than the press in arousing and informing the countryside.

Yet even though they overflowed the weekly press with the Radical Whig message, it was not enough. Their patriotic festivals, and the galleries which they voted to erect in the House of Representatives, "so Noble a School of Political Learning," might encourage the "spirit of virtue" in Boston and its immediate environs, but they were much more symbols of opposition aspirations than they were organs of political instruction.[14] What was needed, they came to believe, was a recognized, systematic method to make sure that every town, and every person in every town was thoroughly acquainted with their rights and the essential features of the constitution. Then if they were properly informed, their duty to maintain and assert their rights would always be self-evident. The ardor of 1765 would rekindle itself. This, at least, was the hope of Boston Whigs.

One further way they found to inculcate political knowledge was through permanent series of orations. Boston, using the anniversary of the Massacre as the occasion, originated the annual town lecture in

13. Samuel Adams to Elbridge Gerry, Nov. 14, 1772, *The Writings of Samuel Adams*, ed. Harry A. Cushing (New York, 1904–1908), II, 348–350.

14. John Adams, diary entry, Aug. 14, 1769, *Diary and Autobiography of John Adams*, ed. Lyman H. Butterfield (Cambridge, Mass., 1961), I, 341; Thomas Young to John Wendell, Nov. 23, 1766, Miscellaneous Photostats, Massachusetts Historical Society. *Boston Gazette*, June 16, 1766, 4:2.

1771. This public performance used the official forum of the town meeting as an instructional vehicle. There orators, always reasoning from first principles, led their listeners out of the state of nature into the voluntary compact of civil society, explaining again and again that society was formed for the defense of basic rights. They repeatedly described the virtuous patriot and self-consciously tried to exemplify his character, pointing with alarm to the standard ways in which tyranny conquered or seduced a free people. These orations, printed and sold in pamphlet form, reached a wide audience.

The technique seemed promising. In March 1772 Braintree adopted Boston's example, voting "To have an oration or lecture in some branch of Government, delivered on the morning of next May meeting day, by some person of a liberal education." [15] It reasoned that the morning prior to the election of the representative would be the most appropriate and useful time for such a lecture, enlivening voters to their public responsibility. Perhaps Braintree would once more set a pattern; it was hoped "that a like public spirited means of preserving a just sense of our invaluable rights and privileges be adopted in every town thro' out the province." [16]

But the only means used to spread the idea was the press. One writer urged that all patriots everywhere use their influence to establish "stated political Lectures, not only in every County, but in every Town and Parish." [17] Yet the idea did not catch on. No voices were raised against it, but towns, concerned as they were in immediate local matters, did not respond. Some recognized the need for political enlightenment and "Answers to all the Doubts arising in our minds," [18] but they lacked a suitable orator. In any case an occasional example like Braintree's, like a casual invitation in the press, was easily ignored. Thomas Cushing, a leader in Boston as well as of the House, saw so little prospect of thoroughly educating or permanently awakening the people, that he thought it would be vain "to place any great dependence upon the virtue of the people in general." He would rely on the assemblies of all the colonies instead.[19]

Yet his associate, Samuel Adams, was not so easily discouraged.

15. Reported in *Boston Weekly News-Letter*, March 19, 1772, 4:1, request that John Adams give the first annual lecture.
16. Editors speaking in *Boston Weekly News-Letter*, March 19, 1772, 4:1.
17. "Fervidus," *Boston Gazette*, May 18, 1772, 1:3.
18. "Vulcan," Petersham, in *Boston Gazette*, March 30, 1772, 1:2.
19. Thomas Cushing to Roger Sherman, Jan. 21, 1772, Mass. Hist. Soc., *Collections*, 4th Ser., IV, 358–359.

Turning the problem over in his mind, discussing it among experienced friends, Adams tried to find a solution that would save not only Massachusetts, but all of Great Britain. Writing to Arthur Lee, author of Junius Americanus' celebrated letters, Adams speculated on a possible remedy:

The Grievances of Britain & the Colonies as you observe spring from the same root of Bitterness & are of the same pernicious growth. The Union of Britain & the Colonies is therefore by all means to be cultivated. If in every Colony Societies should be formed out of the most respectable Inhabitants, similar to that of the Bill of Rights, who should once in the year meet by their Deputies, and correspond with such a Society in London, would it not effectually promote such an Union? And if conducted with a proper spirit would it not afford reason for the Enemies of our common Liberty, however great, to tremble. This is a sudden Thought & drops undigested from my pen. It would be an arduous Task for any man to attempt to awaken a sufficient Number in the Colonies to so grand an Undertaking. Nothing however should be despaired of.[20]

Corresponding societies could furnish an extensive and perhaps potent bulwark of liberty. This conception, however "sudden" and "undigested" it might be for Adams, was neither unique nor original. In fact, among the Anglo-American Whig opposition, this kind of self-constituted society, voluntarily associated to exert influence in a political cause, was a recurrent idea.[21] New York dissenters had used the press to initiate such a series of corresponding societies in 1769. They had formed committees wherever dissenters lived and planned to correspond with a standing committee of dissenters in England, which would help them promote informed, united opposition to the establishment of bishops in America. They planned that each society would have its own standing committee of correspondence. The New York committee began the program by writing to influential persons and encouraging the creation of societies elsewhere.[22] Yet the plan foundered for the reasons antici-

20. Samuel Adams to Arthur Lee, Sept. 27, 1771, *Writings of Samuel Adams*, II, 234.

21. See Carl Bridenbaugh, *Mitre and Sceptre: Transatlantic Faiths, Ideas, Personalities, and Politics, 1689–1775* (New York, 1962). Bridenbaugh describes the origins of the mechanism of committees of correspondence. He discusses the English Dissenters' committees of correspondence dating from the 1730's, as well as the colonial congregational and presbyterian clerics' committees of the 1750's and 1760's. Bridenbaugh believes Samuel Adams consciously borrowed this committee idea, concluding that "the colonial opposition to royal authority . . . took the tried-and-proved ecclesiastical organization of the Nonconformist churches and adapted it to secular affairs with great though hardly surprising success" (pp. 203–204).

22. *New York Gazette and Weekly Mercury*, July 24, 1769, 1:1–3. Society in-

pated by Adams respecting his own scheme: it was too arduous a task, and the intensity of the New York dissenters' interest, struggling as they were with a local Episcopal party, was not matched elsewhere.

Adams and Thomas Young, an Albany physician and son of liberty who had settled in Boston in 1766, together with others in Massachusetts, were in communication with New York dissenters, and undoubtedly witnessed both the rise and fall of this particular scheme. Yet they were not ready to discard the idea. Instead they remodeled it, narrowing its geographic focus, adapting it to their own special needs, and shaping it to accommodate Massachusetts' particular conditions. From their own experience, as well as that in New York, they recognized that the press was not the suitable vehicle to launch such a scheme; it spoke to everyone in general and no one in particular, and therefore could not be relied on to reach the right people in the appropriate manner. Moreover they had learned that it was equally futile to count on many scattered individuals to seize an initiative and assume responsibility for organizing and establishing such societies. The task was too arduous and time-consuming for all but the most zealous. Finally, they believed the Empire was far too large for such an enterprise, unless, in some distant future, political conditions should be radically altered.

Massachusetts, however, was not too large. The organization of societies which Adams and the New York dissenters had envisioned, could be erected within the province, and could furnish the apparatus for education and information which they had long been seeking. But in place of private societies, somehow "formed out of the most respectable Inhabitants," town meetings would establish public committees of correspondence composed of the most respectable inhabitants. Under the proper circumstances, these committees could effectively transform periodic town meetings into a "Society for the Bill of Rights" where many inhabitants perforce, as a matter of duty, would be instructed in political principles and their specific application. The existing institutional structure of local government could easily carry the load of organization, making the immense project of creating a separate structure unnecessary. The means of uniting all the "societies," all the towns, in an annual general meeting already existed in the General Court. Moreover when the assembly was not sitting, or when the governor

cluded Alexander McDougall and William and Peter Livingston among others. Reference courtesy of Professor Richard Buel, Jr., Wesleyan University, Middletown, Conn.

refused to call it into session as he had in September 1768, then the committees of correspondence would furnish an independent means of mobilizing the province.

The possibilities for such a plan were much greater than Adams' first conception of societies of the Bill of Rights. Potentially every town, even the smallest, could be included, and the activities of the committees of correspondence, unlike the Society for the Bill of Rights, would have the recognized public stature of official town committees. They would speak to and for the whole community, not merely a collection of private individuals, however respectable. This would have important consequences outside the province as well as within it, since the professions of the committees would have to be recognized in England as public declarations. Adams was sure they would give the lie to the idea which he believed the governor promoted, that the people acquiesced in submission to Parliament. Moreover they would involve every inhabitant in each community. The "most respectable inhabitants," instead of acting by themselves and enlightening themselves only, would communicate with the rest of the town, providing instruction and leadership under the auspices of town authority. Capable of meeting whenever the need arose, they would be "on call," ready to address themselves to particular political issues as it was necessary. Meanwhile the continuing process of education would go on.

As a result every one would recognize the necessity of untiring watchfulness. Every town would be able to perceive and resist constitutional affronts as Boston already did. All would "vie with one another in love to our country, and in all virtue, and do our utmost, in our proper stations." [23] This spirit would frustrate the insidious designs of ministerial tools wherever they appeared. The existing encroachments would be wiped away by the power of a unified refusal to tolerate their continued existence. This was the ideal.

It was an ambitious, far-reaching plan. Committees of correspondence, long used by colonial assemblies for communication with their agents and among each other, had also been regularly used by merchant groups and other private associations; but they had never been used in the manner that Adams and Young planned. Recognizing the utility of an old, conventional name, "committee of correspondence," they fitted it to their new purpose. Young exulted in the scheme: "we are brewing something here which will make some people's heads reel at a

23. "Fervidus," *Boston Gazette*, March 16, 1772, 2:2–3.

47

very moderate age." Yet they felt the consequences of the plan must still be thoroughly examined, and the means for instituting it carefully considered. "Ripeness for great enterprizes," Young observed, "advances slowly; but perhaps that is the best fruit which requires time to attain its perfection."[24] Their project was not aimed at the immediate future, nor did they anticipate rapid success.

Indeed their immediate expectations regarding the plan were by no means definite. In letters written in the autumn of 1772, Samuel Adams seldom hinted that the committee plan was anything more than an effort to obtain a general expression of protest against Crown stipends for judges of the Superior Court of Massachusetts. Unlike Young, Adams made no boasts about making "heads reel." Instead he characteristically forestalled the risk of publicly appearing to falter in a major project by not giving out that it was anything more than an ad hoc maneuver against the stipends. That more was at stake is apparent from his earlier correspondence and his reported conversations with other Whig leaders.[25] Since Adams and his associates were always careful to maintain maneuvering space and the capability of "improving" opportunities as they arose, they most likely expected the committees of correspondence to reach their fruition by stages, understanding that the rest of the plan might have to be shelved if the situation required.

III

In the minds of its creators, the Boston Committee of Correspondence was never intended to function in isolation. Only as part of a province-wide collection of committees could it begin to perform its services. Conceived as a means to unify the province in sentiments of active alarm, the whole scheme would fail if Boston was separated from the other Massachusetts towns. No matter how brilliant their potential, committees of correspondence would arrive still-born if their inception

24. Thomas Young to Hugh Hughes, Aug. 31, 1772, Miscellaneous Bound Documents, 1765–1775, Massachusetts Historical Society.

25. William Gordon, History of the Rise, Progress, and Establishment, of the Independence of the United States of America (London, 1788), I, 312–314, claims that James Warren of Plymouth originated the idea of committees of correspondence and first suggested it to Samuel Adams. That this was not the case is evident in light of the prior correspondence of Adams and Young. A conversation with Warren on the subject is certainly plausible, and if Gordon is correct as to the substance then it is apparent that a large project was in view.

was improperly timed, or if no justification for their introduction was apparent. Moreover any hurried misstep in promoting the project might furnish the governor's allies with a means to end it.

For these reasons, the idea for committees of correspondence was permitted to ripen gradually, while the appropriate time to begin was carefully awaited. Boston, with its aggressive reputation, must not be the aggressor. The proceedings should be conspicuous for their order and regularity. Any innovation should be well within the structure of political convention, and emerge only as a last resort. Most important, Boston must act on the defensive, since that was the only posture congruent with the ideal of a virtuous citizenry protecting liberty from the strides of power.

In September 1772 an aggressive ministerial stride became apparent. Reliable information from English sources disclosed that the judges of Massachusetts' Superior Court of Judicature, traditionally paid by annual assembly grants, would henceforth be paid by the Crown. Their stipends, it was reported, would be paid out of the American customs revenue.[26] From the English viewpoint this long-needed reform would free the judges from popular influence, rendering them "independent," as were judges in England. Governors and ex-governors of the province had recommended this alteration for years, believing it would prevent harsh treatment of officers of government and end judicial leniency to popular offenders. Stipends for the judges were only part of the reform, for it was believed that the entire civil list should be extended to the colonies, so as to make all officials both fully independent of the people and their assemblies, and fully responsive to Westminster.

Opposition to this civil list reform had been expressed long before the autumn of 1772 by both Whig politicians and friends of the administration in other colonies as well as Massachusetts. Whigs feared that Crown salaries would encourage the appointment of corrupt officials, who "being hackneyed in the paths of deceit and avarice, will be fit tools to enslave & oppress our honest people."[27] More important from a constitutional standpoint, they believed that extension of the civil list would make officials independent of the people over whom they

26. *Boston Gazette*, Sept. 28, 1772, 2:1–2. For an excellent brief discussion of the issue of judicial tenure in the colonies see, Bernard Bailyn, *Pamphlets of the American Revolution* (Cambridge, Mass., 1965———), I, 249–255.

27. Andrew Eliot to Thomas Hollis, Dec. 10, 1767, Mass. Hist. Soc., *Collections*, 4th Ser., IV, 420.

ruled. Such an independence was reminiscent of Stuart tyranny, and could not be explained away as merely "expedient."[28] Even Israel Williams, a particular friend of Governor Hutchinson in Hampshire County saw a threat in the civil list.[29] Richard Jackson, an English ally of the governor and former agent for the province, though he now supported the plan in 1772, had earlier said, "I cannot persuade myself that Governors ought to be independent of the People," even after the Stamp Act disturbances.[30] Discussion of the question had always been sporadic, since the project for establishing stipends had only appeared irregularly. Various ministries had been friendly to the plan, but none had been willing to adopt it unless the American revenue was "found sufficient to defray the salaries."[31] Late in 1771, however, the ministry decided to adopt the program for Massachusetts. They began with the governor's salary.

Intimations of the policy had been circulating for some time before immediate opposition arose within the province.[32] It began in Boston when the town instructed its representatives to oppose the measure. Later the House of Representatives, after first ascertaining the fact directly from Governor Hutchinson, went on to condemn it in a full report. The House argued that a Crown salary to Massachusetts' governor ran contrary to the charter and traditional practice by making him independent of both the people and their assembly. In addition a salary independent of the assembly would remove their check upon the governor, destroying "the balance of power which is essential to all free governments." The House urged the governor to refuse the royal grant, so that they could provide him with his normal provision. They were insulted by the suggestion implied by the stipend, that they would not continue to provide adequately for their executive as they always had in the past. Aiming their thrust indirectly at Hutchinson, they concluded that "The advice, therefore, given to his Majesty, to take upon himself the payment of his Governor, must have been grounded on

28. Samuel Cooper to Benjamin Franklin, July 10, 1771, *Works of Benjamin Franklin*, ed. John Bigelow, Federal ed. (New York, 1904), V, 253–254.

29. Israel Williams to Thomas Hutchinson, May 3, 1769, Hutchinson Letter Books, Mass. Arch., XXV, 308.

30. Richard Jackson to Thomas Hutchinson, July 15, 1767, and Nov. 18, 1766, Hutchinson Letter Books, Mass. Arch., XXV, 187, 105–106.

31. Benjamin Franklin to Thomas Cushing, Feb. 5, 1771, *Works of Benjamin Franklin*, V, 228.

32. *Ibid.*

false information, or proceeded from a temper inimical to the good people of this province." [33]

Nevertheless the governor replied that he would accept the Crown salary since it was the wish of his Majesty. Notwithstanding the House's "unfortunate" arguments to the contrary, Hutchinson said that the charter did not limit the King's power to pay his officials, and the representatives had misunderstood the nature of constitutional checks. The people and their representatives were never intended to check every branch, he said, each branch mutually checked the others by the requirement of concurrence by all in every legislative act. He admonished them: "No state of government is perfect; if we have all that perfection which the state we are in [that is, colonial] will admit of, we have no reason to complain." They could rely on the King who was always tender toward his subjects' rights. [34]

The House vote against the governor's stipend and in favor of their own "report and resolves" had been a one-sided 85 to 19. [35] Seeking to discredit his opposition, Hutchinson assured the world that the House "have not done it from sinister views and purposes, but that they have been induced to form an erroneous opinion of the rights and powers of the several branches of this Legislative. I wish that this may palliate what it is not in my power to justify or excuse." [36] But his opposition remained obstinate in its error. Carrying the argument into the press, they asserted "an INDEPENDENT *ruler*, [is] a MONSTER *in a free state*." [37] Yet as the weeks of July and August 1772 went by, their attack became diffuse, striking at a variety of the governor's offenses, and gradually subsiding. [38]

Meanwhile members of the Boston opposition developed the committee of correspondence plan from Samuel Adams' embryo. They anticipated that an extension of the civil list to the judges of the Superior Court would soon be public news, since there had already been scat-

33. Alden Bradford, ed., *Speeches of the Governors of Massachusetts, 1765–1775* (Boston, 1818), 324–329; also Samuel Cooper to Benjamin Franklin, July 10, 1771, *Works of Benjamin Franklin*, V, 253–254.
34. Bradford, *Speeches of the Governors*, 331–335, delivered on July 14, 1772.
35. *Boston Gazette*, July 6, 1772, 3:2.
36. Thomas Hutchinson, delivered on July 14, 1772, in Bradford, *Speeches of the Governors*, 336.
37. John Adams as "Marchmont Nedham," *Boston Gazette*, July 6, 1772, 2:1–3.
38. See *Boston Gazette*, "An Elector," July 27, 1772; anonymous, Aug. 24, 1772; "Marchmont Nedham," June 29, 1772, and July 6, 1772.

tered hints from England.[39] This they expected, would "inevitably bring matters to a crisis." Even "Gentlemen who have currently passed for friends of what is called government declare this step intolerable, and will freely vote the government dissolved when this is ascertained." This offense against the constitution would be far more provocative than the governor's stipend, since it was at least logical that the King's servant be paid by the King. The governor's dependence on the ministry was already overt, and had always been regarded as natural if undesirable. But the judges of the Superior Court were another matter entirely. For it was an established constitutional principle, defined in England by the Act of Settlement of 1701, that judges should be independent of Crown influence; and in England this was guaranteed by judicial tenure "during good behavior," even though judges were paid by the Crown. In the colonies, however, judges were removable at the "pleasure" of the administration and so it was believed that the constitutional principle of judicial independence was already compromised. In Massachusetts judicial partiality was held in balance by the fact that the legislature paid the salaries of the judges. Therefore if this counterbalance was removed and judges were not only hired and fired but also paid by the Crown, it was expected that the judges would then become utterly dependent on the ministry, and their impartiality would necessarily be totally destroyed. The Boston Whigs thought that, in view of earlier ministerial steps, no one would now be able to doubt "whether the design to enslave us was really fixed." [40]

Earlier efforts to oppose constitutional infringements had failed "for want of a maturated plan." The disorders in Boston had provided the administration with an effective rejoinder to their opposition. But now a "slow and steady manner . . . has stopt the mouths of every bellower against mobing, pulling down houses &c." Moreover the committee of correspondence plan would enable the opposition to resist the encroachments of the administration within "a regular mode of procedure, which with the greatest safety, should promise a full accomplishment of the desired end." With this plan, and the provocation of the judges' salaries, Adams and his associates believed their time had come.[41]

Late in September 1772 a specific report appeared in the Boston press announcing salaries of £400 for the chief justice, £200 for his

39. *Boston Gazette*, June 15, 1772, 3:2.
40. Thomas Young to Hugh Hughes, Boston, Aug. 31, 1772, Miscellaneous Bound Documents, 1765–1775, Mass. Hist. Soc.
41. *Ibid.*

associates, and £150 each for the attorney general and solicitor general of the province.[42] It had been preceded by and was accompanied with a cluster of impassioned attacks on the program in the newspapers. "Americus" rhetorically asked what could be more alarming and humiliating than having the judges, "upon whose decisions depend our lives, our property, and every thing dear and sacred, holding their places at the will of the creature of a favorite, and supported at his discretion, out of monies extorted from the people!" That the present judges were personally virtuous was no consolation: "considering the frailty of human nature, are we to expect they will continue so?" And if miraculously they should remain honest and impartial, then they would surely be removed in favor of "base and mercenary wretches."[43] "Oliver Cromwell" explained that "the independency of our judges has at length compleated the tragedy. Yes, I repeat it, THE INDEPENDENCY OF OUR JUDGES IS THE FINISHING STROKE, and we are as compleat slaves as the inhabitants of Turkey or Japan."[44] When, in mid-October, the Boston Whigs began to circulate a petition for a town meeting on the subject, the petition expressing like sentiments, the governor regarded the whole opposition to judges' salaries as simply another attempt "to promote discontent," another "great clamour."[45]

Judging from previous experience, Hutchinson had every reason to believe this was merely one more effort to encourage resistance to the administration. But for Samuel Adams and his associates it was much more. This "clamour" would open the way for committees of correspondence which could not only resist judges' salaries, but could also demonstrate to the world that the whole province was united with Boston — that Boston was not an isolated town dominated by a dying faction of seditious conspirators. Perhaps the united voice of the province would persuade the judges to "show an Example of public Virtue, in refusing to accept of such Stipends."[46] More important, every town and every person would be educated in the correct principles of a free government and instructed in the immediate relevance of these principles to Massachusetts' immediate situation. "A people as ignorant as the inhabitants of Negro land" would inevitably be vulnerable to the

42. *Boston Gazette*, Sept. 28, 1772, 2:1–2.
43. "Americus," *Boston Gazette*, Aug. 31, 1772, 3:1.
44. *Boston Gazette*, Oct. 19, 1772, 1:2–3.
45. Hutchinson to Lord Dartmouth, Oct. 23, 1772, to Francis Bernard, Oct. 21, 1772, Hutchinson Letter Books, Mass. Arch., XXVII, 397–398, 396.
46. Boston petition of Oct. 14, 1772, in *Boston Gazette*, Oct. 26, 1772, 2:3.

same "external insults or internal abuses and usurpations." But by means of the committees of correspondence, Young hopefully declared, there need be no ignorance and no enemies at all within the province; "we can reduce them to reason, and make them our friends."[47]

The tactics of the Boston Whigs followed exactly the pattern that they had used so effectively in 1768 for the convention of towns. The town of Boston requested information of the governor as it had in 1768 with respect to the troops. Then it asked him to call the assembly into session to deal with the threat. On his refusal, Boston took a further step: in 1768 a circular inviting towns to a convention, now, in 1772, a circular inviting committees of correspondence. The strategy was intended to demonstrate Boston's desire to meet the threat by conventional constitutional means. The governor's refusal to allow such a conventional defense laid any blame on him, and justified Boston's last expedient.[48]

This sequence of events started on October 14 when the petition calling for a town meeting began to circulate. Faced with reports of

47. Thomas Young to Hugh Hughes, Dec. 21, 1772, Miscellaneous Bound Documents, 1765–1775, Mass. Hist. Soc.

48. William Gordon, a contemporary observer of Boston politics, offered the following general description of the management of town politics by Samuel Adams and his associates in his *History*, I, 312–314:

"The prime managers were about six in number; each of whom when separate, headed a division; the several individuals of which, collected and led distinct subdivisions. In this manner the political engine has been constructed: The different parts are not equally good and operative. Like other bodies, its composition includes numbers who act mechanically, as they are pressed this or that way by those who judge for them; and divers of the wicked, fitted for evil practices when the adoption of them is thought necessary to particular purposes, and a part of whose creed it is, that in political matters the public good is above every other consideration, and that all rules of morality when in competition with it, may be safely dispensed with. When any important transaction is to be brought forward, it is thoroughly considered by the prime managers. If they approve, each communicates it to his own division; from thence, if adopted, it passes to the several subdivisions, which form a general meeting in order to canvass the business. The prime managers being known only by few to be the promoters of it, are desired to be present at the debate, that they may give their opinion when it closes. If they observe, that the collected body is in general strongly against the measure they wish to have carried, they declare it to be improper: is it opposed by great numbers, but not warmly, they advise a re-consideration at another meeting, and prepare for its being then adopted; if the opposition is not considerable, either in number or weight of persons, they give their reasons, and then recommend the adoption of the measure."

Whether it was quite so systematic and whether these techniques were employed in managing the committee of correspondence plan cannot now be determined. Gordon's description does, however, suggest the responsive interaction between Boston leaders and the public, and the mixture of planning and spontaneity which went into Boston politics. It appears that in an essentially unstructured situation, Adams and the others achieved their power largely by providing structure.

judges' stipends, it declared that the people should speak their minds, since no "free people" could tolerate such a "judiciary constitution." This establishment would complete "the Ruin of our Liberties." [49] Within a week the petition was offered to the selectmen who consented to a meeting and issued warrants for October 28.[50] When the town convened three active Whigs, Samuel Adams, Joseph Warren, and Benjamin Church, were chosen to draw up an address to the governor inquiring about the truth of the alarming reports. Unanimously the town asked if Hutchinson had "received any such advise . . . which gives you an assurance that such an Establishment has been or is likely to be made." The Whiggish merchant William Phillips, James Otis, and two selectmen, Timothy Newell and Thomas Marshall, were elected to join Adams, Warren, and Church in presenting the openly Whig address to his Excellency.[51]

Hutchinson, affronted by their rhetoric of "fatal evils" and approaching slavery, replied cooly that his correspondence was not a matter for town scrutiny: "This reason alone if your Address to me had been in other respects unexceptionable, would have been sufficient to restrain me from complying with your desire." [52] Hutchinson could not permit Boston's effrontery to go unrebuked. He reckoned that to let it pass would be to condone it. At the same time he did not wish to dignify their attempts by any serious, reasoned rebuttal, since it would only call attention to the turmoil. So his response was restrained to an essential minimum.

But after his answer was read to the meeting on Friday the 30th, the town was ready to petition the governor "to permit the General Assembly to meet at the time to which they stand prorogued," with or without confirmation of the judges' stipends. Otis, Adams, and Thomas Cushing prepared the petition, which after explaining the necessity of judicial impartiality and the historic manner in which England had finally secured it, went on to "request that your Excellency would be pleased to allow the General Assembly to meet . . .; in order that in that *Constitutional Body*, with whom it is to enquire into Grievances and Redress them, the Joint Wisdom of the Province may be employed."

49. Boston petition, *Boston Gazette*, Oct. 26, 1772, 2:3.
50. Thomas Hutchinson to Francis Bernard, Oct. 21, 1772, Hutchinson Letter Books, Mass. Arch., XXVII, 396, says that the Boston selectmen were divided but that the "friends to order" yielded.
51. *Boston Town Records, 1770–1777*, Boston Record Commissioners, *Report*, XVIII (Boston, 1887), 88–90. John Hancock was moderator.
52. *Boston Town Records, 1770–1777*, p. 90.

The same committee which had presented the previous address would present the petition the next day, Saturday. On Monday, November 2, the town would reconvene.[53]

Since the governor was jealous of his prerogatives, with reason, Adams and the Boston Whigs anticipated his negative reply.[54] The governor's right to convene and prorogue assemblies was explicit in the charter. Yet until they had tried all of the old avenues they could not suggest an innovation. Their critics would attack the propriety of their innovation, making that the issue, and frightening cautious minds away from the central question of resistance to unconstitutional encroachments. Samuel Adams believed Boston had to be "so reasonable," that the governor's inflexibility and "high tone" would put him *"in the wrong,"* thereby making the further measure of committees of correspondence "reconcileable even to cautious minds, & thus we may expect that unanimity we wish for."[55]

Governor Hutchinson did not disappoint his Boston opponents. His reply to the petition was to rebuke the town meeting. He pointed out that the charter empowered him to adjourn, prorogue, and dissolve assemblies, and "The Reasons which you [Boston] have advanced have not altered my Opinion" as to when it should meet. Hutchinson argued that he would be violating the royal trust if he were to accede to Boston's wishes: "There would moreover be danger of encouraging the Inhabitants of the other Towns in the Province to Assemble from time to time in order to consider of the necessity or expediency of a Session of the General Assembly or to debate & transact other matters which the Law that authorizes Towns to Assemble, does not make the business of a Town Meeting."[56] Not content with a mere negative, the governor was anxious to point out the limited competence of town meetings. On this point he was adamant, since in his view promiscuous town meetings were a regular fountain of disobedience to the administration.[57] Whigs found his attitude reminiscent of Tudor and Stuart tyranny. His declaration that some matters were beyond town scrutiny sounded like James I's insistence that the prerogative was not a matter for subjects to discuss in Parliament.

53. *Boston Town Records, 1770–1777*, pp. 90–92.
54. Samuel Adams to Elbridge Gerry, Nov. 5, 1772, *Writings of Samuel Adams*, II, 346.
55. *Ibid.*
56. *Boston Town Records, 1770–1777*, p. 92.
57. Hutchinson to Lord Dartmouth, Boston, Nov. 3, 1772, Hutchinson Letter Books, Mass. Arch., XXVII, 402.

In the Boston town meeting this reply called for several readings. After some consideration the town unanimously decided it was unsatisfactory. The towns, they said, had a free right to meet and petition according to their own judgment. They always had. Moreover, they had full right "to communicate their Sentiment to other Towns." Here Adams found a suitable moment to propose committees of correspondence. He moved:

That a Committee of Correspondence be appointed to consist of twenty-one Persons — to state the Rights of the Colonists and of this Province in particular, as Men, as Christians, and as Subjects; to communicate and publish the same to the several Towns in this Province and to the World as the sense of this Town, with the Infringements and Violations thereof that have been, or from time to time may be made — Also requesting of each Town a free communication of their Sentiments on this Subject.

His carefully prepared motion passed unanimously.[58]

58. *Boston Town Records, 1770–1777,* pp. 92–93.

4

The Boston Committee
of Correspondence
Enters Massachusetts Politics

The unanimous vote establishing the Boston Committee of Correspondence was a victory for the Boston Whigs. The governor's friends had tried to discourage interest in the meeting, and had themselves deliberately stayed away. Thus they left the field free to their opponents, a move which had significant results. Had the administration's supporters been present, division would have replaced unanimity in the town votes, and even more important, the membership of the committee might not have been so homogeneous in its opposition to the administration. In that event the work of the committee and indeed its entire career might have been very different. As it was, the committee would become a major vehicle of opposition to the royal administration and all it signified.

Governor Hutchinson, though at first scornful of the Boston Committee of Correspondence and its works, soon came to recognize the threat it created for his objectives in Massachusetts public life. His response was a lengthy public rebuttal of the ideas the committee represented. He challenged the province to decide whether it was prepared to recognize parliamentary sovereignty and accept his leadership. As a result, he joined the Boston committee in stimulating and expanding the polarization of Massachusetts politics.

I

The men chosen to serve on the committee of correspondence were all members of the town political class, men with property or a profession that allowed them time for politics.[1] Although a few of the wealthiest men in Boston declined to serve on the committee, among them John Hancock and Thomas Cushing, its members were generally men of some means. Several were well-to-do merchants and capitalists with diverse investments, two were lawyers, three physicians, and the rest were involved in trade and manufactures with assets of less than £1,000.[2] All had previously served the town in various offices: one, Oliver Wendell, was currently serving as selectman; another, William Greenleaf, was an overseer of the poor. With one third of its members holding degrees from Harvard College, the committee of correspondence was an unusually distinguished town committee.

The social and economic stature of its members are a certain indication of the prestige accorded the committee.[3] But the uniform political persuasion of the members was of much greater significance than their prestige or social background in shaping the committee's course. For as devout Whigs they were prepared to recognize Samuel Adams, the Boston representative, as their leader; and Adams could rely on their fundamental devotion to liberty as he understood it, even though differences might arise. Moreover many of the members had previously worked together in opposition to the Stamp and Townshend Acts. Having taken active parts in promoting and enforcing nonimportation, they could all be confident of one another's commitment to the cause of Massachusetts rights.

1. *Boston Town Records, 1770-1777*, Boston Record Commissioners, *Report*, XVIII (Boston, 1887), 93: James Otis, Samuel Adams, Joseph Warren, Benjamin Church, William Dennie, William Greenleaf, Joseph Greenleaf, Thomas Young, William Powell, Nathaniel Appleton, Oliver Wendell, John Sweetser, Josiah Quincy, John Bradford, Richard Boynton, William Mackay, Nathaniel Barber, Caleb Davis, Alexander Hill, William Molineux, Robert Pierpont. The issue of opposition to the meeting is touched on in Samuel Adams to Arthur Lee, Nov. 3, 1772, *The Writings of Samuel Adams*, ed. Harry A. Cushing (New York, 1904-1908), II, 342-345.
2. Boston Tax Return, 1771, Massachusetts Archives, CXXXII, 92-147.
3. For the close correlation between socioeconomic status and political office-holding in Boston see James A. Henretta, "Economic Development and Social Structure in Colonial Boston," *William and Mary Quarterly*, 3d Ser., XXII (1965), 75-92.

Equally significant, the membership of the committee linked it closely to the existing institutions of Boston politics, so closely that it was hardly separate. At least eight of the twenty-one members also belonged to the North End Caucus, a private political club which met regularly to discuss and to influence Boston affairs.[4] Members also participated in several Boston congregations, in both of Boston's Masonic lodges, the fire companies of several wards, as well as a variety of private clubs. Personal and professional connections attached them to virtually every circle in Boston, political or otherwise, excepting the governor's circle. Consequently the Boston Committee of Correspondence was a town committee par excellence, even though its ambitions were primarily directed toward the province at large.

Adams, and perhaps others, apparently intended that John Hancock, Thomas Cushing, and William Phillips, Boston's other representatives, would serve on the committee. Their presence would have enhanced its stature considerably; and since Cushing and Hancock were well known and respected throughout the province, it could have made the committee more impressive and attractive to the lesser ports and the country towns. Cushing, the speaker of the House, together with the remaining Boston representatives, might even have added a quasi-provincial aspect to the Boston committee which it lacked in their absence. Hancock, Cushing, and Phillips had each been nominated at the town meeting, but each had declined owing, they said, to private obligations. Tories argued that their refusal to serve was a tacit expression of their distaste for the project. The similar refusal by Selectmen John Scollay and Benjamin Austin lent color to their charge. They asked if it could be coincidence that five of the wealthiest, most eminent Whigs declined to serve on the committee of correspondence. Tories spread the word that the Boston Whigs were divided.[5]

Yet even though several prominent Whigs did not serve on the committee, evidence supporting the Tory claim is at most circumstantial. Since the information regarding the judicial stipends was not official, some may have been reluctant to commit themselves publicly and to embark on a project which, if it failed, would leave Boston isolated. Cushing, moreover, had recently expressed his strong preference for opposing British measures through the colonial legislatures, since he

4. North End Caucus minutes, March 23, 1772, in Elbridge H. Goss, *The Life of Colonel Paul Revere* (Boston, 1891), II, 635–637.
5. "Q.E.D.," *Boston Weekly News-Letter*, Nov. 12, 1772, 3:1–2.

doubted the popular will to resist.[6] Thus it is possible that there was some division over tactics. Yet this possibility must be measured against the readiness of a score of Boston Whigs, many of them prominent, to serve on the committee. Furthermore, though Cushing had declined to serve as a regular member of the committee, Samuel Adams later reported privately that Cushing "frequently met with the Committee and appears to be hearty in forwarding the Measure." Adams, who recognized too late the mistake of nominating Hancock, Cushing, and Phillips without prior knowledge of their intentions, himself believed they "were unaware of the evil Tendency of their Conduct," and he did not believe it especially significant.[7]

Whatever their reasons, there is no doubt that their absence diminished the committee's prestige. For even though some of its members were wealthy, their assets were measured in thousands not tens of thousands of pounds; none was in the first rank for wealth. James Otis and Samuel Adams were well known all over Massachusetts, and Josiah Quincy, Jr., had gained a reputation in the "massacre trials" of 1770, but the other members of the committee were virtually unknown outside of Boston. The absence of Hancock and Cushing especially deprived the committee of a dazzling array of Whig heroes committing their personal prestige to the project. At the same time the fact that they publicly declined to serve the committee furnished the governor's party with "proofs" to disparage both the measure and the "divided" opposition party.[8]

6. Thomas Cushing to Roger Sherman, Jan. 21, 1772, Massachusetts Historical Society, *Collections*, 4th Ser., IV (1858), 358-359.

7. Samuel Adams to James Warren, Dec. 9, 1772, *Warren-Adams Letters, Being Chiefly a Correspondence among John Adams, Samuel Adams, and James Warren*, Massachusetts Historical Society, *Collections*, LXXII–LXXIII (1917-1925), I, 14-15. John C. Miller, in *Sam Adams: Pioneer in Propaganda* (Boston, 1936), 264-265, accepted the Tory argument at face value and used the idea of Whig division to emphasize Samuel Adams' individual role as founder of the committees of correspondence. He suggests that Adams was ready to "go it alone." But such behavior would not have been characteristic of his political leadership, and since there is substantial evidence supporting the view that many Boston Whigs favored the plan, Miller's hypothesis must be rejected. Robert E. Brown argues that a split had developed between Hancock and Samuel Adams during the spring of 1772, culminating in an attempt by Hancock to prevent the election of Adams to the House. Brown's evidence is inconclusive, but the possibility cannot be dismissed (*Middle-Class Democracy and the Revolution in Massachusetts, 1691-1780* (Ithaca, 1955), 365-366).

8. "Q.E.D.," *Boston Weekly News-Letter*, Nov. 12, 1772, 3:1-2. Thomas Hutchinson's significant but erroneous recollection of divisions in this meeting may be found in *Additions to Thomas Hutchinson's "History of Massachusetts-Bay*," ed. Catherine B. Mayo (Worcester, 1949), 51. His recollection that Otis opposed the measure is contradicted by various contemporary sources including his own letters.

II

Before the ramifications of this tactical failing were wholly evident, the committee of correspondence began its work. Its first meeting was held on November 3, 1772, the day after the town had created it. Meeting at the representatives' chamber in Faneuil Hall, with James Otis in the chair, they started by reading the resolve of the town which prescribed their duties. Before proceeding further they unanimously chose William Cooper, the Boston town clerk, as their clerk, to keep a regular record. Then they voted unanimously "that each Member of the Committee be desired to declare to the Chairman, that he does hold himself bound in honor, not to divulge or make known any part of the Conversation of this Committee at their Meetings to any Person whatsoever," excepting official statements authorized by the committee. All the members immediately declared they would follow this rule of secrecy.[9] The reasons for this secrecy rule were never explained, but the purpose was apparently defensive and intended to guard against the likelihood that fragmentary reports of their activities would provide the basis for rumors which might be debilitating to the committee's operations. At the least, the spread of rumors would require the committee to occupy itself in answering them, and if the committee was divided on an issue or engaged in choosing among several proposals, public access to the information might make their deliberations more difficult. The public itself never seems to have expected the committee to operate in any other manner.

Having framed essential rules for its activity, the committee assigned specific tasks. First, they must prepare a statement of "the Rights of the Colonists and of this Province in particular, as Men, as Christians, and as Subjects." James Otis, Josiah Quincy, and Samuel Adams were appointed a subcommittee to prepare the statement and to report it back to the committee "as soon as possible."[10] Their selection for this purpose from among the twenty-one was deliberate. Otis, the brilliant theorist of *The Rights of the Colonies* (1764), had been recognized as the foremost Whig political thinker in Massachusetts for a decade. Though recently he had been troubled by his recurrent mental disorder, he continued to command respect among Whigs for his erudition in

9. Boston Committee of Correspondence, minutes, Nov. 3, 1772, Minute Book, I, 1–3, New York Public Library, photostats at Massachusetts Historical Society.
10. *Ibid.*, I, 2.

constitutional thought and his sharp wit. In contrast to Otis, Josiah Quincy's reputation was of recent origin. Adams had recognized his talent several years earlier and had quickly drawn him into the circle of active opposition to Bernard, Hutchinson, and the ministry. In 1770, at the age of twenty-six, he had made his first official contribution by drafting the Boston instructions, and later in the year he had gained distinction by his association with John Adams in defending the soldiers involved in the Massacre. By late 1772 Whigs saw him as a rising star, a fervid orator as well as a superior lawyer, perhaps a new, more balanced Otis. The third member of the subcommittee, the fifty-year-old Samuel Adams, was not known for either his profound learning or his spark-ling rhetoric. His literary gift was primarily clear exposition and straight-forward, easy-to-follow argument. For years he had turned out persua-sive essays for the press, representatives' instructions, assembly addresses, and an occasional pamphlet. No one knew better than Adams how to distill the essence of an argument into readily understood logic. To-gether Otis, Quincy, and Adams could be expected to produce a sound theoretical essay which townspeople throughout the province would find convincing.

A second subcommittee, Joseph Warren, Joseph Greenleaf, and Thomas Young, was appointed to prepare the list of "infringements and Violations" of the colonists' rights, both those "that have been, or from time to time may be made."[11] They too were particularly well suited to their assignment. Doctor Warren, nine years out of Harvard, was a long-time contributor to the press and had given the March 5th Oration earlier that year. He was a master of evocative, alarming rhetoric, and Whig grievances, which the governor claimed no one could see or feel, were palpable and shocking when painted by Warren. Joseph Greenleaf, a printer who had recently moved to Boston from Abington where he held an appointment as justice of the peace, had established his standing in Whig circles in 1770 as the author of Abington's resolves declaring the Townshend Acts "a mere nullity," and sending troops to Boston to enforce them was "an open declaration of war" against American liberty. A year or so later Greenleaf had been deprived of his office as justice of the peace because he had made no attempt to suppress an inflammatory piece by Warren in Isaiah Thomas' Spy. Greenleaf's immediate reply had been a vigorous demand for a free press. Though he was not an exceptional writer, he was able and

11. Ibid., I, 3; Boston Town Records, 1770–1777, p. 93.

had already acted out his deep concern with informing and alerting the people.[12] The third member of the subcommittee on infringements was Thomas Young, another physician. Young had been continually active in the Whig cause ever since his arrival from New York in 1766. With an apparent taste for controversy, he had argued boldly and confidently in both the press and public meetings, always in opposition to imperial measures and their defenders in the province. Together, Warren, Greenleaf, and Young could be expected to provide a vivid description of grievances and their consequences for the cause of liberty.

The committee of correspondence plan was given to Benjamin Church, Nathaniel Appleton, and William Powell, who were assigned to draft a "letter of correspondence." Church, like Josiah Quincy and Joseph Warren, had been drawn into the opposition party by Samuel Adams.[13] A physician, like Warren and Young, he was perhaps the most sophisticated of Whig writers. Possessing a broad acquaintance with English letters, adept at exposition and argument, he had long been a master of Whig theory. His companions Appleton and Powell were earnest, respectable Whigs. Powell, a merchant, had not previously written in defense of liberty, but Appleton, son of the well-known Cambridge pastor, Nathaniel Appleton, Sr., had contributed to the press from time to time and had published a tract attacking Negro slavery in 1767.[14] His experience in the Whig cause would be useful in preparing the letter that would invite towns to meet, discuss, and communicate with Boston.

The committee, having divided its assignment among nine members, adjourned to the evening of November 13 at the selectmen's chamber where hereafter they would meet regularly. How much discussion had accompanied the formation of the subcommittees and their assignments remains unknown. Like all town records of the period, the committee

---

12. Benjamin Hobart, *History of the Town of Abington* (Boston, 1866), 271. In an article in the *Boston Gazette*, Jan. 13, 1772, 1:1–2, defending his conduct as justice of the peace, Greenleaf offered a passionate defense of a free press to inform the public. At various times Greenleaf operated a press himself, for a while with Isaiah Thomas, and after Thomas gave up publication of the *Royal American Magazine* in mid-1774, Greenleaf published it alone for several months. Greenleaf was an old friend of Robert Treat Paine, their friendship dating at least from the mid-1740's, and in 1749 Greenleaf had married Paine's sister.

13. John Adams to William Tudor, Feb. 9, 1819, *The Works of John Adams, Second President of the United States*, ed. Charles Francis Adams (Boston, 1850–1856), X, 364–365.

14. So far as I have found, Powell had never previously written. Appleton was the author of *Considerations on Slavery* (Boston, 1767).

minutes report only formal actions, not the discussion surrounding measures. The oath of secrecy and the easy means of verbal communication among the members gave assurance that accounts of the meetings would not leak out in letters. As a result discussions within the meetings have been lost.

When the committee convened once more on Friday, November 13, Otis, Adams, and Quincy alone reported a completed draft. Warren's grievance committee gave a partial report, while Church's letter committee was not yet ready to present a draft. Whether these delays resulted from divisions over content is not known. In any case the committee requested that a draft of the letter be reported to them the following morning, together with a revised and completed statement of grievances. The next day Samuel Adams wrote Elbridge Gerry that "our Committee are industrious, and I think I may promise you, they will be ready to report to the Town in two or three days." [15] His optimistic mood suggested that any difficulties or disagreements which might have arisen were minor and easily resolved.

After the meeting of Saturday the 14th, the committee adjourned to Monday when they gave final approval to the letter of correspondence. The list of grievances was still incomplete; the committee discussed it once more, ironing out the remaining problems. When they were finished they were confident that the job was all but complete, so they voted to ask the selectmen to call a town meeting as soon as possible to receive their report. They adjourned to the 18th, when each of the subcommittees presented its finished draft, gaining unanimous approval from the whole committee. As a final step chairman James Otis was requested "to bring the three reports into one." [16]

On receiving the committee's request for a town meeting, the selectmen ordered warrants posted for the morning of Friday, November 20. The warrants specified that the purpose of the meeting was to consider the report of the committee of correspondence, yet the governor's supporters once more absented themselves. Although the committee was careful to meet beforehand to prepare the presentation of its report, Hutchinson believed the whole project contemptible: "to keep up a correspondence through the Province by Committees of the several Towns . . . is such a foolish scheme that they must necessarily make

15. Samuel Adams to Elbridge Gerry, Nov. 14, 1772, *Writings of Samuel Adams*, II, 348.
16. Boston Committee of Correspondence, minutes, Nov. 18, 1772, Minute Book, I, 4.

themselves ridiculous."[17] His attitude, apparently shared by his friends who opposed the committee of correspondence and stayed away from the meeting, provided the Whigs with another uncontested victory in the town meeting.

At this meeting John Hancock was first elected moderator, and thus he became part of the proceedings after all. Then the whole report was twice read aloud, and each part separately voted. The first, *"The state of the Rights of the Colonists,"* was accepted unanimously. The second part, *"The Enumeration of the Violations of our Rights,"* was not entirely satisfactory, so it was sent back to the committee "for some Additions relative to the Lieutenant Governor, Attorney General & Soliciter Generals Salaries," as well as the customhouse fees. After an adjournment to permit the committee to add these grievances to its list, the meeting convened again in the afternoon. Now the revised list was unanimously adopted. The "Letter of Correspondence to the other Towns," was read over again, then it too passed unanimously. Afterwards the town voted to print a pamphlet of their proceedings, and directed the committee to distribute six hundred of them "among the Selectmen of the several Towns, and such other Gentlemen as the Committee shall think fit." The town clerk, William Cooper, was directed to attest the proceedings and to sign the letters of correspondence before sending them out. The town, having unanimously endorsed the committee of correspondence's revised report in its entirety, gave it no further instructions.[18]

When the committee met again on November 30, the pamphlet containing their report to the town was ready. After reading over the town's order to distribute the pamphlets as they saw fit, the committee agreed to furnish each Boston selectman with six copies, each representative of Boston twelve, and every member of the Boston clergy, of whatever denomination, with one. Hancock, as moderator of the meeting, should get six more, so that as selectman, representative, and

17. *Selectmen's Minutes, 1769–1775*, Boston Record Commissioners, *Report*, XXIII (Boston, 1893), 150. Order given on Nov. 17, 1772; Boston Committee of Correspondence, minutes, Nov. 19, 1772, Minute Book, I, 4; Hutchinson to John Pownall, Nov. 13, 1772, Thomas Hutchinson Letter Books, Massachusetts Archives, XXVII, 412.

18. *Boston Town Records, 1770–1777*, p. 94. The report as presented to the town in its original state may have been printed because Charles Evans lists a copy in the Harvard College Library. But this copy, if it exists, is lost and the editor of the microcard set of *Early American Imprints* has not been able to locate a single copy. So Evans' entry may be a "ghost."

moderator, this prominent Whig who had earlier declined service on the committee of correspondence would receive in sum twenty-four copies for distribution. As planned, one would be sent to the selectmen of every town and district in Massachusetts, and a subcommittee of five was chosen to assist William Cooper in forwarding the pamphlets. Before adjourning, the members of the committee were asked to prepare lists of persons who could be "best intrusted" to deliver the pamphlets to the selectmen of each of the 260 towns and districts.[19]

Their decisions in allocating the pamphlets pointed to Boston, the province, and beyond. The selectmen of Boston together with the clergy could reach virtually everyone in the town who was willing to receive the message. Boston would be saturated. The representatives, who were allotted twice as many as the selectmen, could distribute them to important people all over Massachusetts. Hancock, with extensive connections outside the province as well as within it, was best suited to place the pamphlet in prominent hands on both sides of the Atlantic. Moreover at a subsequent meeting the committee itself decided to send the pamphlet to "several Noble Lords & Gentlemen."[20] But although they sought to plead the colonial cause in England, they concentrated on Massachusetts. Only a small fraction of the pamphlets were sent outside the province, and the committee took special precautions to make certain that the pamphlets would actually reach their fundamental audience in the towns. The pamphlet, formally titled *The Votes and Proceedings of the Town of Boston*, was written for Massachusetts.

The subcommittee charged with sending out the pamphlets worked quickly, but they did not rush. Putting the pamphlet in the right hands was more important than speed alone. Yet within two weeks Samuel Adams reported that the *Votes and Proceedings* "has been forwarded to four fifths of the Gentlemen Selectmen in the Country, the Representatives of the several Towns, the Members of his Majesty's Council and others of Note."[21] Apparently the subcommittee, with a surplus of over two hundred pamphlets above the distribution assigned by the committee, had decided itself to send them to the representatives and

19. Boston Committee of Correspondence, minutes, Nov. 30, 1772, Minute Book, I, 4–6. Subcommittee: William Greenleaf, John Sweetser, Samuel Adams, John Bradford, Nathaniel Appleton; Boston Committee of Correspondence, minutes, Dec. 8, 1772, Minute Book, I, 8–9, has space for entry of list of persons entrusted for delivery, but the list is omitted.

20. Boston Committee of Correspondence, minutes, Dec. 12, 1772, Minute Book, I, 9.

21. Samuel Adams as "Candidus," *Boston Gazette*, Dec. 14, 1772, 2:3.

councillors. In addition, members of the committee sent them to their own personal connections. When the distribution was completed, the pamphlet had been placed in the hands of hundreds of opinion leaders, especially elected public officials, all over the province.

Generally the committee of correspondence was pleased with its efforts and proud of the pamphlet. Adams could not "help entertaining some sanguine hopes that the measures we have pursued will have a happy event," and Thomas Young was elated. Young boasted to a New York Son of Liberty that "when our plan is completed and ex- plain'd you will join the general voice in proclaiming the Bostonians the saviors of America." [22] The governor, however, held a different view. He found the pamphlet "miserable," proving that "the restless faction" of Boston was desperate.[23] Though at first he had believed it would have "little or no effect," when he saw "this doctrine of Independence is every day spreading and strengthening itself," he became disturbed. Though the pamphlet was no worse in his eyes than many earlier publications, it was apparently enjoying outrageous success among the people.[24]

III

The Votes and Proceedings of the Freeholders and other Inhabitants of the Town of Boston, In Town Meeting assembled, According to Law, called the "Boston pamphlet," by contemporaries, has been regu- larly ignored by historians.[25] Otis' *Rights of the Colonies* and Dickin- son's *Farmer's Letters* have attracted critical attention because they contained original theoretical statements on parliamentary sovereignty and the taxing power; but the Boston pamphlet, merely a summary of rights with a catalogue of grievances, defining no new stage in the discussion of taxation and representation, has not called for closer scru-

22. Samuel Adams to Elbridge Gerry, Dec. 23, 1772, *Writings of Samuel Adams*, II, 389; Thomas Young to Hugh Hughes, Dec. 21, 1772, Miscellaneous Bound Docu- ments, 1765–1775, Massachusetts Historical Society.
23. Hutchinson to Richard Jackson, Dec. 8, 1772, Hutchinson Letter Books, Mass. Arch., XXVII, 428.
24. Hutchinson to Francis Bernard [?], Dec. 8, 1772, to Francis Bernard, Nov. 26, 1772, to Richard Jackson, Dec. 8, 1772, to ?, Dec. 13, 1772, Hutchinson Letter Books, Mass. Arch., XXVII, 426, 417, 428, 429–431.
25. *The Votes and Proceedings of the freeholders and other inhabitants of the town of Boston, in town meeting assembled, according to law*, [Published by order of the town.] To which is prefixed, as introductory, an attested copy of a Vote of the town at a preceding meeting. Boston: Printed by Edes and Gill in Queen-Street. And T. and J. Fleet, in Cornhill. [1772.] pp. iv, 43. 8 vo.

tiny. Since similar repetitions of old grievances against theoretical rights had regularly appeared in Edes and Gill's *Boston Gazette* for years, historians have been inclined to agree with Governor Hutchinson that the Boston pamphlet was simply more of the same.

Yet wholly apart from considerations of the originality of its substance, the Boston pamphlet was a significant event in Revolutionary politics. Boston had produced pamphlets before, the *Appeal to the World* in 1769 and the *Short Narrative* in 1770, but each of these had been written for an audience of English merchants and politicians. In contrast the Boston pamphlet of 1772 was explicitly directed toward a Massachusetts audience. Where the pamphlets of 1769 and 1770 had sought to gain redress by influencing English politics, telling Englishmen about the governor's false accusations and the violence perpetrated on an innocent town by rapacious troops in league with avaricious customs officials, the pamphlet of 1772 recognized that the primary effective audience was provincial, not English. Presumably the Massachusetts towns, the target of the pamphlets, were themselves capable of providing a means of redress.

The substance of the pamphlet is equally noteworthy. For though it contained no new theory or analysis of either colonial rights or the constitution, the effect of its particular formulation was revealing. It showed which ideas were believed essential and relevant in Massachusetts, illustrating the province's constitutional "priorities." [26] The statement of grievances, even though many were not new, was vital because it explained not only the immediate efforts of particular encroachments, but, more important, their ultimate consequences. The pamphlet provided a thorough, connected explanation of affairs, and appealed directly to the towns for redress. It assumed the necessity of constitutional discussion and a statement from every community. Passive, acquiescent political behavior, the contemporary English standard, was represented

26. I am not prepared to say whether the views contained in the pamphlet differed significantly from attitudes expressed in other colonies. In their broad outlines the constitutional arguments and grievances expressed in the pamphlet appear similar to articles which appeared in 1772 in the colonial press outside the province, however there may well have been significant variations. Until we have a detailed study of the attitudes common in other colonies in the early 1770's, it will be an open question whether the substance of the Boston pamphlet was typical or unique. One circumstance which suggests that its appeal was specialized is the fact that it was never reprinted, nor did it develop a wide audience outside Massachusetts even though it was sent to Whigs in other colonies. But any argument based on these circumstances must be tenuous at best because one might plausibly argue that the pamphlet aroused little interest elsewhere simply because its contents were already seen as being conventional.

as a grave political sin in the pamphlet. Neither was this idea entirely new, but as an official town statement broadcast openly throughout the province, it marked a new stage in political affairs and a reversal of the conception which had prevailed prior to 1760.

Finally, the effects of the Boston pamphlet on Massachusetts politics were considerable, according to observers of diverse political loyalties. As a result of its publication, dozens of towns met all over the province, and the governor, though he found the pamphlet contemptible, came to believe that it must be finally answered and obliterated. He grew convinced that unless its doctrines were thoroughly refuted they would be sanctioned in the minds of the townspeople, even though its doctrines contained nothing new. It was not brilliance or originality which Hutchinson feared in the pamphlet, it was its effective simplicity.

When Otis, Quincy, and Adams set out to prepare the statement of colonial rights as men, as Christians, and as subjects, they felt no need to innovate because they could draw upon a host of recognized authorities, ranging from seventeenth-century figures like Coke, Grotius, and Locke, to eighteenth-century Radical Whigs.[27] To be novel or original would have been superfluous — or worse, it might arouse suspicion. All the Boston Committee of Correspondence needed was to express the familiar essentials, making the necessity of their defense self-evident.

Their statement of natural rights — the "State of Rights" — was directly grounded on the common Whig assumption that society is formed

27. Traditionally historians have attributed the "State of the Rights of the Colonists" to Samuel Adams, the "List of the Infringements and Violations of Rights" to Joseph Warren, and the "Letter of Correspondence" to Benjamin Church. These attributions rest on the assumption that, since each of the three was an important political writer, and since each was assigned to one of the three subcommittees drafting the report, each must have written one of its sections. There is no conclusive documentary evidence either confirming or refuting this view.

Yet the general organization and activity of the committee of correspondence suggests that group authorship of each section was in fact the case. Four arguments support this view. First, the committee chose subcommittees of three men, not single individuals, and thus it expected group authorship. Second, if one man was to write each section there was no point in assigning Otis, Adams, and Quincy — three of the most esteemed writers — to one subcommittee. Third, individual authorship would not have required the consultations and postponements which delayed the presentation of two of the sections to the full committee. Finally, the principle of solitary authorship ran directly contrary to the general policy and practice of the committee, which was joint consultation, criticism, and review. Since single letters prepared by the committee were frequently composed by three or four of its members, it seems most unlikely that each part of its most important production was left to the judgment of a single author. Indeed the sum of the committee's literary production suggests that it considered group authorship, where able writers revised and polished each others' sentences, as the best means of producing effective yet judicious political statements.

by voluntary compact, and government ruled by consent of the governed. They began with the indisputable first law of nature, self-preservation, explaining that the natural rights to life, liberty, and property were constituent parts of "the Duty of Self-Preservation." Moving step-by-step in paragraphs of one or two sentences, avoiding the use of Latin terms, they pointed out that in any voluntary compact men retained the "Right to demand and insist upon the Performance of such Conditions and previous Limitations" as they had originally set. If the compact was formed to preserve essential rights, then it must preserve them or men were free to withdraw from it or dissolve it and form another. Society was merely a device for protecting essential natural rights.[28]

Everyone recognized that natural liberty was bound to be abridged when men entered society, but only to the extent "necessary for the great End of Society, the best Good of the Whole."[29] Life, liberty, property could not be abridged, neither could liberty of conscience. Reason and religion required the free exercise of religion so long as it was not, like Roman Catholicism, subversive of the ends of society. Such emphasis on toleration, which "all good and candid Minds in all Ages have ever practiced," was unusual, especially in the context of the conflict with Britain.[30] Yet liberty of conscience was critical for Massachusetts. Congregationalists felt continual anxiety over projections of an American episcopate, while Baptists, regarding themselves as a persecuted minority in Massachusetts as it was, had a special zeal for toleration.

From a conventional English viewpoint, the most extraordinary part of the statement of natural rights was the description of the people's relation to their rulers. In place of the usual model of a wise magistracy leading an obedient people, the pamphlet likened the people to masters who employ servants to work at a wage. In the analogy, governors served as arbiters hired to dispense impartial justice. They were entitled to honorable support, this was their right "from the same Principle 'that the Labourer is worthy of his Hire.'" But they remained servants. Their master, the community where they served, had a master's natural right to fix their wages. Moreover, while governors were hired to arbitrate among people and rule the community, they did not,

28. *Votes and Proceedings*, 2. Latin is used once in the text (page 4), "*imperium in imperio*"; it is translated into English in a footnote as "A Government within a Government."
29. *Ibid.*, 5.
30. *Ibid.*, 3.

nor could they assume any of the people's rights.[31] Society, government, existed for its people, and any contrary tendency violated "the eternal Law of Reason." They concluded that "the Right of Freedom being the Gift of GOD ALMIGHTY, it is not in the Power of Man to alienate this Gift, and voluntarily become a Slave." [32]

Their statement of the colonists' rights as Christians stressed the right of liberty of conscience once more. For after asserting that their rights as Christians could be best understood by careful study of the New Testament, the pamphlet turned to a description of the guarantees of worship according to conscience. In England there was the Toleration Act; in Massachusetts the province charter guaranteed freedom of worship to all Christians except Papists. The unstated implication was that the Toleration Act did not apply in the colonies. Magna Carta and Blackstone, authorities which spoke of the equal natural rights of all free men, they interpreted as further legal recognition of the right to freedom of worship. Having thus established its natural and legal foundations, they had no further rights as Christians to discuss.[33] They turned to the rights of the colonists as subjects.

Of the entire statement of rights, this section was particularly offensive to the governor, since it seemed to accept Parliament as the supreme power and then deny categorically its competence to tax the colonies. Such a brazen contradiction was infuriating to Hutchinson. He believed they were defending *imperium in imperio*, the patent absurdity of a government within a government. Moreover they introduced a concept of individual rights which contradicted the whole idea of sovereignty as he understood it.

Englishmen, they asserted, like all freemen in or out of society had certain *"absolute Rights,"* principally life, liberty, and property. As they had already stated, these rights could be neither seized nor given away. Most important, these rights controlled and defined the "Legislative Power." The legislative had "no Right to absolute arbitrary Power over the Lives and Fortunes of the People," such power belonged only to God. Quoting Locke, they described further limitations on legislative power. It could not arrogate power to itself, but was bound to see justice dispensed according to known laws. The legislative must make certain that judgments were given by independent judges, "Independent as

31. *Votes and Proceedings*, 6.
32. *Ibid.*, 7.
33. Samuel Adams to Elbridge Gerry, Nov. 14, 1772, *Writings of Samuel Adams*, II, 349, says "rights as Christians" was included to stir clergy.

far as is possible, of Prince and People." Otherwise there could be no impartial justice. Selecting one of Locke's more pointed maxims, they concluded: *"There should be one Rule of Justice for Rich and Poor; for the Favourite at Court, and the Countryman at the Plough."* [34]

Having circumscribed the legislative power by individuals' *"absolute Rights,"* and laid down the rule that independent judges were necessary for that essential function of government the equal distribution of justice, they emphasized one more essential point. "The Supreme Power," a synonym for Parliament, "cannot justly take from any Man, any Part of his Property without his Consent, in Person or by his Representative." [35] Its supremacy was limited, not absolute.

The statement of rights concluded with a summary exhortation. The principles which had just been explained all applied directly to Massachusetts' relation to Parliament. The House of Commons could not deprive them of the natural rights explicitly guaranteed in the charter. They quoted the charter to establish their point. Parliament had "assumed a Power to dispose of their Lives, Liberties and Properties," but it had no more right "than to chuse an Emperor of China!" [36] Implicitly denying the legislative competence of Parliament in the colonies, they declared that the American continent did not consent to be ruled by Parliament, and that it was foolish to suppose it could ever be properly represented there. In the future, when their posterity would outnumber the English, Scotch, and Irish put together, no one, they said, would be able to pretend otherwise. Parliament, whose natural interest conflicted with the colonies, was not merely unrepresentative, it was effectively bribed against them by the self-interest of Britons. If it could take away money now, what would prevent it from taking the land? Yet when colonists complained of such treatment they were called "Traitors and Rebels." Closing on a note of restraint, they asked how long such treatment should be borne. [37]

Except for several sentences in the closing paragraph, Otis, Quincy, and Adams had expressed colonial rights coolly, without an emotional appeal. Alluding to the grievance of the judges' salaries only by indirection in their treatment of rulers, people, and justice, they had tried to describe the essence of government and its consequences for the colonists' relation to Britain. Throughout their discussion one funda-

34. *Votes and Proceedings,* 9–10.
35. *Ibid.,* 10.
36. *Ibid.,* 11.
37. *Ibid.,* 12.

mental assumption ruled: the colonists had inviolable, unalienable rights. This fact determined the merely practical relationship of people and rulers, and the limited character of supreme power. They built the structure of the constitution upward from the individual's absolute rights. From the perspective of the committee of correspondence and Massachusetts Whigs, other aspects of the English constitution were only the superstructure, not the foundation.

The "List of Infringements and Violations of Rights" prepared by Warren, Greenleaf, and Young was less original and more emotive than the statement of rights. Only a few of the grievances were new, and the committee's glosses all carried a familiar message. However the list was comprehensive. Longer by half than the statement of rights, it was a handbook, cataloguing, explaining, and connecting Massachusetts' grievances. The evils it portrayed flowed from two sources, Parliament and the ministry. At the moment most were merely troublesome, but they might become disastrous to the liberty of Massachusetts and its inhabitants, since behind the infringements lay the sinister motive of colonial enslavement. Why else, they asked, would the Parliament and ministry create invidious distinctions between the English and the colonists? Why else would the rights and interests of Englishmen be recognized and defended as superior to those of the Americans? People must be awakened to the fact that if Britain deprived the Americans of equal liberty they would indeed be slaves.

Conveniently, the committee opened the list of infringements and violations by assuming the point they wished to make. They were sure that the list would "excite the Attention of all who consider themselves interested in the Happiness and Freedom of Mankind in general, and of this Continent and Province in particular." Moreover to "every candid Person" the grievances would surely justify whatever measures had been taken, or might be thought proper to be taken in order to gain redress.[38] Professing humility in the conventional manner, they began by sketching the sins they saw in Parliament.

First, the Parliament had "assumed" the power to legislate for the colonies in "all Cases whatsoever." The necessity of consent had been ignored. Parliament was using this assumed power to raise revenues, taking property without even the pretense of consent.[39] The outrage

38. *Votes and Proceedings*, 13.
39. They regarded the conception and arguments supporting "virtual representation" as too ridiculous for serious argument.

74

was exacerbated in their eyes by the belief that the Parliament was aware of what it was doing. For the House of Commons itself jealously maintained its own exclusive right to grant money in England, at the very time they denied it to the colonies. Even the Romans had shown more decency to their conquered provinces, only demanding a sum, letting each one raise it as they wished.

In order to collect the unconstitutional revenue, new officers had been sent to the province, even though the charter between King William III and the people of Massachusetts empowered the General Court to appoint all officers not otherwise specified in the charter. Moreover the powers given these officers were as unconstitutional as the offices themselves. Customs officers were given authority to enter any house merely on suspicion. Readers were invited to picture the consequences: "Our Houses, and even our Bed-Chambers, are exposed to be ransacked, our Boxes, Trunks and Chests broke open, ravaged and plundered, by Wretches, whom no prudent Man would venture to employ even as menial Servants." They might almost commit murder with impunity.[40]

To support "these unconstitutional Officers in collecting and managing this unconstitutional Revenue," fleets and armies were brought to the province. The people were thus subjected to a standing army in a time of peace, once again without their consent.[41] As if this were not grievous enough, the revenues taken from the province were unconstitutionally used to support its royal officers. In time this would inevitably destroy Massachusetts government, since like every mixed government, its freedom depended on a constant equilibrium among its parts. The governor's royal stipend, together with those of the lieutenant governor, the attorney general, and the solicitor general, all paid out of the American revenue, destroyed the balance. Unchecked by the assembly and responsible only to the Crown for their bread as well as their places, royal officials would no longer share mutual interests with the people and the province. Instead they would possess an interest in exploiting Massachusetts.

Here the list came to its climax. All these infringements, together with the judges' stipends, would "compleat our Slavery." Taxed without consent, governed by men independent of the province and depen-

40. *Votes and Proceedings*, 16–17. Following this the customhouse fee was added as a grievance at the town's request.
41. *Ibid.*, 18.

dent on the unconstitutional revenue, with the colonists' lives, liberty, and property at their governors' mercy, in view of "the depravity of mankind," they could only look "with horror on the danger to which we are exposed!" Once again they pointed out that it was the British, who knew full well the necessity of an independent judiciary and rulers supported by the people, who were depriving them of the very rights which were cherished for Britons.[42]

Nor did the infringements stop there. The instructions to the governor made him, "the first branch of our legislature . . . meerly a ministerial Engine."[43] By instructions from the ministry he had delivered the provincial fortress, Castle William, to the troops, "at a time when they were menacing the slaughter of the inhabitants of the town, and our streets were stain'd with the blood they had so barbarously shed." Instructions and a stipend had made the governor an instrument to thwart the other branches of the legislature, rendering their efforts for redress "futile." In New York an instruction had even been used to suspend the assembly entirely.[44]

Extending the jurisdiction of the courts of vice-admiralty beyond the limits maintained in England was yet another example of the inferior status they saw being fixed for Americans. In England revenue cases were tried by a common-law court, but in the colonies they were being tried by the vice-admiralty courts, without juries and according to civil law, so their right to trial by jury was, they said, being arbitrarily cut back.[45] The Dock-Yards Act displayed the full consequences of such an invasion. For by its provisions any man suspected "or pretended to be suspected" could be transported to wherever the Crown wished for trial. He would be tried by strangers, instead of his peers of "*the Vicinity*," and his costs from time lost and transportation would ruin him even if he should be acquitted.[46] No "candid Person" could doubt the evil intentions behind the plan.

The final grievances exposed in the pamphlet were miscellaneous in character, but the committee tied each of them to the main theme of colonial enslavement and exploitation it had been developing. One, the threat of an American episcopate, had appeared frequently in colonial

42. *Votes and Proceedings*, 19–21.
43. *Ibid.*, 21.
44. *Ibid.*, 22–23.
45. Carl Ubbelohde, *The Vice-Admiralty Courts and the American Revolution* (Chapel Hill., N.C., 1960), 145–146. On pages 12–17 Ubbelohde describes the jurisdiction of colonial vice-admiralty courts prior to the reforms.
46. *Ibid.*, 25–26.

discussion. Its inclusion in the pamphlet, its authors hoped, would awaken the clergy to the need for political activity. As a grievance, the American episcopate was entirely potential, rather than accomplished. Yet even English planning for it was regarded offensive, since "doing or attempting to do any thing which has even the remotest tendency to endanger this Enjoyment [of free exercise of religion], is justly looked upon a great Grievance; and also an Infringement of our Rights; which is not barely to exercise, but peaceably and securely to enjoy, that Liberty with which CHRIST hath made us free." [47] From an English viewpoint this argument claiming that the mere suggestion of an epis-copacy as practised in England was an "Infringement of our Rights," seemed ludicrous. But the people of the province regarded the argu-ment soberly. Their ancestors had, they believed, fled England because of episcopacy. The suggestion that it might now be introduced gave them pause, especially in view of the context of its appearance.

Another of these grievances, the parliamentary prohibitions of cer-tain manufacturing activities like slitting mills for iron, had not received much colonial attention or obedience earlier, and its economic conse-quences had been minor.[48] But the committee noted that the idea of suppressing the colonists' rights to manufacture gave further evidence that Parliament treated the colonists as inferior and aimed to exploit them. At least one town was to respond to this grievance vehemently, saying that here the English served the Americans as the Philistines did the Israelites.[49]

The final grievance, changes in provincial boundaries, was a special problem of northcentral and western Massachusetts communities, but like the threat of an episcopate it was generally disquieting. "Frequent" alterations in colonial boundaries by the King and his Council had arbitrarily placed Massachusetts inhabitants within the governments of New York and New Hampshire without their consent. People had been forced to re-establish title to their lands, an expensive, uncertain business. Military force had even been used to compel their obedi-ence.[50] Most of the the province had never been inconvenienced by

47. Samuel Adams to Elbridge Gerry, Nov. 14, 1772, *Writings of Samuel Adams*, II, 349; *Votes and Proceedings*, 27.
48. Arthur C. Bining, *British Regulation of the Colonial Iron Industry* (Phila-delphia, 1933), ch. 5.
49. South Hadley, Jan. 18, 1773, Letters and Proceedings received by the Boston Committee of Correspondence, photos, 776–777, New York Public Library, photostats at Massachusetts Historical Society.
50. *Votes and Proceedings*, 28–29.

border changes, yet their consequences when projected against the future could be alarming. If land titles should prove as fragile as recent innovations had shown their other rights to be, then general enslavement would be a certainty. This emphasis on the future consequences of existing English policy, stressing the colonists' precarious situation, was characteristic of the entire list of grievances.

With the way prepared by the "State of Rights" and the "List of Infringements," the "Letter of Correspondence" drawn by Church, Powell, and Appleton provided a carefully wrought explanation of the purpose of the whole pamphlet, together with a delicately phrased request to join in seeking redress. Adopting a stance of fraternal confidence, their letter alternated argument with straightforward information and hortatory rhetoric. Scrupulously avoiding any hint of condescension, flattering here and there, they presented their case vigorously.

Boston was alarmed to witness "the Plan of *Despotism*, rapidly hastening to completion." The town's restraint had been exhausted by the "constant, unremitted, uniform Aim to inslave us." [51] The letter assumed that the "Plan of *Despotism*" was generally understood; the list of grievances had described the evidence and no one would question their interpretation of it. The judges' stipends were the last straw. The letter repeated in condensed, evocative prose the familiar arguments. Then, as introduction to Boston's remedy, they asked without immediately answering: "What can withstand the Attacks of mere Power? What can preserve the Liberties of the Subject, when the Barriers of the Constitution are taken away?"

Boston had asked the governor for information in the crisis. But he had declined it. It had requested that the General Court might be permitted to consult on the question, yet the governor refused. His Excellency had given no satisfaction, so Boston decided to recapitulate its own sentiments and lay them before each town so that the crisis might be properly weighed, "and the collected wisdom of the whole People, as far as possible, be obtained." They assumed there was no need to demonstrate the legitimacy or reasonableness of this idea. But there was a further cause for explicit, widespread, general expression on the subject. Great pains had been taken to persuade the British administration, "that the good People of this Province in general are quiet and undisturbed at the late Measures; and that any Uneasiness that appears, arises only from a few factious designing and disaffected men." Com-

51. *Votes and Proceedings*, 30.

munication of each town's sentiments, explicit declarations of "the sense of the People," would settle the question.[52]

Then the letter artfully made its most direct appeal. If the towns concurred, finding their rights and the infringements properly stated, they would "doubtless think it of the utmost Importance that we stand firm as one Man." Together they would seek to defend and recover their rights by instructing their representatives, or taking whatever other measures "your Wisdom and Fortitude shall dictate." Of course a town might not concur; its inhabitants might not believe they possessed the rights stated in the pamphlet, or that their rights had not been violated, or that they were not worth defending. But Boston could not believe that the "generous Ardor for Civil and Religious Liberty" of their ancestors had died completely. Using a rich, emotional metaphor, "the Iron hand of Oppression is daily tearing the choicest Fruit from the fair Tree of Liberty," the letter expressed confidence that "we have yet some Share of public Virtue remaining: We are not afraid of Poverty, but disdain Slavery." Sweden had recently become so debased and vicious that it rejoiced in its chains. But America would be jealous, sure "to keep an Eagle Eye upon every Inovation and Stretch of Power." Concluding, the committee called upon their brethren to disappoint the tyrants and to vindicate themselves by living up to the standard of their forefathers.[53]

The Boston pamphlet did not make a direct appeal to the towns to form committees of correspondence. Instead, perhaps as part of the committee's self-effacing role, it relied upon the force of example. The pamphlet had opened with the Boston resolution creating the committee of correspondence, and included the names of its members. Hancock's name appeared in large roman capital letters across the middle of the first page of text, helping to emphasize the authority and respectability of the example. Boston's open invitation to the towns to communicate their sentiments and to collect the sense of the people to discover effective means for redress all but asked them to form committees of correspondence. Yet the Boston committee had stopped short of an actual request, mentioning only representatives' instructions specifically. All the same, the example, coupled with the suggestion to seek other means of redress, could be and was readily interpreted as an invitation to join together in committees of correspondence. The Boston Committee of

52. *Ibid.*, 28–33.
53. *Ibid.*, 33, 34–35.

Correspondence could achieve its ends without seeming to dictate, because it could rely upon a shared body of political habits and ideas. Given the same information, towns would all tend to form the same conclusions, and recognize the value of committees of correspondence. At least this seems to have been the committee's hope.

For this reason the pamphlet had been able to assume the premises of its case against Parliament and the ministry throughout. The committee's interpretation merely required repeated illustration of the relevance of events to the deeply felt beliefs of Massachusetts subjects. To provoke political activity it had only to emphasize the consequences latent in each innovation. The call to action, embellished with noble phrases, relied upon Massachusetts inhabitants' profound sense of duty, duty to themselves and their ancestors. Posing its questions in moral terms, calling for an exhibition of virtue, the committee touched especially sensitive aspects of its audience's political beliefs. Massachusetts towns, aspiring to a public virtue which could measure up with that of their celebrated ancestors, might at least be expected to listen to Boston's call.

IV

While the Boston Committee of Correspondence was formally occupied with preparing the pamphlet, informally its members began to promote support in other towns. Samuel Adams, who spent all of his time "employed in the public Service," seems to have been most active. Among his regular correspondents in the province were Elbridge Gerry in Marblehead, Joseph Hawley, in Northampton, Joseph Otis in Barnstable, and James Warren at Plymouth.[54] All had been active in the General Court, and were influential in their own towns. They might bring their towns to act even before Boston had made its direct appeal in the pamphlet.

Adams wrote Gerry on October 29, four days before Boston established the committee, suggesting that Marblehead meet and consider the judges' salaries immediately. Since the Superior Court would be meeting at Salem the following week, the town of Marblehead might take the opportunity to ask the judges formally whether or not stipends had been assigned. And, as Gerry had initially suggested, Marblehead

54. John Adams, Dec. 30, 1772, *Diary and Autobiography of John Adams*, ed. Lyman H. Butterfield (Cambridge, Mass., 1961), II, 74.

might even request that the judges demonstrate their attachment to constitutional liberty by refusing Crown salaries. Some action Adams believed was imperative, because "every day strengthens our oppressors and weakens us." Gerry would no doubt agree that "if each Town would declare its Sense of these matters, . . . our Enemies would not have it in their power to divide us, in which they have all along shown their dexterity." Without any mention of committees of correspondence, he urged Gerry to promote activity in Salem and the other nearby towns.[55]

On November 4, after the Boston Committee of Correspondence had been formed and had begun its work, Adams sent similar encouragement to James Warren, a Plymouth selectman and representative with whom he had earlier discussed the committee of correspondence project.[56] Adams wished "our Mother Plymouth would see her way clear to have a meeting and second Boston by appointing a Committee of Communication and Correspondence." The more activity shown outside the capital, the better it was for morale all over the province. It was even useful within Boston where, he explained, "our timid sort of people are disconcerted, when they are positively told that the sentiments of the country are different from those of the city."[57]

In his explanations of the benefits deriving from communication among the towns, Adams repeatedly emphasized the need not only for united sentiments, but for a self-conscious public union of sentiment. To Warren he wrote: "Whenever the friends of the Country shall be assured of each others *Sentiments*, that Spirit which is necessary will not be wanting." "Therefore," he told Gerry, "a free communication with each town will serve to ascertain this matter; and when it once appears beyond contradiction, that we are united in sentiments there will be a confidence in each other, & a plan of opposition will be easily formed, & executed with spirit." The people must be made conscious that their whole strength lay in their own virtue. English support was fickle, even Lords Chatham and Shelburne were not always dependable. Once the people were awakened to the realization that they need bear "insults and oppression no longer than until they feel in themselves

55. Samuel Adams to Elbridge Gerry, Oct. 29, 1772, and Nov. 5, 1772, in *The Writings of Samuel Adams*, II, 341–342, 347.
56. William Gordon, *History of the Rise, Progress, and Establishment, of the Independence of the United States of America* (London, 1788), I, 312.
57. Samuel Adams to James Warren, Nov. 4, 1772, *Warren-Adams Letters*, I, 12; Samuel Adams to Elbridge Gerry, Nov. 5, 1772, *Writings of Samuel Adams*, II, 346–347.

strength to shake off the yoke," redress would lie within their reach. For the moment it was crucial that some towns make public declaration; these doings reported in the press would raise morale, encouraging widespread participation. Otherwise, if Boston raised its voice alone, Adams feared it would once more be singled out as the discontented seat of faction; and the "tory" claim that legitimate grievances were "imaginary" or "seditious" would be accepted in England as the general voice of Massachusetts.[58] Even worse, towns which shared Boston's view might be persuaded that they were indeed in a minority, and that their own views were at least unorthodox if not wholly incorrect.

The first news from Marblehead, Newburyport, and Plymouth encouraged the Boston committee. In Marblehead a petition for a town meeting was rapidly drafted and circulated, and Gerry was confident his town would "give a spring" to Boston's proposal.[59] In Plymouth the political pulse was "beating high," and Warren was able to assure Adams that he would "have no difficulty in getting a meeting here and carrying the point to second you as proposed." Yet in early November most other towns remained quiet. Their silence raised questions in Warren's mind; he wondered whether it was part of the Boston committee's plan. Perhaps it was Boston's intention to complete its proceedings in advance of the other towns, so they might be able to "have before them a full view of the Transactions of the Metropolis" before they acted. However this general quiet, broken only by the stirrings of half a dozen towns, certainly was not Adams' or the committee's wish.[60]

The towns' reluctance to act immediately seems to have resulted from several causes. First, though Samuel Adams and the Boston committee had acquired reliable private information that the judges' stipends had been settled, the rest of the province was uncertain. Even the most zealous towns hesitated. Should the newspaper reports prove mistaken, if the salaries had not been confirmed, or if the judges had declined to accept them, then a town would be acting prematurely, risking its good

58. Samuel Adams to James Warren, Nov. 4, 1772, *Warren-Adams Letters*, I, 12; Adams to Elbridge Gerry, Nov. 5, 1772, to Arthur Lee, Nov. 3, 1772, *Writings of Samuel Adams*, II, 346–347, 348, 344–345.

59. Samuel Adams to James Warren, Nov. 4, 1772, *Warren-Adams Letters*, I, 12; Adams to Elbridge Gerry, Nov. 14, 1772, *Writings of Samuel Adams*, II, 349–350; Elbridge Gerry to Adams, Nov. 10, 1772, Samuel Adams Papers, New York Public Library.

60. James Warren to Samuel Adams, Nov. 8, 1772, *Warren-Adams Letters*, II, 399–400; Adams to Elbridge Gerry, Nov. 14, 1772, *Writings of Samuel Adams*, II, 350.

name.[61] More important, almost every town was reluctant to make itself stand out as opposed to the administration unless it could be sure of general support. In addition, towns felt it would be presumptuous for a smaller, less important town to act ahead of Boston, the customary leader. It was recognized that Boston, the "metropolis," closest to information and to acts of government, should act first.[62]

The Boston committee, of course, was thoroughly acquainted with these prevailing attitudes. It had developed its whole plan to arouse activity in conformity with the assumptions and habits of the towns. It knew that the people in the province would not act hastily; it recognized that "they must see thro' the matter to its utmost termination; they must be satisfied how many ways it may probably terminate, and compute the chances with the nicety of a De Moivre, before they will engage in anything dangerous." At the same time the committee believed it could be confident that "when they are satisfied they will proceed gently, but with constancy, and finally attain their end." Though the committee members would have preferred to "see the flame bursting in different parts of the Country & distant from each other" immediately, they had not expected it; as it was they were pleased by the vigor of the handful of towns which had begun to stir.[63]

The governor's friends, however, were heartened to see that Boston's attitude of resistance was almost unique. Hoping to contain this spirit, they attacked and disparaged both the Boston committee and the town meeting which had created it. In the press, articles appeared pointing to the supposed thinness of the town meeting, to the unwillingness of eminent persons to serve on the committee, and to the foolishness of the alarm.[64] It was argued that if the people in Boston were too busy to attend the meeting and to serve the committee, then certainly the country people would be "exceeding busy." Ridiculing the plan to correspond with the other towns, its opponents described it as merely

61. Samuel Adams to Elbridge Gerry, Oct. 27, 1772, *Writings of Samuel Adams*, II, 339–340; Elbridge Gerry to Samuel Adams, Oct. 27, 1772, Elbridge Gerry Papers, Massachusetts Historical Society.

62. Above comment based on the contents of subsequent replies.

63. Abraham De Moivre (1667–1754) was a Huguenot mathematician who settled in England, and was a friend of Isaac Newton, and author of *The Doctrine of Chances* (London, 1716). Thomas Young to Hugh Hughes, Dec. 21, 1772, Miscellaneous Bound Documents, 1765–1775, Mass. Hist. Soc.; Samuel Adams to Elbridge Gerry, Nov. 14, 1772, *Writings of Samuel Adams*, II, 350.

64. The first charge was authoritatively answered by the Boston selectmen in the *Boston Gazette*, Dec. 7, 1772, 3:2. They asserted the attendance was above three hundred persons.

"another channel for conveying their stale harangues to the Publick." To those allied with the governor, it seemed likely that the whole "political Manoeuvre will be frustrated."[65]

Yet as responses to Boston's lead appeared in the last weeks of November, even before the *Votes and Proceedings* were printed and sent, the scorn of the "friends to government" became mixed with a more serious concern. Invective directed at the committee in the press became sharper and less good-natured. The Boston committee was stigmatized as "a set of Atheists or Deists, men of profligate manners and profane tongues." To counter the activity of Boston and Plymouth, it was asserted that "the best men" in both towns had taken no part in the proceedings, and that everywhere the people of Massachusetts and all the colonies were "really tired of quarrelling." The new ministry led by Dartmouth, they claimed, was the best that rational men could expect. Massachusetts' governor, Thomas Hutchinson, a native, was also the best man the province could wish for. They said he not only possessed the love and admiration of Massachusetts, but also the respect of the English. They reported that his speech to the assembly during the previous summer was being regarded as "a most perfect master-piece" in England, "one of the finest portraits (notwithstanding its brevity) of the nature and end of the British constitution that ever was penned."[66]

In the courts, where Adams and Gerry had hoped the towns would seize the initiative, the administration took the offensive. Yet Gerry found that its efforts only reinforced Boston's position. Exulting, he described the session at Salem:

Such extraordinary Pains are taken by the Governor, Judges & ordinary Justices to lull the people & reconcile these "Establishments" that they begin to be fully convinced the Crown is strengthening itself by raising Monies out of them gradually, & converting these Revenues to bribe every Officer in the Government on its Side. Nothing serves to bring such full Conviction as the Charges to the grand Juries; for instead of instructing the grand Jurymen &c in their Offices & Duty, the Judge tells them "*that* the Governor is a fine Man, *that* they must submit to Government. *That* the Non Importation Agreement was contrary to the Laws of God & Man"; & such

65. "Q.E.D.," in *Boston Weekly News-Letter*, Nov. 12, 1772, 3:1–2; also Ann Hulton, Nov. 21, 1772, *Letters of a Loyalist Lady, 1767–1776* (Cambridge, Mass., 1927), 55; "Q.E.D.," *Boston Weekly News-Letter*, Nov. 19, 1772, 2:2.

66. Aaron Davis, Jr., *Boston Weekly News-Letter*, Nov. 26, 1772, 2:1–2; "I.H.," *Boston Weekly News-Letter*, Nov. 26, 1772, 2:2; *Massachusetts Gazette and Boston Post-Boy*, Nov. 16, 1772, 2:2.

untrue & designing Inculcations are advanced, as are too gross for our Children, much more so for the grand & petty Juries of this province — [67]

The newspapers, in spite of the praise for the governor and the attacks on the Boston committee, were encouraging action by people all over the province simply by describing the activity in Marblehead and New-buryport, Cambridge and Plymouth, as well as Boston.[68] The handful of towns "in motion of their accord" excited the hopes of the Boston committee as it prepared to send out the pamphlet.[69] The "tories" had not only been thrown on the defensive strategically, it now appeared that the committee of correspondence had judged the public climate accurately. Now with the harvest over, and snow-free and mud-free roads permitting the best overland communication, their pamphlet would be placed in waiting hands all over Massachusetts.

V

Governor Hutchinson watched this affair with growing alarm. His early scorn had quickly changed to serious concern as he saw Boston's activity catch on elsewhere. He believed he saw the "doctrine of Independence upon the Parliament and the mischiefs of it every day increase."[70] For several years he had been urging Parliament to take some effective steps to squelch this absurdity. But as time went on he came to feel he was waiting in vain. The longer the opinion was tolerated — and the silence and inactivity of Parliament meant toleration — the more the opinion spread. Soon it would become impossible to eradicate. The "delusion" must be answered directly, explicitly, and officially, or, he was convinced, Massachusetts would never return to good government and order.[71]

Having already waited years for Parliament to act, he feared that in the present crisis he could not afford to wait any longer. So he

67. Elbridge Gerry to Samuel Adams, Nov. 18, 1772, Samuel Adams Papers, New York Public Library.
68. Elbridge Gerry to Samuel Adams, Nov. 18, 1772, and Nov. 19, 1772, Samuel Adams Papers, New York Public Library; James Warren to Samuel Adams, Nov. 17, 1772, *Warren-Adams Letters*, II, 400.
69. Samuel Adams to Arthur Lee, Nov. 31, 1772, *Writings of Samuel Adams*, II, 379–380.
70. Thomas Hutchinson to Richard Jackson, Dec. 8, 1772, Hutchinson Letter Books, Mass. Arch., XXVII, 428.
71. Hutchinson to Lord Dartmouth, Dec. 22, 1772, Hutchinson Letter Books, Mass. Arch., XXVII, 431.

decided to call the assembly. When it convened in January 1773, he would put the question to it in an address, and force the House and the Council either to avow or disavow these town proceedings "tending to mutiny and rebellion." He would confront them with his own "calm and dispassionate State of the case." For once, he thought, he would take full advantage of his position of eminence and authority, and use the forum of the General Court to answer finally the specious arguments of the opposition. Hutchinson was confident that if his speech could not convince the entire assembly, "yet it would have a good effect with many of the people who . . . were every day through the unwearied pains of the Leaders of Opposition made Proselytes to these new opinions in Government." The press had proved insufficient; indeed he believed that "seven eighths of the people" only read Edes and Gill anyway.[72] The judges' charges to the grand and petty juries had not fulfilled their purpose. Recognizing the necessity of a properly informed public, sure of his ability to explain and interpret the constitution, the governor decided to take his case to the people through a speech to their representatives in the General Court.

From a logical as well as a political standpoint, his position was precarious. In order to maintain the authority of government as he understood it, he was forced to attempt to convince the public that their rights as colonists could not in all respects be equal to those of the English, and that they themselves must recognize the practical limits of their rights and restrain themselves within those bounds. His whole speech of January 6, 1773, the official "answer" to the Boston pamphlet, would indirectly acknowledge the primary assumption of the committee of correspondence — that government in Massachusetts actually did rest on the beliefs of the people, the active consent of the governed.

To rebut the Boston pamphlet Governor Hutchinson regarded only one point as essential — the supremacy of Parliament. If he could firmly establish that point, he believed his other conclusions would prove incontrovertible. Therefore, rather than dilute his efforts by arguing over the specific rights or the particular grievances asserted in the pamphlet, the governor attempted to explain Massachusetts' subordina-

72. Hutchinson to Dartmouth, Dec. 22, 1772, to Dartmouth, Jan. 7, 1773, to Francis Bernard, Aug. 12, 1770, Hutchinson Letter Books, Mass. Arch., XXVII, 431, 436–437, XXVI, 534–535.

tion to Parliament, in the clearest, most direct terms. Adopting a tone of candor and conciliation, he led the assembly and the province through his own reasoning on the subject.

He began by apologizing for making a speech. But when he considered "the government is at present in a disturbed and disordered state," his duty to the King and the province required him to communicate his sentiments. Speaking with the authority of an expert on Massachusetts history, he described the province's subordination to Parliament from the earliest days when the original settlers had taken possession of the colony under a grant from the Crown (not the King) of England. From the outset, he said, both the settlers and the kingdom had understood that the settlers would "remain subject to the supreme authority of Parliament."[73] Moreover this authority had been exercised by Parliament, and acknowledged by the assembly for generations. Indeed, until recently, it had never been questioned. Massachusetts law and Massachusetts courts had always recognized acts of Parliament as binding in the province. This, the governor said, was a matter of fact.

Nor could it be otherwise. It was a universal law of nations that colonies remained subject to the government of the parent state. The fact that English colonies had their own legislatures could not alter that central truth. These legislatures, living testimony to the remarkable spirit of liberty inherent in the English constitution, could only exercise "subordinate powers." The imperial relationship was hierarchical, and Parliament was at the top of the hierarchy. For generations, he said, the colony had been happy under this arrangement.[74]

But now, suddenly, "a number of inhabitants," assuming "the name of legal town meetings," were denying all this and alienating the people from their King. They had even formed "committees of correspondence . . . in several of those towns, to maintain the principles" which ran so contrary to reason.[75] They were making absurd claims: that a subordinate legislature, the General Court, could possess exclusive powers, wholly beyond the competence of the supreme power; and that the subjects in a colony could possess "all" the liberties of Englishmen in England. Their arguments, based on the charter, were entirely specious according to Hutchinson. The charter made no mention of any exclusive legislative powers, it merely authorized legislation which

73. Alden Bradford, ed., *Speeches of the Governors of Massachusetts, 1765–1775* (Boston, 1818), 336, 337; whole speech at 336–342.
74. *Ibid.*, 338.
75. *Ibid.*

was not repugnant to the laws of England. The charter guarantee of colonists' rights, although it did include "all the liberties and immunities of free and natural subjects, to all intents, constructions and purposes whatsoever, as if they had been born within the realm of England," merely indicated that emigrants and their offspring were not to be regarded as aliens. The governor asserted that it was obviously "impossible" for all Englishmen everywhere to enjoy identical rights.

Such claims, he argued, were based upon a fallacious conception of rights. Rights were neither absolute nor inalienable. If someone voluntarily left the realm to settle in a colony where he could not be represented, then he relinquished the right to representation. The case was clear, either the emigrant gave up his right, or the government was deprived of its authority over the subject. It could not be the latter; emigrants could not simply remove themselves from subjection to government. Nor could they properly claim violations of their "natural rights." For it was in the nature of every government, necessarily, to deprive its subjects of natural rights. To complain of infringements of natural rights was, he said, to object to the "state of government" itself.[76]

Hutchinson brought his appeal to a dramatic climax by posing what he regarded as the essential alternatives: "I know of no line that can be drawn between the supreme authority of Parliament and the total independence of the colonies."[77] He meant to shock Massachusetts back to its senses. He felt sure that if the people of the province would recognize that these were the only alternatives they would cease their restless opposition. It was self-evident that the colony could not survive independent, and no one would be so perverse as to suggest that it would be better off under Spanish, French, or Dutch rule; therefore the people would have to accept parliamentary supremacy. Everyone, he thought, would agree that everything of value to the province depended on its connection to England.

Once the people in Massachusetts accepted these principles, "contentment and order" would return. When Parliament's authority was accepted, there could be no more complaints about "the mere exercise of this authority." He exhorted the assembly and the people to return to "the same principles, [by which] our ancestors were easy and happy for a long course of years together."[78] Here was the correct constitu-

76. Bradford, ed., *Speeches of the Governors of Massachusetts*, 340.
77. *Ibid.*
78. *Ibid.*, 341.

tional path; and from a practical standpoint he offered this as their best hope. It would permit them to continue to "enjoy as great a proportion" of English and natural rights "as can be enjoyed by a plantation or colony." Massachusetts would be restored to that tranquillity which could once more unite it with England and the other colonies.[79]

The governor's appeal to the province had been thoughtfully prepared. There were no Latin phrases and no authorities cited to overawe the reader. The language was as simple and direct as the logic was easy to follow. The argument ran in short, straight lines to sensible, practical conclusions. The governor's tone expressed absolute certainty. He meant to convince his audience, and like the Boston Committee of Correspondence, he assumed that the province shared his premises. His long and varied experience in provincial affairs, his thorough study of Massachusetts' past, the universal applause his *History* had received, all led him to believe that he could understand the province if anyone could. He never considered that his own fundamental political beliefs might not be generally held. It was only a "delusion" which had spread through Massachusetts in recent years, an infatuation promulgated and exploited by a handful of his own "blackhearted," cynical enemies. They had succeeded because the towns were "perfect Democracies" where inhabitants, every one of them, came to regard themselves as legislators. In these forums the false, flattering ideas of the "faction" could hold sway over the "true principles" of government. The people were duped into mouthing and voting for ideas which they could not understand. His speech might at least set the leaders of towns, men of "worth," back on the proper path.

When he concluded his speech, Governor Hutchinson was not at all sure what its effect might be. He did not expect to silence the assembly since it was led by "the faction," but he believed he had forced it to reflect upon its actions. He found that the speech had "amazed" three fourths of the representatives, men so ignorant of "their Constitution" that they had simply "taken for granted that all that had been done by parliament was arbitrary and unconstitutional." When and if the House or Council should choose to reply to his arguments, the emphasis he had placed on the supremacy of Parliament would force them to either yield to his logic, or to expose publicly their extravagant view of "independence" to both the province and to their troublesome allies in English politics. In the latter case his own hand would be strengthened,

79. *Ibid.*, 341, 342.

since it would "make apparent the reasonableness and necessity of coercion and justify it to all the world."[80]

As the weeks went by the governor became convinced that his speech had been successful. If he had not restored orthodox political ideas to Massachusetts, he had at least blocked the committee of correspondence "plan." His speech, he believed, had forced the House to consider constitutional questions, and had thereby diverted it from its supposed intention to send a circular letter to the other assemblies inviting them to join in its principles.[81] Within the province he believed he had properly reasserted authority, and as a result he thought "I certainly have put a stop for the present to the progress of the Towns and Districts."[82] He reported to Dartmouth that only "one or two have called a meeting of their Inhabitants since my Speech appeared in print." His friends assured him he had done a "great service, by opening people's eyes."[83] Now, he believed, if Parliament would actively and consistently maintain its supremacy, the people could be brought to believe in subordination to Parliament as the only way to restore a spirit of mutual harmony.[84]

Governor Hutchinson repeated this estimate of the effect of his speech on Massachusetts in more than half a dozen letters in February and March 1773. But he was seriously mistaken. Nowhere in the province was there any hint of a popular return to orthodoxy as Hutchinson understood it. Towns continued to meet, pass resolves, and make their own elaborations on the Boston pamphlet. His assessment of the impact of his speech, like the arguments he had propounded in the speech itself, was based upon assumptions which differed profoundly from those common in Massachusetts. Ironically, the speech which had given the governor fresh hope when he first saw it in print in the newspaper, was subsequently published by his opponents Edes and Gill in a pamphlet together with the Council and House replies.[85] His adversaries found that it explicitly confirmed their contentions.

80. Thomas Hutchinson to ?, Jan. 7, 1773; to John Pownall, Jan. 7, 1773, Hutchinson Letter Books, Mass. Arch., XXVII, 438–441.

81. Hutchinson to James Gambier, Feb. 19, 1773, to John Pownall, Feb. 24, 1773, to General Mackay, Feb. 23, 1773, Hutchinson Letter Books, Mass. Arch., XXVII, 448–449, 457–458, 454–455.

82. Hutchinson to Israel Mauduit, Feb. 20, 1773, ibid., 450–451.

83. Hutchinson to Dartmouth, Feb. 22, 1773, ibid., 451–452.

84. Hutchinson to Israel Mauduit, Feb. 20, 1773, ibid., 450–451.

85. Thomas Hutchinson, The Speeches of his Excellency Governor Hutchinson, to the General Assembly of the Massachusetts-Bay. At a session begun and held on the 6th of January 1773. With the answers of his Majesty's Council and the House of Representatives respectively (Boston, 1773).

In part the governor's error may be explained by his need to justify the strategy of his speech, both to himself and the ministry. In addition his information about the sentiments of various towns was frequently distorted. His friends usually sent word that the people in their towns were quiet and agreed with the administration. Those who were not his friends did not communicate. Draper's *Boston Weekly News-Letter*, the administration gazette, stopped printing town proceedings in January; and Edes and Gill's *Boston Gazette* misled him because its policy of printing town proceedings at the direction of the Boston committee in the order they were received meant that they were printing January proceedings throughout February and March, and even as late as August. As a result the governor could readily believe that the progress of the Boston pamphlet had been stopped, and that his opponents were merely printing old material in order to create the impression that activity was continuing in the towns, even though they were silent. Believing the towns to be quiet, Hutchinson could assume that by their silence they acquiesced with the government, a conventional assumption of contemporary English politics.

5

The Emergence

of Local Opinion

Beginning in January 1773, and continuing into the spring and even the summer, scores of towns met to consider the Boston pamphlet. Their responses, though primarily concerned with the issues raised by the Boston committee, also served as replies to Governor Hutchinson's position. Indeed most of them were prepared and voted after the governor's speech had been delivered and after the representatives who had listened to it had returned home. These local responses, however, were more than merely replies to the Boston committee or the governor. They comprised the most elaborate general expression of provincial opinion that Massachusetts had ever witnessed, revealing the catalytic role of the Boston Committee of Correspondence in the development of a broadly-based revolutionary movement in Massachusetts.

Still, Governor Hutchinson's judgments about public assumptions had been accurate in several respects. The people of Massachusetts more than joined in his appreciation of the correctness of their ancestors' behavior; and they were anxious to follow the path their forefathers had chosen. Moreover they also agreed that harmony with Great Britain was essential to their well-being, and that separation from the mother country was a fearsome danger. Like the governor, they shared a profound belief in the necessity of order. But the governor's central premise

Note: An earlier version of chapter 5 appeared as "Massachusetts Towns Reply to the Boston Committee of Correspondence, 1773," *William and Mary Quarterly*, 3d ser., XXV (1968) 22–39.

about the nature of individual rights and parliamentary supremacy was not similarly shared. It conflicted with common provincial beliefs that rights were more valuable than order and that order must rest on the constitution. Public virtue was dearer than tranquillity.

In local replies most people in Massachusetts rejected Governor Hutchinson's solicitude for the rights of authority. Their primary interest, as they were to express it, lay in the rights of individual subjects. When the governor rhetorically asked whether a subject could voluntarily remove himself from subjection to Parliament, he expected an emphatic "No." But his audience in Massachusetts was to answer "Yes." Where the governor saw natural rights, including the right to taxation by consent, as mutable, the province regarded the eternal protection of such rights as the government's sole reason for existence. Time and again they would repeat that their ancestors, by emigrating from England, had not relinquished their right to consent to taxes as the governor so easily assumed.

The parliamentary supremacy described in the governor's speech meant that Parliament enjoyed absolute legislative authority in the colonies as well as England. However in Massachusetts, even though people allowed that Parliament was the highest legislature in the empire, they regarded all legislative authority as limited, limited by inviolable constitutional safeguards. Supremacy did not, in their eyes, mean unlimited competence or an ability to overturn essential rights. The powers which Hutchinson attributed to Parliament, wholly apart from questions of its proper sphere of competence, most people believed could not be properly assigned to any legislature whatsoever.

The governor's final pragmatic assumption that colonial status necessarily involved a diminution of subjects' rights, a fact which he regarded as self-evident, was fundamentally opposed to the all but universal belief that subjects in Massachusetts should enjoy precisely the same rights as subjects in any county in England. People in the province regarded it as self-evident that their ancestors would not have undergone the hardships of settlement in exchange for a reduction in their rights. They took the words of the charter literally; and the grievances which Hutchinson called insignificant were especially outrageous because they deprived the inhabitants of equal liberty with their fellow subjects in England. As a result, persuasive as the speech of January 6 appeared to its author, it could not persuade its intended audience.

Instead the local answers to the Boston pamphlet vindicated the Boston committee's efforts. Towns did not merely accept the pamphlet as legitimate, they were frequently enthusiastic in answering its call for statements of political principles. Now, for the first time, under the impetus of the Boston committee a majority of Massachusetts towns met to consider and to formulate their basic political beliefs. Their opinions were not uniform, and they varied in significant ways. Yet beneath their variations the local proceedings exposed the elements of a consensus built around the idea that in an immediate, practical sense, sovereignty lay with the people organized in towns not Parliament or even the General Court. The local proceedings revealed that in Massachusetts at least, the Revolution would be created from a broad local base.[1]

I

The torrent of town and district proceedings which deluged Massachusetts in the first months of 1773 represented, at least superficially, the voice of the people. In scores of communities and in every county in the province the thousands of inhabitants who normally participated in local affairs considered the Boston pamphlet and voted on it, one way or another. How far these votes and proceedings represented truly popular views cannot be known with exactitude. Indeed several scholars have argued plausibly that this outpouring of opinion in the name of the people actually expressed the views of a relatively small, homogeneous political elite spread in a thin layer all over the province. The people at large, it is said, were too little informed in political theory to have possessed any clear ideas, and so they voted in ignorance for the opinions presented to them by a handful of local leaders, either leaders tied to the Boston radicals or else simply the traditional local leaders.[2]

In some towns this elitist interpretation can be more persuasively

1. These remarks will be supported by the body of information which follows in this chapter.

2. One variant of this view is presented by Lawrence H. Gipson, *The British Empire Before the American Revolution* (New York, 1936–1967), XIII, 450–451, which stresses the role of Boston leadership. Another version was offered in 1918 by Arthur M. Schlesinger, *The Colonial Merchants and the American Revolution, 1763–1776* (New York, 1957), 259–260, where he referred specifically to the response to the Boston committee: "Groups of extremists in the various localities engineered town meetings, which approved the Boston resolutions or adopted others more radical, and appointed standing committees of correspondence composed of radicals." More recently Richard V. Buel, Jr., suggested in letters to me (Jan. 10, 1967, Jan. 27, 1967) that in his view "the shared sentiments of the leadership in the General Court . . . were behind many of the town replies." In his judgment the prominent leaders assumed the active role and the rest of the town assented to their actions.

Map of New England, Carrington Bowles, London, 1771.

Blow-up view from Paul Revere's 1774 View of Boston. The major buildings are, from left to right: Old South Meeting-House, King's Chapel, Beacon Hill Beacon, Old Boston Town House, Province House (Old State House), Brattle Street Meeting-House, Faneuil Hall, New North Brick Meeting-House. At the lower right can be seen the beginning of the Long Wharf, and at the far left the foot of Fort Hill. *Royal American Magazine* (1774).

View of Faneuil Hall, engraving by Paul Revere for *Massachusetts Magazine* (March 1789). Courtesy, Massachusetts Historical Society, Boston.

Thomas Hutchinson by John Singleton Copley (?). Courtesy, Massachusetts Historical Society, Boston.

Samuel Adams by John Singleton Copley. Courtesy, Museum of Fine Arts, Boston.

Joseph Warren by John Singleton Copley. Courtesy, Museum of Fine Arts, Boston, bequest of Dr. Buckminster Brown.

James Otis, Jr., by Joseph Blackburn. Courtesy, Mrs. Carlos Hepp and Museum of Fine Arts, Boston.

BOSTON, *May* 12, 1774.

GENTLEMEN,

BY the laſt advices from London we learn that an Act has been paſſed by the Britiſh Parliament for blocking up the Harbour of Boſton, with a Fleet of Ships of War, and preventing the Entrance in, or Exportation of, all Sorts of Merchandize, on Penalty of Forfeiture of the Goods and the Veſſels which carry them : And not only the Goods and Veſſels are to be forfeited, but the very Wharfinger who ſhall aſſiſt in lading or diſcharging ſuch Goods or Merchandize, ſhall forfeit treble their Value, at their higheſt Price, together with his Cattle, Horſes, Carriages, Implements whatſoever, made Uſe of in lading or landing them.

And under theſe grievous and unheard of Impoſitions are we to remain till his Majeſty in Council ſhall be certified by the Governor or Lieutenant Governor, that a *full Obedience* is yielded to the *Laws* of a Britiſh Parliament, and the Revenue duly collected ; and alſo that the Eaſt-India Company have received full Satisfaction for their Teas, and the Revenue Officers, and others for their Sufferings, by their Endeavours to fix the Tea Duty upon us. And even then, the whole Port of *Boſton* with all its Wharves, Quays, &c. ſhall be under the abſolute Controul of his Majeſty, and no Article of Merchandize landed on or laded from any of them, but ſuch as he ſhall licence, on the Penalty aboveſaid.

By this Means, even in Caſe of the moſt abject Submiſſion, and unconditional Obedience, the private Property, in moſt of the Wharves which ſurround this great Town, is raviſhed from the rightful Owners, and rendered uſeleſs, to the utter Ruin of many worthy Citizens, in Revenge to the Patriotiſm of ſome, whom probably this Clauſe was inſerted to puniſh.

To this alarming Situation has the Machinations of our Enemies here and in Great-Britain reduced us : And as this is a Cauſe ſo intereſting to *all* America—A Cauſe which has been hitherto ſo nobly defended by ALL, we cannot entertain a Thought ſo diſhonorable to our Friends, that in this Criſis *we* ſhall be left to ſtruggle *alone.*

We are, Gentlemen,

Your Friends and Fellow Countrymen,

By Order of the Committee,

William Cooper *Clerk*

P. S. As it has been induſtriouſly and wickedly propagated that the patriotic Col. BARRE had become our Enemy, we can aſſure you that in a Speech on this Bill he expreſſed himſelf in theſe emphatic Terms, " *America is ſtamped upon every Loom and Anvil in Great-Britain.*" In plain Engliſh, let America diſcontinue its Trade, and the Britiſh Manufacturer muſt *emigrate* or *ſtarve.*

N. B. This Letter was written in Preſence of and with the Concurrence of the Committees of Correſpondence for the Towns of Dorcheſter, Roxbury, Newtown, Lexington, Brooklyn, Cambridge, Charleſtown and Lynn.

Boston Committee of Correspondence to Salem, May 12, 1774. Courtesy, Massachusetts Historical Society, Boston.

applied than in others, but at the moment neither interpretation, elite or popular, can be conclusively confirmed or refuted. Certainly it is true that when the towns spoke, their statements were drawn up by a small group or even a single individual who was not necessarily speaking accurately for a majority of the townspeople, though a majority may have voted in town meeting. Yet in view of the variety of local opinions and their widespread appearance, it is hazardous to postulate the existence of any connected provincial elite operating in the towns. On the contrary, it seems safer for the moment to assume that if a town voted, its vote did reasonably express the views of local townspeople. How these people formed their views is another question, one which will be considered in a later chapter. It was only after an increasing number of towns established their own standing committees of correspondence that one begins to see fragmentary evidence which at least suggests the dynamics of opinion-formation at the local level.

The pattern of provincial opinion as declared by the towns, however, became visible almost immediately. By April 1773 at least 119 of the 260 towns and districts in Massachusetts had taken some action, and at least 25 more responded within the succeeding five months, making a majority. These figures are somewhat lower than the exact figures because they are drawn primarily from the records of the Boston Committee of Correspondence which are incomplete. The committee records have been supplemented by information found in the local records of a representative sample of 93 towns and districts of every size and in every part of every county in the province, one third of the total. This sample reveals more fully than can the records of the committee alone the actual response of the province to Boston's initiative, since the committee records include only the local proceedings that were sent to Boston, received by the Boston committee, and still survive. Together, the records of the committee and the information from the sample permit at least a rough analysis of the incidence of local responses to the Boston Committee of Correspondence.

The most important correlation these records demonstrate is that local behavior in early 1773 was closely related to previous patterns of action or inaction on questions touching provincial and imperial politics. Judging on the basis of towns and districts in the sample, in which town meeting records were examined from 1765 to 1775, it is apparent that towns where the events of the 1760's like the Stamp Act or the non-importation movement had produced responses, much more frequently acted on the Boston committee pamphlet; whereas inactive towns were far more likely to remain inactive. Among the towns in the sample which considered the Boston pamphlet, two thirds had acted in relation to some provincial or imperial issue at least twice between 1765 and 1771.[3] In contrast, towns where the pamphlet was never taken up in town meeting normally had a history of ignoring such questions. More than half of them had never considered any of the issues which had aroused the province from the Stamp Act onward, and only one fifth had acted as often as twice before. Thus, the towns already "engaged" in provincial politics were most responsive to the Boston committee's appeal.

At the same time, however, it is significant that the efforts of the Boston Committee of Correspondence exercised an immediate impact on the political awareness of some previously "apolitical" communities. One sixth of the responding towns had never before considered a provincial or imperial issue, and another sixth had acted only once before, mostly in connection with the Convention of 1768. Therefore, although it is clear that the Boston committee aroused the most general response from towns where interest in extraordinary provincial issues had already been demonstrated, it also stimulated activity in localities where such interest had seldom if ever appeared before.

This primary correlation between previous activity and responsiveness to the Boston pamphlet overlaps with two other factors, population and location, which also distinguished the responsive from the unresponsive towns. Larger towns and those nearest to Boston were far more active than tiny, faraway districts. Yet this correlation holds only at relatively extreme ends of the spectrum, for communities of less than 700 inhabitants and the handful of those with over 2,700 people. The great majority of towns were between these extremes, and though there was some connection between population and activity it was not very marked and there were numerous exceptions.

Geographic location, which overlaps somewhat with population, appears directly related to local responsiveness from one perspective, since

3. These assertions and those which follow are based on the records of the ninety-three towns listed in the Appendix and on the records found among the papers of the Boston committee. The provincial-imperial issues on which towns might have acted (in every case at least several did) between 1765 and 1771 were: 1765, Stamp Act; 1766, question of compensation to Stamp Act riot sufferers; 1767, movement to encourage manufacturing and discourage luxuries, boycott movement; 1768, approval or disapproval of vote to rescind circular letter, Convention of Towns; 1769, boycott movement; 1770, boycott movement, Boston Massacre.

65 percent of the towns and districts east of Hampshire County responded, while in the western counties of Hampshire and Berkshire only 22 percent responded. Here, regional political habits probably exercised some influence. Eastern Massachusetts had always been more closely associated with Boston than the western counties, and in 1768 only three of the delegates to the Convention of Towns had come from Hampshire and none came from Berkshire. Robert J. Taylor believes that western towns were normally reluctant to follow Boston; yet Taylor also reports that the pamphlet "made a real dent in the conservatism of the west," so the political implications of the low response from Hampshire and Berkshire are ambiguous.[4]

Location alone, clearly, does not provide a satisfactory explanation for the disproportionately low response rate of the westernmost counties. The fact that Hampshire and Berkshire contained the highest proportion of brand-new, tiny (under five hundred people) frontier communities — towns which were less likely to participate in provincial affairs regardless of their location — appears important in light of the correlations of size and prior activity discussed earlier. Further evidence that mere proximity to Boston was not a crucial determinant comes from the pattern of responses among other counties. The response rate in Boston's own county, Suffolk, ran 15 percent lower than Middlesex, while two counties of roughly equal distance from Boston, Bristol and Barnstable, showed response rates which differed by 25 points. Most striking of all, Cumberland County in Maine exhibited a response rate 35 points above its neighbor York, even though York was actually closer to Boston.[5]

Geography does have a part in explaining some of these disparities. In the case of Bristol County, much of its commerce and communica-

4. Delegates to the Convention of Towns are listed in Richard D. Brown, "The Massachusetts Convention of Towns, 1768," *William and Mary Quarterly*, 3d Ser., XXVI (1969), 103–104; Robert J. Taylor, *Western Massachusetts in the Revolution* (Providence, 1954), 34, 37, 62.

5. Population statements are based on the censuses of 1763–1765 and 1775, which appear in Joseph B. Felt, "Statistics of Population in Massachusetts," American Statistical Association, *Collections*, I, pt. ii (Boston, 1845), 121–214, census of 1763–1765 appears on 148–157; and in Stella H. Sutherland, *Population Distribution in Colonial America* (New York, 1936), 16–20.

The percent of towns in each county which responded to the Boston Committee of Correspondence pamphlet prior to September 1773 is as follows: Nantucket, 100 percent; Middlesex, 89 percent; Essex, 80 percent; Cumberland, 75 percent; Suffolk, 74 percent; Barnstable, 67 percent; Worcester, 64 percent; Plymouth, 62 percent; Lincoln, 50 percent; Bristol, 42 percent; York, 40 percent; Hampshire, 22 percent; Berkshire, 20 percent; Dukes, 0 percent.

tion centered on Providence, Rhode Island, rather than Boston. And towns in Hampshire and Berkshire were likely to trade with Hartford, the major commercial center for the entire Connecticut River valley. But even these general patterns of commerce and communication do not provide conclusive explanations because several counties and many individual towns do not fit this mold. Indeed there were nearly fifty towns, including thirty in Bristol, Hampshire, and Berkshire, which had sent representatives to the current session of the General Court and yet, according to the data in hand, did not respond in any way to Boston's invitation. Their inaction may be explained in various ways, but absence of direct communication with Boston is not one of them.

The governor, of course, thought that the impression made by his speech to the assembly had stopped local responses. For some of these fifty towns this may indeed have been an indirect result of the governor's speech, since after the House and Council had finished rebutting the governor and stating their own fundamentally Whig position, some believed that further local statements were redundant. After all, the highest representative authorities, the House and Council, appeared to have said it all in their 20,000 words of closely-reasoned argument.[6] In towns where sending a representative comprised the normal maximum of local participation in provincial political activity, there seemed no need to explore these issues in town meeting.

However, in some of the large towns like Springfield in Hampshire and Middleborough in Plymouth, it is clear that the decision to ignore the Boston pamphlet or even suppress it was a deliberate political act of repudiation. Often it appears that the decision was made by local leaders allied to the Hutchinson administration. The governor had powerful allies in Bristol, Hampshire, and Berkshire, and of the ten Hampshire representatives who represented twenty Hampshire towns, most were "connected" to Governor Hutchinson. Thus the dent that Taylor described in western "conservatism" was merely a dent; the Boston pamphlet did not produce a radical alteration in the orientation of Massachusetts' two westernmost counties. From the governor's standpoint no response was probably the best "response" of all, although a handful of towns actually reacted to the pamphlet by voting to either ignore it or else criticize it in some way.

This brief, summary analysis of the incidence of local responses does

6. Alden Bradford, ed., *Speeches of the Governors of Massachusetts, 1765–1775* (Boston, 1818), 342–364, 381–398.

not, certainly, provide a full explanation of why towns acted as they did. However it should indicate that local decisions were not necessarily motivated by ideology or self-conscious partisanship, and that blanket generalizations do not readily fit the actual pattern of behavior. Personal and political factors like local leadership and tradition, the demographic and geographic circumstances of size and location, as well as casual factors such as the timing of the pamphlet's delivery if it was delivered at all — any or all of these could play a part in determining whether or not a town acted on the issues raised by the Boston pamphlet.

Local responses, in the majority of cases a direct reply to the Boston committee, cannot have been totally representative of opinion in Massachusetts. Too many towns were silent, and the views of those that did speak were confined within the relatively compressed formal structure of town meeting resolves. Still this was a larger, more detailed expression of provincial opinion than had ever before been articulated. Moreover the replies revealed the ways in which provincial towns of a few hundred or a few thousand inhabitants related the large questions of imperial policy and constitutional government to their own sphere of political responsibility. Their contents rewarded the efforts of the Boston committee, whose basic assumptions concerning politics and the constitution were not merely confirmed but elaborated in scores of communities.

II

Early in 1773 it became apparent that Boston and its pamphlet had begun what was developing into a general re-examination of the constitutional role of the judges and other officials. At the most sophisticated level John Adams carried on a successful, scholarly newspaper war of attrition with William Brattle over whether or not Massachusetts Bay judges held office "at pleasure" or "during good behavior." Brattle's argument that tenure was "during good behavior," and that therefore royal stipends would assure impartiality, had begun in the Cambridge town meeting.[7] Adams answered him in the *Boston Gazette*, where, with a stupefying display of erudition, Adams proved that tenure was in fact "at pleasure," further arguing that Crown stipends would end

7. See William Brattle's notes of Cambridge town meeting, Dec. 14, 1772, in "Letters and Documents relating to Harvard College and Cambridge," 78, Boston Public Library.

all hopes of impartial justice. Brattle, out-quoted, out-cited, and mistaken, quickly lost interest in the argument and stopped replying to Adams' essays.

Both Adams and Brattle started from the assumption that judges should be as impartial as possible, free from every external influence except justice and the law. Brattle argued that removing their salaries from the assembly's annual appropriation would help serve that purpose. Adams said that to put their salaries in the hands of those who appointed them would bind them like servants to the ministry. The towns agreed with Adams, but there was some uncertainty over whether or not the judges should be entirely impartial after all; and, as it developed, there was also considerable resistance to the idea that judges, or indeed any officer of government, ought to be independent of the people.

The Boston pamphlet, in its objections to the innovation of stipends, paid homage to the conventional principal that judges should be "as independent as possible both on the Prince and People." [8] Many towns concurred, but some disagreed, and a large number were not satisfied with merely resisting the innovation. Most often towns instructed their representatives to investigate the whole matter of judicial salaries and if the reports were true that judges were underpaid, they concluded that the assembly should raise salaries to a level befitting the dignity of the bench.[9] Several towns even went so far as to urge that the salaries be raised immediately.[10] Samuel Adams and the Boston committee opposed these propositions since they would reward the governor's appointees, enhance their stature, and divert attention from the "real issue," the ministerial threat.[11]

Some towns followed the consequences of the discussion even further. On one side a town proposed that the General Court establish a permanent fund so as to secure permanent salaries for the judges; in

8. *Boston Town Records, 1770–1777*, Boston Record Commissioners, *Report*, XVIII (Boston, 1887), 102.

9. E.g. Wrentham, Jan. 11, 1773, Boston Committee of Correspondence, Minute Book, IV, 288–290, New York Public Library, photostats at Massachusetts Historical Society; Bradford, Jan. 7, 1773, *ibid.*, II, 141–142; Beverly, Jan. 5, 1773, Letters and Proceedings received by the Boston Committee of Correspondence, photos 76–78, New York Public Library, photostats at Massachusetts Historical Society.

10. E.g. Scarborough, Leicester, Spencer, Paxton.

11. Samuel Adams to James Warren, Dec. 9, 1772, *Warren-Adams Letters, Being Chiefly a Correspondence among John Adams, Samuel Adams, and James Warren*, Massachusetts Historical Society, *Collections*, LXXII–LXXIII (1917–1925), I, 14–15.

that way they would be truly independent of both Crown and people.[12] In contrast, more than a few towns rejected the whole principle of independent officials, arguing that all magistrates, including judges, were servants of the people and ought to be dependent on, not independent of, them. Generally towns developed the idea that popular control of official salaries was a constitutional check, a proper balance to the power of rulers. This idea, although it had been inherent in some earlier provincial discussions, was a novelty with particularly important consequences.

In the Boston committee's statement of rights governors had been described as servants, hired by the people and paid by them. No town had taken issue with this formulation, and many had embellished it. However in the minds of some there were differences concerning its precise meaning. The town of Bristol applied the idea to judges and other government officials, "Saving His Excellency the Governor and Council." Applying English constitutional theory to Massachusetts, they believed it proper that the governor and Council, paralleling the King and House of Lords, should be independent of the people.[13] The townspeople of Mendon, however, saw the danger of disequilibrium in the legislature itself, where the governor's stipend would have "a necessary tendency to destroy that balance of Powers which ought to exist between the several branches of the Legislature."[14] They reasoned that the governor himself must be checked by the people's representatives.

Most towns recognized no such distinctions. As the district of New Salem noted, all governors were "trustees" of the people and therefore their interests must be kept identical to those of the people. The relationship was exactly the same as a private trust. To insure their fidelity, trustees ought to be dependent on the people for their salaries; "likewise . . . all trustees are in reason answerable to those who have lodged a trust in their hands."[15] Properly speaking, the governors ought to

12. Roxbury, Dec. 23, 1772, Boston Committee of Correspondence, Minute Book, I, 19–21.

13. Bristol, March 9, 1773, Letters and Proceedings received, photo 109.

14. Mendon, March 1, 1773, *ibid.*, photos 327–328.

15. New Salem, Feb. 15, 1773, *ibid.*, photos 565–569. Such expressions of the proper relation of rulers to the people suggest that the old paternal conception of authority was being supplanted. There is parallel evidence supporting this view in the struggles over the dismission of clergymen in the 1770's. Here the congregations asserted the right to dismiss ministers in the same way that a town would dismiss its officers. A general examination of the problem is in Alan Dawley, "The Political

be united with the people as their guardians; if they became independent they would develop distinct, contrary, alien interests.[16] Braintree summarized this viewpoint: "All civil officers are or ought to be Servants to the people & dependent upon them for their official Support; and every instance to the Contrary from the Governor downwards tends to crush & destroy civil liberty."[17] So far as Governor Hutchinson and the ministry were concerned, this application of the idea was new, radical and destructive of constitutional equilibrium. It destroyed the traditional balance of the three orders in Parliament by making the popular order dominant. It was not the "mixed" government of England, but rather a democratic form of republicanism. Not every town shared this idea, certainly not in such explicit terms. However the overwhelming tendency of resolves, instructions, and letters was in this republican direction — toward a government entirely responsible to the inhabitants of the province — for it was said, "in all civil Governments all power under God is Derived from the People both Legeslative and Executive and such Persons who are thus Invested are no more than the most Dignify'd Servants of the people."[18]

By raising the question of judges' salaries, by discussing the role of officials, by even replying to the Boston committee's pamphlet, towns were implicitly disputing the governor's position. But in some communities, more than a dozen, such an indirect response to the governor's speech was regarded as insufficient, and direct rebuttals were voted either as endorsements of the published replies of the House and Council, or else in their own words, point-by-point. Such responses underlined the divergence between essential public assumptions about government and those held by the governor.

The first point was the towns' right to meet and consult on any matter. Generally townspeople acted on the belief that they could consider any subject and express an opinion individually or as a body. This right had been continually exercised by generations of Massachusetts settlers and was so widely accepted that in the past it had rarely been discussed. It had not been included in the Boston pamphlet, nor had it

Theory of Church Government: Ministerial Dismissions of the 1770's" seminar paper, Harvard University, 1966.

16. Tewksbury, March 4, 1773, Boston Committee of Correspondence, Minute Book, III, 252–255; Holliston, March 1, 1773, Letters and Proceedings received, photo 349.

17. Braintree, March 1, 1773, *ibid.*, photo 99.

18. Petersham, April 3, 1773, *ibid.*, photo 430.

been subject to controversy since the time of Governor Edmund Andros. Yet Governor Hutchinson had opened the question while rebuking the Boston town meeting for its petition and addresses on the subject of judicial salaries. His declaration that "the Law that authorises Towns to Assemble, does not make the business of a Town Meeting . . . to consider of the necessity or expediency of a session of the General Assembly or to debate and transact other matters," suggested that the towns had no right to meet, and that the law permitted consideration of local town business alone.[19] When the governor later elaborated on this theme in his speech, he was not only challenging Boston but all the towns, and so some of them formulated a defense for what had previously been an uncontested, practical right.

Actually, every town that considered Boston's pamphlet tacitly affirmed the right of every community to meet freely and discuss any political question, but on this point some were more direct. Lancaster, a town which Boston Whigs regarded as slightly Tory, signified the importance of this right in its first resolve: "That this and Every other Town in this Province have an undoubted right to meete together and consult upon all matters interesting to them when and so often as they shall Judge fit and it is more especially their Dutey So to Do when any Infringement is made upon their civil or religious liberties."[20] The people of Lexington regarded it as "their unalienable Right, and a Duty they owe to themselves and Posterity, as a Town, as well as Individuals to take these Matters into serious Consideration," notwithstanding the governor's strictures.[21] They were sure that selectmen could call a meeting whenever it was wanted by the inhabitants, and that towns had the further right to correspond at will.[22] Cambridge argued that in the speech the governor had "aimed a blow at the whole Province through the Sides of Boston." It answered by asserting that the town meetings were legal, the resolves were legal, and so were committees of correspondence.[23] Lynn found the governor's proposition absurd: "it appears to be a Principle with his Excellency, that the Representa-

19. *Boston Town Records, 1770–1777*, p. 92. Hutchinson's phrases are inverted.
20. Lancaster, Jan. 13, 1773, Letters and Proceedings received, photo 372; Samuel Adams to James Warren, Dec. 9, 1772, *Warren-Adams Letters*, I, 14–15.
21. Lexington, Dec. 31, 1772, Letters and Proceedings received, photos 396–397. See also Rochester, Jan. 11, 1773, *ibid.*, photo 662; Brimfield, Jan. 21, 1773, *ibid.*, photos 102–104; Sudbury, Jan. 18, 1773, *ibid.*, photos 808–809; Groton, Jan. 25, 1773, Boston Committee of Correspondence, Minute Book, III, 186.
22. Lexington, Jan. 5, 1773, Letters and Proceedings received, photos 396–399.
23. Cambridge, May 3, 1773, Letters and Proceedings received, photo 123.

tives in General Assembly have Authority to determine *some Points* which their Constituents have no Authority to show their Sentiments upon." How, they asked, could a representative have more rights than the very constituents who delegated his power? Surely, they said, the constituents had full "Right to communicate freely our Sentiments to our Representative in General Assembly." [24] Servants could not have a competence broader than their masters; the argument proceeded from the same principles that had been used in describing the relationship of governors and governed.

The Boston "State of Rights" and Governor Hutchinson's speech, both dealing with general constitutional problems, and especially the relationship of Massachusetts to Parliament, called forth lengthy constitutional statements from the towns. Samuel Adams wryly observed, "it must be placed to the credit of the governor, that he has quickened a spirit of enquiry into the nature and end of government, and the connexion of the colonies with Great Britain." [25] Virtually every town denied Parliament's ability to tax the province, and most went considerably futher, directly rebutting the governor's assertion of Parliament's universal legislative competence.[26] Gorham complained that he was merely repeating "the Declaritory Act of Parliament to bind the Colonies in every respect whatsoever," [27] and his argument that the colonists could only expect a "proportion" of the rights of Englishmen was equally outrageous. Many towns found the idea inconceivable, since it was common knowledge that their ancestors had left England to settle the "howling wilderness" with the single purpose of a fuller enjoyment of English and natural rights, civil and religious. Massachusetts inhabitants must enjoy equal rights with inhabitants of Britain.[28] The charter was absolutely clear and explicit on this point. Such a compact "must be Plain & Easily understood it being of such vast Consequence: we know the Deed's of our Lands Though of infinitely less Consequence, will hold no more than what is Plainly Expressed in them." The governor was using "Ambiguous words," "Dark Riddles," and an obviously one-sided explanation to support an incredible view.[29] The concept of unequal, proportional rights was incomprehensible. Perhaps, they felt,

24. Lynn, May 19, 1773, Letters and Proceedings received, photo 429.
25. Samuel Adams to Arthur Lee, May 6, 1773, *The Writings of Samuel Adams,* ed. Harry A. Cushing (New York, 1904–1908), III, 36–38.
26. Mendon, March 1, 1773, Letters and Proceedings received, photo 327. Mendon emphasized that God, not Parliament, was "the supreme Legislator."
27. Gorham, May 14, 1773, *ibid.,* photo 277.
28. E.g. Ashby, June 10, 1773, *ibid.,* photos 30–31.
29. Bellingham, May 19, 1773, *ibid.,* photos 58–59.

"proportional rights" was no more than a courtier's euphemism for slavery.

The heart of their disagreement with the governor lay in towns-people's literal and comprehensive understanding of the meaning of government by the consent of the governed. Consent, the towns repeated over and over again, was the only lawful basis for government; "The People of new England have never given the People of Britain any Right of Jurisdiction over us Consequently we Deem it to be the most unwarrantable Usurpation & view it as an *insufferable insult* in the British Parliament that they assume a Legislative Authority over the American Colonies." [30] If the colonies, New England, or Massachusetts had ever made a compact placing themselves within Parliament's jurisdiction, they demanded to know "when Was it made, in what Year, or What King's Reign, or in what Book Is it Recorded." [31] Plainly, no such compact existed, so Parliament's pretensions were entirely "unconstitutional." The idea that consent might operate in some symbolic manner, or that subjects might exercise such a crucial right in a merely tacit way, appeared so unreasonable in many towns as to be absurd.

The profundity of this difference with the governor can be measured in the statement voted by Pownallborough, a Lincoln County community of 1,400 people which had never previously participated in any provincial politics. Pownallborough chose to answer the governor directly on the question of whether subjects could remove themselves from English jurisdiction, stating that their ancestors had indeed done so on the ground that their liberty of conscience had been violated. Moreover by removing themselves from England they had ended their allegiance to it. "Allegiance," the town continued, "is a relative Term & like Kingdoms and commonwealths is local and has its bounds . . . we doubt not, our Forefathers soon as they landed here considered themselves as beyond the Jurisdiction of the Supream Authority of the Relm of England." [32] The only relation between Massachusetts and England was that stipulated in the charter. From the Massachusetts perspective blood was not thicker than water, so presumably the violations of province rights might lead the sons to tread the same path as their fathers and withdraw their allegiance from Britain.

Yet few towns went so far as Pownallborough's explicit consideration

30. Holden, May 20, 1773, *ibid.*, photo 347.
31. Bellingham, May 19, 1773, *ibid.*, photos 58–59.
32. Pownallborough Resolves, March 31, 1773, in Records of the Town of Wiscasset, vols. 1–2, 31, Wiscasset, Me.

of the question of allegiance. The Boston Committee of Correspondence had not touched the issue, and most towns took their lead from the Boston pamphlet rather than the governor's speech. Their resolutions illustrated not only their divergence from the governor's position, but also their essential agreement with the Boston committee's outlook. Again and again the town resolves supported the Boston committee's assumptions.

One way in which towns reinforced the committee was in their widely expressed desire for a spirit of union among the towns. Often they went beyond the contents of the pamphlet. Recognizing that all were "engaged in one Common Cause, Viz. that of Asserting and Maintaining our Rights," Marlborough citizens hoped "that each Town assisting and Uniting Like a band of Brothers may Banish Tyranny from our Land."[33] They believed, as the committee believed, that union would provide the power to gain redress. Other towns extended the union even beyond the province by aspiring to "Stand firm as one man" with colonists all over the continent.[34] These attitudes, expressed almost without exception in town proceedings but not in the pamphlet, were apparently not implanted by the Boston committee but had been common for some time. In fact this already existing aspiration for unity partly explains the popular welcome given the Boston pamphlet and the applause bestowed "on the means pursued to unite the hearts of the People," the pamphlet and the correspondence among towns.[35]

The Boston committee aimed to promote widespread political education. Its pamphlet was an expression of the belief that an informed citizenry would see the need for continuous defense of political liberty. Often, after examining the pamphlet carefully in public meetings, towns asserted the committee's own implicit assumptions about the importance of political education. Political action was not reserved to elected or appointed officials, or the assembly, or even the towns: "There is a loud call to every one to awake from security and in earnest strive to secure his Liberty, least he politically perish."[36] As Dorchester suc-

33. Marlborough, Jan. 7, 1773, Letter and Proceedings received, photo 503.
34. Medway, Jan. 11, 1773, ibid., photos 518–519. See also Shirley, Jan. 11, 1773, ibid., photo 760; Salisbury, Dec. 28, 1772, ibid., photos 716–718; Sandwich, Jan. 26, 1773, ibid., photos 732–736; Abington, Jan. 11, 1773, ibid., photos 1–2; Cambridge, Dec. 14, 1772, Boston Committee of Correspondence, Minute Book, I, 15–19; Plymouth, Nov. 26, 1772, ibid., 7–8; Templeton, Jan. 11, 1773, ibid., II, 111–115; Wilmington, Jan. 28, 1773, ibid., IV, 352–354.
35. Wilmington, Jan. 28, 1773, Boston Committee of Correspondence, Minute Book, IV, 352–354.
36. Westborough, Jan. 4, 1773, ibid., II, 171–173.

cinctly put it, "It is incumbent upon the People to be watchful." [37] It was "necessary that every Member of this Community qualified to vote in Town Affairs should at all times have a proper sense of them [their rights and the infringements] especially as the future happiness of his Family as well as himself depends greatly on their [the infringements] being removed." [38] Frequently towns expressed no limitation at all on those who should be informed so as to defend their rights; or, setting the most comprehensive limits, they called for "the attention of all well disposed People, and a mutual Connection and joint adherence" in sustaining their rights.[39] At least one town directed that the Boston pamphlet be read to its inhabitants annually so as to stimulate an enlightened, lasting jealousy of their rights.[40]

The necessity of resistance to encroachments on constitutional rights was perhaps the most essential assumption made by the committee of correspondence. Resistance, possessing a glorious history dating from the ouster of Governor Edmund Andros, had been a matter of common practice since the Stamp Act. The pamphlet presented it as a duty to the towns, which gave it widespread endorsement. Towns regarded resistance as a corollary of watchfulness. And, once tyranny was perceived, they concluded that "opposition becomes a Duty." [41] Frequently resistance became a matter of honor no less than duty: "The Dog the more he is beaten the more he fawns, but . . . A Noble Mind Defends to the last, and every Stripe Stimulates his efforts." [42] The Boston pamphlet had complained that the people of Boston and Massachusetts were being castigated as traitors and rebels merely for remonstrating; South Hadley District in Hampshire County, defending the province, revealed how thoroughly the right of resistance could be regarded as natural, even instinctive. It asked, "What if Som imprudencies have hapned in time past and Exceptionable proceedings have been perpetrated when we were almost Desperate and Ruine at the Dore; what

37. Dorchester, Jan. 4, 1773, Letters and Proceedings received, photos 205–206.
38. Westborough, Jan. 4, 1773, Boston Committee of Correspondence, Minute Book, II, 171–173.
39. Princeton, Jan. 25, 1773, Letters and Proceedings received, photos 651–652. See also Plymouth petition, Nov. 13, 1772, in *Boston Weekly News-Letter*, Nov. 26, 1772; Roxbury, Dec. 14, 1772, Boston Committee of Correspondence, Minute Book, I, 25–28; Marlborough, Jan. 1, 1773, Letters and Proceedings received, photos 493–495; Lunenburgh, Jan. 18, 1773, *ibid.*, photos 418–419; Salisbury, Dec. 28, 1772, *ibid.*, photos 716–718; Sandwich, Jan. 26, 1773, *ibid.*, photos 723–726.
40. Marblehead, Dec. 15, 1772, Letters and Proceedings received, photos 473–474.
41. Westborough, Jan. 4, 1773, Boston Committee of Correspondence, Minute Book, II, 171–173.
42. Princeton, Jan. 25, 1773, Letters and Proceedings received, photos 651–652.

man will not Sudenly throw out his Arm to prevent his Neighbour from thrusting his Finger into his eye, even altho his arm might hapen to Strike the face of his Superior; must wee therefore be allways after be Stigmatized on that account." [43] Resistance was far more important than political decorum; it was "the first and highest social Duty of this people," and God and Nature warranted "the use of every Rightful art, and energy of policy, stratagem and force." [44] Within such a climate of belief, attested by the actions and professions of scores of towns since 1765, the proposals of the Boston pamphlet were modest indeed.

Frequently towns greeted the Boston pamphlet with applause, voting their approval and general agreement with it. It had opened "the Eyes of many who have not the opportunity of informing themselves concerning these important matters." [45] At least one town met and "adopted" the pamphlet verbatim.[46] Several found it so useful, so clear and complete, that they recommended it to their representatives for "careful perusal." [47] Yet in spite of the general agreement with it, there were significant variations among towns on particular points. And among the measures recommended for gaining redress there were both important differences and considerable uncertainty. These elements demonstrate conclusively that the town replies were not merely automatic reflexes. Towns acted independently, often choosing to follow Boston, but not in every detail.

On the question of the "rights" of the colonists, several towns dif-

43. South Hadley, Jan. 18, 1773, Letters and Proceedings received, photos 776–777.
44. Petersham, Jan. 4, 1773, *ibid.*, photo 622. According to William Gordon, the Petersham resolves incorporated fragments of a set of resolves which Josiah Quincy, Jr., had previously drawn up for Boston. Gordon reports that a resident of Petersham solicited them from the obliging Quincy and that these fragments comprise about 25 percent of the Petersham resolves. If Gordon's story is true, then this is the only known instance when a member of the Boston committee provided a town with ready-made resolves. From the Boston committee's standpoint this was a risky step because the major purposes of the whole endeavor would have been compromised and laid open to devastating political attack if members of the committee furnished towns with resolves prepared in Boston. The quotation here cited was, according to Gordon, drafted by Quincy. The quotations from Petersham elsewhere in the chapter are from portions of the resolves which were *not* by Quincy. See William Gordon, *History of the Rise, Progress, and Establishment, of the Independence of the United States of America* (London, 1788), I, 315–319. See also Marlborough, Jan. 1, 1773, Letters and Proceedings received, photos 490–495; Lunenburgh, Jan. 18, 1773, *ibid.*, photos 418–419; Gloucester, Dec. 28, 1772, *ibid.*, photos 266–267.
45. Westford, Jan. 12, 1773, Boston Committee of Correspondence, Minute Book, I, 88–90.
46. Shrewsbury, Jan. 4, 1773, Letters and Proceedings received, photo 770.
47. Medford, Dec. 31, 1772, *ibid.*, photos 510–511; Scarborough, Jan. 14, 1773, Boston Committee of Correspondence, Minute Book, II, 163–165.

fered with Boston. Two asserted that their rights were founded on "Divine Revelation" in the Bible, and not merely on the laws of nature, the British Constitution, and the charter as the pamphlet had stated.[48] A more important difference was expressed by Attleborough, which argued the contrary, that their rights took "their rise merely from nature," thus ignoring the constitution. Because the colonists had freely emigrated from Britain at their own expense, Attleborough townspeople reasoned, their subjection to Britain was purely voluntary, and "known only by the Stipulation Between us and the King of Great Britain Expressed in our Charter." Beyond the Massachusetts charter, they "utterly disalow[ed] any Right of Government over us" by Britain, to whom they had "no natural or necessary Connection."[49] At the time, January 1773, such an explicit declaration was radical. Certainly the argument of the committee of correspondence was much more circumspect, grounding discussion merely on the "equal liberty" of the colonists with Englishmen. Yet, extreme as the Attleborough formulation may have seemed to some contemporaries, it rested on the same assumptions as the Boston pamphlet and the other town proceedings. Attleborough merely used the historical aspect of the conventional Massachusetts Whig argument by itself — the colonists had freely settled, formed their society, and entered into a compact with King William III. Where others went on to discuss a relationship with Parliament, acknowledging its "supremacy," Attleborough went no further than the charter in defining the connection with England. Most other towns, including Boston, were not prepared to carry the consequences of the same historical argument to such a limit.

The Boston committee's letter to the towns had requested proposals for seeking redress. The committee had mentioned instructing the representatives, and by its own example suggested a union of towns via committees of correspondence. Most towns that wrote readily adopted the first suggestion, and nearly half of them established local committees of correspondence. But in addition they experimented, initiating a variety of other suggestions. Some of these, like the idea of committees of correspondence, implied that existing institutions had proved to be incapable of providing for redress.

In Marblehead an idea circulated arising out of the frustrations cre-

48. Brookline, Jan. 4, 1773, Letters and Proceedings received, photos 113–115; Sherborn, Jan. 25, 1773, ibid., photo 752.
49. Attleborough, Jan. 18, 1773, ibid., photos 36–37.

ated by colonial governors' proroguing and dissolving the assemblies. It was privately suggested that every town establish "a committee of grievances, to act at all times when the assembly is prevented from meeting." These committees would continually invent methods for gaining redress, and "communicate their sentiments to a grand committee at Boston." The grand committee at Boston would review proposals and "communicate such as are approved to their respective towns," until the grievances were finally removed. Merely instructing the representatives was inadequate, since even though the House had regularly fulfilled its duty, its constituents still remained oppressed.[50]

The idea was vague and incomplete. Yet its similarity to Samuel Adams' conception of the committees of correspondence showed that his thoughts were shared by others in the province. Moreover, dissatisfaction with the traditional modes of seeking redress was not confined to a few towns. Indeed this readiness to experiment seemed to be general.[51] Lynn, for example, suggested a general consultation of towns, "either by Letter or a Convention of the respective Comittees of the Towns."[52] Ipswich proposed that the assembly send a separate agent to London, to be supported independently of the province treasury by proportional town grants,[53] while three small towns in Worcester County proposed that the assembly undertake "an Intercourse with the Sister Colonies on this Continent on these Matters, as we are all embarked in one common Cause."[54] Most remarkable of all was the advice from Petersham, also in Worcester County, recommending that the House "call in the aid of Some Protestant Power or Powers Requesting that they would use their Kind and Cristian Influence with our Mother Country," so as to restore harmony.[55]

Nevertheless, while most of the towns were ready to experiment, their own suggestions most often looked directly to the assembly and traditional approaches. Several believed that "the General Court is the only proper Body" to seek redress.[56] Most, however, were not so re-

50. Elbridge Gerry to Samuel Adams, Nov. 26, 1772, in James T. Austin, *The Life of Elbridge Gerry* (Boston, 1828-1829), I, 21-22.
51. For instance, Marlborough, Jan. 1, 1773, Letters and Proceedings received, photos 493-495.
52. Lynn, Jan. 20, 1773, *ibid.*, photos 425-426.
53. Ipswich, Dec. 28, 1772, *ibid.*, photos 359-360.
54. Leicester, Spencer, Paxton, Jan. 4, 1773, *ibid.*, photos 382-384.
55. Petersham, Jan. 4, 1773, *ibid.*, photos 620-621.
56. Chelmsford, Jan. 21, 1773, Boston Committee of Correspondence, Minute Book, III, 199-201; also Falmouth, Jan. 1, 1773, Letters and Proceedings received, photo 241; Beverly, Jan. 5, 1773, *ibid.*, photos 76-78.

stricted, although old ways were all that occurred to them. Since many had learned of Lord Hillsborough's replacement by the "virtuous" Lord Dartmouth, they thought that an assembly petition to the King might now at last be successful.[57] Others thought additional petitions should be sent to the House of Commons and to the whole Parliament.[58] Several, taking a position directly contrary to the Boston Whigs, said it was important that the governor be persuaded to join in the petition and in any choice the House might make of an agent.[59] Another advised that all the colonies jointly petition the King for redress. With respect to the specific grievance of the judges' stipends a large proportion recommended that the assembly review judges' salaries and, if necessary, raise them, so as to prevent the Crown from paying them.[60] Here, too, towns were taking a contrary line, since Boston Whigs opposed enhancing the judges' stature by raising their salaries.

The diversity of opinion surrounding the appropriate means for seeking redress appears to have reflected a basic uncertainty on strategy. A number of towns, apart from whatever else they might have proposed, used their initiative to call for a day of fasting and prayer in Massachusetts.[61] It would promote virtue, and God might open their eyes to an effective means to remedy their predicament. Many of the more remote towns expressed confidence in Boston, and a willingness to follow whatever it recommended.[62] "What measures to take we are at a loss," Chatham confided. "But as you are the Metropolis and have all the acts of the Government and of the British parliament and the Bills of Rights with you we hope you will use your joint Endeavors in a constitutional way to save from impending ruin this distressed people."[63]

57. Malden, Jan. 21, 1773, Boston Committee of Correspondence, Minute Book, II, 165–171; Westborough, Jan. 4, 1773, *ibid.*, 171–173; Acton, Jan. 18, 1773, Letters and Proceedings received, photos 17–18; Lancaster, Jan. 19, 1773, *ibid.*, photos 372–375; Charlestown, Dec. 28, 1772, *ibid.*, photo 143.

58. Leicester, Jan. 4, 1773, *ibid.*, photos 382–386; Gloucester, Dec. 28, 1772, *ibid.*, photos 266–267.

59. Westborough, Jan. 4, 1773, Boston Committee of Correspondence, Minute Book, II, 171–173; Sudbury, Jan. 18, 1773, Letters and Proceedings received, photos 808–809.

60. Bradford, Jan. 7, 1773, Boston Committee of Correspondence, Minute Book, II, 141–142; Scarborough, Jan. 14, 1773, *ibid.*, 163–165; Malden, Jan. 21, 1773, *ibid.*, 165–171; Medford, Dec. 31, 1772, Letters and Proceedings received, photos 510–511; Beverly, Jan. 5, 1773, *ibid.*, photos 76–78.

61. For example, Marlborough, Jan. 1, 1773, Letters and Proceedings received, photos 493–495.

62. For example, Townshend, Jan. 6, 1773, Boston Committee of Correspondence, Minute Book, II, 132–135.

63. Chatham, Dec. 29, 1772, Letters and Proceedings received, photos, 163–164.

Westford was "determined to coincide with the Town of Boston in any measures which may be concluded on as best for the removal of the Burdens we at present labour under; this we think we can safely do." [64] It seemed logical since "your Situation puts you upon an Eminence to decry our Dangers, and your Abilities set you uppermost to point out the Remedies." [65] The most direct expression of this readiness to follow Boston came from the people of Lenox in Berkshire County, who admitted that "as we are in a remote wilderness Corner of the Earth; and almost the remotest and youngest Town in the Province we know but little of the Circumstances of the Affairs you write to us upon . . . Therefore as we are Children about five Years old we depend on you, our Fathers, to dispose of Things we know so little about." They agreed with Boston's statement of their rights, and believed that "as Children" it was not for them "to state the Facts, but to trust you, our Fathers to do that for us." [66] Thus, in some towns at least the pamphlet had enabled Boston and the committee of correspondence to achieve an effective position for informing and instructing.

The thorough approval accorded the basic assumptions of the Boston pamphlet is especially evident when one considers the opposition it faced in a handful of towns. For none of the criticisms touched its essential points. In Cambridge William Brattle led a vain attempt to block action, mistakenly arguing that the judges' tenure was already during good behavior, so that Crown stipends would insure their independence. [67] In Roxbury opponents of the pamphlet, after failing to defeat the measure to second Boston and form a committee of correspondence, fell back on the argument that Moderator William Heath had peremptorily forced the measures through the town meeting. [68] They did not attempt a rebuttal of the pamphlet or the formation of a committee of correspondence on their merits. In Marblehead, where "friends to government" protested the town's enthusiastic resolves, their whole criticism was directed at the uncharitable and, to their minds, dangerous tone of the proceedings, which would expose the town to official repri-

64. Westford, Jan. 12, 1773, Boston Committee of Correspondence, Minute Book, I, 88–90.
65. Brimfield, Jan. 22, 1773, Letters and Proceedings received, photos 102–103.
66. Lenox, Jan. 4, 1773, ibid., photos 392–393.
67. William Brattle's notes of Cambridge town meeting, Dec. 14, 1772, in "Letters and Documents relating to Harvard College and Cambridge," 78, Boston Public Library.
68. There seems to have been substance to the charge. See "minority report" in Boston Weekly News-Letter, Dec. 31, 1772, 2:2–3, and continuing controversy reported ibid.

mand if not reprisal.[69] Chelmsford and Stockbridge, two towns which expressed general agreement with the pamphlet and applauded Boston, also took exception to the tone of some of Boston's thrusts. Yet even their criticism underscored their basic agreement, since they advised that "those who are obliged by their stations, to be the unhappy instruments in the hands of ministers of state of enforcing their unconstitutional mandates, & grievous acts of Parliament," should not be subjected to "invective, reilery, calumny, outrage, malice, & every other irrational injury."[70] There was little here or anywhere else in the towns' replies to comfort the governor.

In his speech the governor had argued that once the supremacy of Parliament was admitted, "grievances" must evaporate. If Parliament had supreme authority, then it would be foolish to dispute the "mere" exercise of that authority. However, the towns did not admit Hutchinson's parliamentary supremacy, so the grievances remained urgent. All of the towns mentioned them. Most listed several specifically, in the manner of the Boston list of grievances. No town was ready to join Hutchinson by easily dismissing them.

Several towns actually found omissions in the list of grievances. One, proposed by Marblehead, suggested an embarrassing potential. For, "without entering into the right of parliament to impose duties" on products imported from Spain and Portugal, the townspeople complained of the expense, inefficiency, and hazards they suffered in being required to bring their imports to England for payment of duties, rather than bringing them directly to America, where the duties could as well be paid.[71] This request, that these duties be collected in America, was an anomaly in view of their other constitutional grievances. Certainly the Boston committee would have preferred its omission.

Generally, however, the grievances of which the towns complained gave the Boston committee no cause for embarrassment. All complained of taxation without representation and then generally went on to recite abbreviated or slightly altered versions of the Boston list. A few described unusual complaints involving customs administration, land titles, Negro slavery,[72] and provincial representation, but these were

69. Marblehead protest, *ibid.*, Dec. 24, 1772, 2:3.
70. Stockbridge, Jan. 4, 1773, Letters and Proceedings received, photos 787–788; Chelmsford, Jan. 21, 1773, Boston Committee of Correspondence, Minute Book, III, 198–201.
71. Marblehead, Dec. 8, 1772, Boston Committee of Correspondence, Minute Book, I, 9–12.
72. Complaints against Negro slavery were primarily a response to a circular

exceptions. When the governor claimed that the Boston committee taught grievances to the towns he had been partially correct. Many, for example, had never heard of the Dockyards Act and were interested to learn its provisions. Yet although towns relied on Boston for some specific information, the grievances were generally familiar. Originally the administration had scoffed at the pamphlet because it contained so little that was new. The towns, applauding the pamphlet, sometimes refrained from listing infringements for the very same reason. The grievances, they said, were so well known and so often recapitulated that they would not repeat them. Yet though many of the grievances were familiar, and though they did not deprive Massachusetts inhabitants of their livelihood or material well-being, they were not, as the administration urged, illusory. The towns believed they were real and that they were even more dangerous because they often lacked immediate, practical consequences which would raise an alarm in the localities of Massachusetts. The grievances provoked their fears since they possessed immediate significance for every town within the Radical Whig chain of reasoning.

This chain of logic expressed by the towns was identical to that which had inspired Boston Whigs to create committees of correspondence. It was built on the same series of beliefs about the corrupt nature of man and society. On the personal level they believed men must strive to preserve virtue from their own vicious tendencies. In society, on the public level, they must seek to preserve liberty from the continuous, insatiable appetite of power. Public virtue was the only fundamental defense of liberty in general and of the constitution in particular. Moreover resistance was regarded as an expression of public virtue. In view of these beliefs, townspeople found that in the current situation there was only one appropriate course open — they must speak out and resist. Their thoughts, which the committee gave to the *Boston Gazette* to be printed, echoed and re-echoed in Massachusetts, further confirming the townspeople in their beliefs.

In the Boston pamphlet this outlook toward man and society had not been stated explicitly, it had been part of the background, appearing in patches here and there. The pamphlet had alluded to the interrelationship of virtue, jealousy, and resistance, but it had pointed the discus-

letter sent to all representatives by a "committee" of slaves in April 1773. It may have been drawn in conjunction with Samuel Adams and John Pickering (of Salem) who were forwarding efforts toward ending slavery. See pp. 173–174 below.

sion toward the specific grievances and their constitutional significance, particularly the consequences of official stipends paid out of "extorted" revenues. The towns had spoken to these points, but frequently they gave equal or even greater attention to developing the moral implications of political affairs. Indeed some were certain that "GOD will not suffer this Land, where the Gospel hath flourished, to become a Slave of the world." He would defend it by the resistance of individuals and communities: "He will stir up witnesses of the truth — And in his own time spirit his people; to stand up for his Cause, and deliver them." In 1689 He had delivered England and New England. Many towns felt sure He would deliver them again, for "in a similar belief, that Patriot of Patriots, the Great ALGERNON SIDNEY, lived and Died, and Dying breathed a like Sentiment, and prophesy touching his own and the then approaching times." [73]

Marlborough translated the whole matter of political conduct and political salvation into biblical terms, thus making its moral obligation absolute. Using a passage comforting to those who believed themselves oppressed, the town instructed its representative to follow the example of Shadrach, Meshach, and Abednego, who refused to submit to the tyrant Nebuchadnezzar, and instead chose to remain true to their religion, trust God to preserve them. Cautiously, or perhaps coyly, it made no more specific application than to call Shadrach, Meshach, and Abednego "three true Sons of Liberty." [74]

The Boston committee had posed the question of political action in moral terms, sharing the assumption of other towns that politics should express the moral duty of a people. Political and religious concepts often coincided in the minds of many, nor were they clearly differentiated. As a consequence liberty was cherished as a kind of temporal salvation, public virtue was seen as part of the broad category of Christian virtue, while political apathy and acquiescence had their counterparts in religious backsliding and corruption. It is no wonder then that so many towns responded vigorously, displaying a desire to exhibit their own virtue in bold, bright colors. Here they were not only acknowledging the efficacy of public virtue for defense, they seemed anxious to rationalize their own political activity by describing their worldviews. They seemed anxious to offer a full "confession of faith" to their fellow countrymen. As communities their mood was highly self-

73. Petersham, Jan. 4, 1773, Letters and Proceedings received, photos 622–623.
74. Marlborough, Jan. 1, 1773, *ibid.*, photos 490–491.

conscious. Each town seemed to believe that it was standing before its peers in the province and in the colonies, before God and mankind, before the watchful souls of their ancestors and the millions of their yet unborn posterity. They envisaged themselves acting on the center of the stage of history.

Their ancestors had been heroes. They had come "to the Wilds of America," suffered "innumerable fatigues and dangers," and undergone a "vast expense of Treasure and Blood," in order to build their settlements "here among the Savages of the Desert." The fruit of their labors had been a "prodigious Accession of Wealth and Power to the Mother Country." [75] Britain had "Wrested" the first compact, the 1629 charter from them and their heirs; but even so their ancestors had shown a "Humble Submissive Temper . . . in Receiving another which Abridged them of Many very many Valuable & Reasonable Rights." [76] Now the present generation must preserve those very rights for which their forefathers "Dyed in the Bed of Honour as Martyrs." [77]

Their ancestors' purpose in settling had been the full enjoyment of civil and religious liberty. They "Chose a wild Desert with Liberty Rather than the fruitfull Fields and beautiful Gardens of their Native Land with Slavery." [78] In order to maintain liberty, the rights which secured it must be maintained absolutely. For every essential right, taxation by consent, legislation by consent, impartial justice, trial by jury, was connected to the others, and together they preserved each other and liberty. If one was eliminated, then in time they would all vanish. Without them the lives and property of individuals were wholly exposed to violation; they would be slaves.

Slavery, as they understood it, was not limited to the chattel slavery of Negroes. Anyone, however rich, however high in rank, might be a slave if he or his property was exposed to the depredations of someone or some organization with superior power. In their view every Frenchman, every Spaniard, and now every Swede, was a slave. All men possessed the same rights, but not their enjoyment. Frenchmen, Spaniards, Africans had either yielded their rights voluntarily, or they had lost them by usurpation or conquest. Here the distinction was critical, and because of it towns felt an obligation to speak.

It was a sin to acquiesce in one's own enslavement. It was "very Crim-

75. Mendon, March 1, 1773, Letters and Proceedings received, photo 328.
76. Petersham, Jan. 4, 1773, *ibid.*, photo 620.
77. Gorham, May 14, 1773, *ibid.*, photo 277.
78. Holden, May 20, 1773, *ibid.*, photos 347–348.

inal" to keep silent in the face of attacks.[79] For it was "self-suicide" and ran "counter to the Will of the great Author of Nature, the supreme Legislator."[80] Everyone was obligated to resist, however God might dispose of the event. By standing up and speaking out, towns knew that they were God's witnesses giving testimony to their own virtue. Public statements were palpable evidence of virtue. Towns spoke so that "whether our Endeavours shall be successful or not posterity might know that we understood our Rights and Liberties and were neither afraid nor ashamed to assert & maintain them and that we ourselves May have (at least) this Consolation in our Chains that it was not through our neglect that this People were enslaved."[81]

This self-conscious heroism was nowhere more elegantly or obviously expressed than by the town of Attleborough in Bristol County. Beginning their proceedings with "The Preamble," the townspeople saluted the King and the Protestant succession. Then, after comparing themselves to the "Israelitish nation," and calling attention to the mortality of kings, they set forth American valor in order to vindicate the colonists to their King. They thought that "to set things in a Clearer Light, we may be Justly intitled to a few notes of Exaltation." Their "few notes" revealed the wisdom of the Boston committee in wondering aloud whether virtue was dead in Massachusetts:

In the Year 1745, when the British Trumpets Sounded war from Beyond the Seas to the Americans, no Sooner did our american Parliament understand the Certain Sound of the Martial Trumpet, but Instantaneously a Political Convocation was called . . . Forthwith orders are Issued out to the Colonels, and from the Colonels to the Captains, and at the beat of the Drum, volunteers Parade the Ground Like well harnessed Soldiers, with Courage bold, Like the war horse, mocked at fear, march with their Commanders to the high Places of Louisbourgh, storm their Entrenchments, made a Discovery of their Subterranean mines and Galleries, beat down the Strong hold, Brake the Jaws of the Gallick Lion, and made Conquest of the City to the Crown of Great Britain. And in the Late war that hath been upon us, have Joined our British Brethren, warring and Fighting through Seas of Blood, until we Subdued all the Canadian Provinces to the Crown of our Sovereign.

After such a display of valor they would not be "conjugated [yoked], Inslaved and Ruined." Britain should take warning: "Fathers Provoke

79. Holden, May 20, 1773, *ibid.*, photos 347–348.
80. Mendon, March 1, 1773, *ibid.*, photo 327.
81. Stoughton protesters, March 31, 1773, Boston Committee of Correspondence, Minute Book, III, 239–240.

not your Children unto Wrath . . . Since there is no new Discovered America for us to flee unto, we are almost Ready to think that we will let go our Plow Shares and Pruning hooks, — to be maliated on the anvel." [82] Such a response went well beyond Boston.

Gorham, in the District of Maine, was anxious to display its virtue in an even more specific manner than Attleborough. It took as a starting point the Boston pamphlet, which had argued that Massachusetts rights must be maintained as a duty to "our Fathers," heroes who had, "in the Face of every Danger" and "at the Expense of their Treasure," planted "the fair tree of Liberty" in the wilderness, watering it "with their Blood." [83] Although recognizing this debt, Gorham, preferred to dwell on more immediate history:

Not only may we say That we enjoy an Inheritance Purchased by the Blood of our forefathers; But this Town was settled at the expence of our own Blood! We have those amongst us whose Blood streaming from their own Wounds watered the soil from which we earn our Bread! Our Ears have heard the infernal yells of the Native Savage Murderers. Our Eyes have seen our young Children weltring in their gore in our own Houses, and our Dearest Friends led into Captivity by Men more Savage than the Savage Beasts themselves! We many of us have been used to earn our Dayly Bread with our Weapons in our hands. Therefore we cannot be supposed to be fully acquainted with the mysteries of Court Policy, but we look upon ourselves as Able to Judge so far concerning our Rights as Men, as Christians, and as Subjects of British Government, as to declare that We apprehend those Rights as settled by the good People of the Town of Boston do belong to us, and that We look with horror and Indignation on the Violation of them; we only add that our old Captain is still living, who for many years has been our chief Officer to rally the Inhabitants of this Town from the Plough, or the Sickle to defend their Wives, their Children and all that was Dear from the Savages. Many of our Families have been inured to the Danger and fatigue of flying to Garrison. Timber of our Fort is yet to be seen, and many of our Women have been used to handle the Cartridge, and load the Musquet, and the Swords which we whet and brightened for our Enemies are not yet grown rusty.[84]

The final remark, that their swords remained ready for defending their rights, like Attleborough's warning "Fathers Provoke not your Children," was an aggressive sign of confidence. Boston's correspondence had offered them an opportunity to re-examine their own past and to justify it

82. Attleborough, Jan. 18, 1773, Letters and Proceedings received, photos 36–37.
83. *Votes and Proceedings of the Freeholders and other Inhabitants of the Town of Boston. In Town Meeting Assembled* (Boston, 1772), 34.
84. Gorham, Jan. 7, 1773, Letters and Proceedings received, photos 274–275.

in a ringing declaration. Recognizing their political responsibility, they could transform the obscurity of their village into glorious eminence. Like the citizens of many another town they were more than ready to put themselves on permanent record as informed, aroused, and ready to resist — beacons of public virtue.[85]

Later, in the spring of 1773, another less self-righteous facet of their concept of individual virtue and public life would emerge in local reactions to the news that Governor Hutchinson had secretly advised restraints on Massachusetts liberties in letters to the ministry.[86] Unlike the Boston committee, towns did not gloat over the disclosure or express great malice toward Hutchinson. They expressed their gratitude to "divine Providence in discovering the Designs of the Enemies"[87] of Massachusetts, which they saw "tends to the Subversion of our Civil Constitution."[88] They regarded God's providence in making the letters known as a sign that He still saw some virtue remaining in Massachusetts and would "protect us still."[89] Some hostility appeared — one town called the governor a "homebred viper," and another was "greatly Surprised at the ingratitude of the man, who is Exerting Every Nerve to inslave a people, that by *their indulgence have Raised him* to the highest pitch of Grandeur."[90] But an equal amount of comment was turned inward by the towns.

The disclosure of Hutchinson's "treachery" exposed the fall of a great man, once much respected and admired. Members of the Boston committee might have axes to grind, but not the inhabitants at large. They saw in Hutchinson's willingness to abridge colonial rights, treachery, the weakness of men corrupted by prestige and power. Hutchinson's evil was potentially in them all. They hoped "there may not be many more such among us," and one town concluded "that the State of america in general actually agrees with the estate of every man in particular. Our worst Enemy is in our Bosom."[91] This understanding was part of the impetus which moved towns to vindicate their rights

85. See also Lexington, Jan. 5, 1773, *ibid.*, photos 396–399; Plymouth, Dec. 14, 1772, *ibid.*, photos 638–640; Newton, Jan. 4, 1773, *ibid.*, photos 572–576; South Hadley, Jan. 18, 1773, *ibid.*, photos 776–777; Pepperell, Jan. 18, 1773, *ibid.*, photos 614–615.
86. See pp. 143–146.
87. Gloucester, July 29, 1773, Letters and Proceedings received, photo 270.
88. Littleton, Oct. 6, 1773, *ibid.*, photo 416.
89. Gloucester, July 29, 1773, *ibid.*, photo 270.
90. Cambridge, May 3, 1773, *ibid.*, photo 123, italics added.
91. Gloucester, July 29, 1773, *ibid.*, photo 270; Chatham, July 6, 1773, *ibid.*, photo 166.

in a public declaration. Thomas Hutchinson's renunciation of Massachusetts' rights was an example of the fall they wished to avoid.

It is clear, then, that by posing political questions within the framework of morality and asserting that a statement of principles was a matter of duty, the Boston committee had touched a super-sensitive area of popular belief. No community would betray itself, its ancestors, and posterity when, by calling a meeting, choosing a committee, and voting resolves, its people could demonstrate that they were friends of liberty and adamant enemies of slavery. Indeed some towns could envisage a glorious future if the people would stand up in defense of liberty. They could, as Samuel Adams had privately hoped, save Britain from her own corruption while saving liberty in America. Their prayers would raise Britain "from the Depth of Political Lethargy." By asserting their own freedom they would be saving their brothers "the People of Britain (our old Natural ally)." For if America was enslaved, Britain could not long resist tyranny. Raising their voices against unconstitutional infringements, they would save the Empire:

We are therefore ambitious of Transmitting our names to all Posterity as favoured instruments in the hand of God of having Preserved Britain from Destruction Therefore we supplicate the Throne of Mercy that God would Excite his People in Britain and America to a Reformation of Morals because as Sin is the Reproach & Ruin of a People so Righteousness Exalteth a Nation to the Summit of Happiness and Glory.[92]

Virtue and liberty were inseparably connected. The towns would lead the general struggle for their public revival.

III

The Massachusetts response to the Boston pamphlet reveals something other than political acquiescence or an automatic reflex set off by familiar rhetoric. The range of town behavior, from silent repudiation to admiring applause, suggests an independence of action which cannot be described as either domination or manipulation by the Boston committee. Indeed the town responses indicate a level of local political awareness and self-consciousness which contemporaries had scarcely recognized before. These replies to the Boston pamphlet demonstrate that many towns were prepared to think about their rights and were tentatively seeking a satisfactory means of gaining redress for their

92. Holden, May 20, 1773, Letters and Proceedings received, photos 247–248.

grievances. Moreover, the publication in the press of their hundreds of resolves early in 1773 reflected and at the same time stimulated a growing recognition of local political responsibility and power.

The diversity among the local responses furnishes even more explicit evidence that towns acted consciously, to suit their own ideas. Some formed committees of correspondence in imitation of Boston, but more were content merely to formulate and publish their political principles. Some proceeded cautiously, grounding their statements wholly on traditional constitutional arguments, while others went beyond Boston, arguing from natural rights and provincial history, virtually bypassing constitutional details. Most gave Boston enthusiastic applause, but a few chose to criticize in spite of their general theoretical agreement. The various methods proposed for gaining redress, ranging from conventional petitions to an appeal for foreign diplomatic intervention, emphasized the individual character of local decisions.

Yet the diversity was limited, confined within a general agreement about basic political principles. The towns that spoke at all spoke the same language, used the same conventional phrases of Whig resistance, and shared the same assumptions about political behavior. All agreed on the necessity of defending their rights, defined in what was for them a traditional manner. They looked first to traditional remedies within the framework of established forms and institutions. Yet at the same time most shared a willingness to experiment if necessary to gain genuine redress. These towns were not passive, unthinking pawns manipulated by Boston, but they did share like opinions and they were prepared to follow its lead. Indeed some were more than ready to take up Boston's call—they were anxious to reply in ringing declarations. Towns that chose to act showed no signs of reluctant acquiescence. Rather, they embraced the opportunity to express their views enthusiastically, and gloried in assuming the active role proposed by Boston. Acknowledging Boston as the leader among towns, they recognized their own political roles in imperial politics, asserting their power as independent, jealous guardians of liberty.

6

The Boston Committee's

Role in Local and

Provincial Politics

The breadth and vigor of local response to the Boston pamphlet altered the pattern of Massachusetts politics, permitting the Boston committee to expand its role. As a result the committee gradually emerged as a co-ordinator of local activity, working with both the towns and the House of Representatives to promote aggressively what it regarded as the defense of liberty. Consequently the level of local interest and participation in the politics of constitutional rights increased significantly, with the Boston committee developing a leading role in the movement. None of this became apparent overnight, but by June 1773 the new pattern was emerging.

The prominence of the Boston Committee of Correspondence in provincial politics was never based on any tightly organized network of local committees of correspondence. The local committees themselves were not the "revolutionary cells" some scholars have imagined.[1] In 1773 they were organized in fifty-eight communities, less than 40 percent of the towns actually in correspondence with Boston, and only one quarter of all the towns in Massachusetts. Here they did not covertly mastermind local activity, but rather worked to articulate local beliefs.

1. Crane Brinton, *Anatomy of Revolution* (New York, 1956), 42, first published in 1938; Arthur M. Schlesinger, *Prelude to Independence: The Newspaper War on Britain, 1764–1776* (New York, 1958), 16.

Indeed, when one considers them in the light of the general pattern of Massachusetts behavior, it is clear that the town committees of correspondence were merely part of a larger process of local political expression. The Boston committee had not merely encouraged participation in colonial political controversy, it had stimulated a broadly based movement in which communities worked out the implications of their views in town meetings as an effort to rationalize political action. This process revealed the radicalism latent in local beliefs; the Boston committee was not so much instructing as it was drawing out the expression of common assumptions.

The Boston Committee of Correspondence did succeed in establishing relationships with particular communities, but its ties were primarily the loose, informal fraternal relations of sharers in a common body of beliefs, not close political alliances. The Boston committee's leadership capacity developed as a consequence of this catalytic role in forming a larger provincial community based on the expression of common beliefs. Within this community of shared interests and beliefs the Boston committee enjoyed a central role, a role which was to provide the committee with a broad base to lead the province by the time the Tea Act was introduced to Massachusetts.

The Boston committee itself seems to have been surprised by the increase in town activity and its members became enthusiastic as they saw the public ardor and political expressions of the countryside exceed their hopes. One member commented in astonishment that, "We seem to have a Solon or Lycurgus in every second or third town and district." [2] Samuel Adams reported with pleasure that Boston's effort had been successful: "Every Art & every Instrument was made use of to prevent the Meetings of the Towns in the Country but to no purpose." [3] Boston had obtained "the explicit political Sentiments of a great Number of the Towns in this Province; and the Number," he said in April, "is daily increasing." [4] Adams was so impressed by the spirit the committee had stimulated, that in a letter to Richard Henry Lee, a member of the Virginia Committee of Correspondence organized in March

2. Thomas Young, sentence deleted from letter of Boston Committee of Correspondence to New Salem, April 6, 1773, Letters and Proceedings received, photo 570; similar comments in other Boston committee letters suggest the surprise of the writers.

3. Samuel Adams to Arthur Lee, April 9, 1773, in letter of April 12, 1773, *The Writings of Samuel Adams*, ed. Harry A. Cushing (New York, 1904–1908), III, 18–25. Adams enclosed a sample of town proceedings for publication in England.

4. Samuel Adams to Richard Henry Lee, April 10, 1773, *ibid.*, 25.

1773, he proposed "the Establishment of Committees of Correspondence among the several Towns in every Colony," in order "to promote that General Union, upon which the Security of the whole depends."[5] The Boston committee was beginning to believe that the pattern of activity in Massachusetts might eventually become a general colonial movement.[6] That, however, was merely a future possibility and in the meantime the Boston committee continued its work, quietly developing and institutionalizing its functions, shaping a role in provincial affairs.

I

The Boston town meeting that had created the committee and directed it to prepare and send the pamphlet had not given it further instructions, but it seems to have been generally assumed that the committee would continue in existence even after these tasks were complete, and that it would answer whatever communications Boston might receive from the other towns. On the several occasions when towns did direct their letter and proceedings to the Boston selectmen or town clerk, they referred them directly to the committee of correspondence for reply. Presumably the committee was competent to send whatever letters it saw fit, without any prior scrutiny by the town meeting or the selectmen. At any rate that was the pattern which developed as the committee began to deal with its most immediate task in the first half of 1773, responding to the scores of town proceedings that were pouring into Boston.

At the beginning the committee devoted intensive consideration to each separate letter of reply. It assigned James Otis, Samuel Adams, and Oliver Wendell as a subcommittee to prepare the first reply, to Plymouth. They were directed to submit a draft for consideration by the whole committee.[7] However as more and more proceedings arrived, a special subcommittee of experienced writers, Adams, Warren, Appleton, Joseph Greenleaf, and Young,[8] was chosen to prepare answers for all the communications received.[8] The efficiency provided by this arrangement made it permanent. At the same time group authorship,

5. Samuel Adams to Richard Henry Lee, April 10, 1773, *Writings of Samuel Adams*, III, 25.
6. See crossed-out passages in Boston committee to New Salem, April 6, 1773, Letters and Proceedings received, photo 570.
7. Boston Committee of Correspondence, minutes, Dec. 1, 1772, Minute Book, I, 6–8, New York Public Library, photostats at Massachusetts Historical Society.
8. Boston Committee of Correspondence, minutes, Dec. 25, 1772, *ibid.*, 14.

so cherished by the committee, was retained, each letter receiving careful scrutiny and the benefit of several expert judgments before it was presented to the whole committee. The committee maintained complete control of its correspondence, which was sent not by the author(s), but by the clerk, William Cooper, who signed the letters. In this way the committee protected itself and its mission from any ill-judged, hasty, or intemperate remarks.

In order to carry its load of work the entire committee met at least once every week. Normally it met in the early evening, between five and seven, at the Selectmen's Chamber in Faneuil Hall. The tone of the meetings was informal, perhaps leisurely. The members jointly purchased and consumed Rhode Island beer. By late March they found their meetings so expansive that it was necessary to formally agree to "break up" at half-past nine in the evening.[9] By this time the process of answering town proceedings had been thoroughly mastered, and a distinctive, sophisticated reply policy had become apparent.

The care which the committee of correspondence devoted to each of its replies emphasized its belief in their importance for establishing a relationship of confidence between Boston and the other towns.[10] Drafts of replies were frequently edited and corrected by one or more members, and on occasion the committee itself directed amendments. Each reply was prepared with the individual town in mind, and the letter normally included a specific reference to the town's proceedings. In this way the committee hoped to make each letter especially relevant to its intended local audience, while eliminating every possibility of giving offense.

The letter the committee sent to Charlestown on January 5 illustrates the attention that could be given to a composition of less than 250 words. The basic draft had been prepared by Joseph Greenleaf, but by the time it was sent out Adams and Warren had made sufficient additions and deletions to make it as much their work as Greenleaf's. Charlestown's letter and proceedings, expressing alarm over the grievances, had supported Boston although its words contained a hint of jealousy over Boston's initiative. Charlestown did not immediately

9. Boston Committee of Correspondence, minutes, Feb. 2, 1773, Minute Book, III, 181; March 30, 1773, *ibid.*, 213–214.

10. It might be said that the committee was seeking to erase old suspicions of Boston, and this may be. But although the idea that the countryside was suspicious of Boston activism has often been stated, positive evidence to support this view is lacking. Moreover the pattern of Boston leadership in the House suggests the reverse, a traditional confidence in Boston.

choose a committee of correspondence, and it voiced confidence that the new ministry headed by Dartmouth would now hear Massachusetts' petitions and provide redress. Although Charlestown appeared fervid in the cause of Massachusetts rights, it seemed less than anxious to follow Boston. The committee recognized these sentiments and dealt with them in its letter.

At first Greenleaf's draft ignored the question of Charlestown's jealousy and simply expressed Boston's pleasure at receiving Charlestown's full support. But Warren caught the omission and discreetly added that Charlestown "justly" considered itself "equally interested with us in the common cause of natural & constitutional liberty." Greenleaf had been ready to answer Charlestown's hopes respecting Dartmouth with scorn, saying "you seem to flatter yourselves with a prospect of Redress" from the change in the ministry, when in fact, "however pious or Virtuous Lord Dartmouth may be" his letter to Rhode Island establishing an unconstitutional commission to investigate the *Gaspee* incident had shown him ready "to further the detestable plan of the present British administration." Greenleaf went on to explain these latest infringements specifically, but his polemical tone was ill-suited to polite persuasion, so Adams deleted the offending passage. Instead, Adams admitted that Dartmouth's appointment "may have at first been flattering to us"; but considering his recent letter to the governor of Rhode Island, Massachusetts' "expectations from this change must be totally annihilated." By joining Boston's own expectations to those of Charlestown, Adams could tactfully dismiss their hopes from Dartmouth.[11]

In general the committee of correspondence used its letters to reinforce particular ideas and beliefs already expressed by the towns. Flattery, more or less restrained, was usually directed to this purpose. The letter subcommittee developed an especially effective technique by excerpting portions of a town's proceedings and then quoting them back to the authors with approval. Frequently it would accentuate the contribution of the particular town by assuring it that Boston joined in the quoted sentiment.[12] Another common method of flattery was to point to a town's proceedings as evidence "that the spirit, wisdom, &

11. Boston committee to Charlestown, Jan. 5, 1773, Letters and Proceedings received, photos 145–148.
12. E.g., Boston committee to Petersham, Jan. 12, 1773, Letters and Proceedings received, photo 624; to Newbury, Jan. 12, 1773, *ibid.*, photo 625; to Framingham, April 13, 1773, *Writings of Samuel Adams*, III, 34–36.

piety of our illustrious ancestors still survives & flourishes in America." [13] Where smaller towns had produced unusually ambitious proceedings, the committee's praise was even more enthusiastic and direct.

This flattery was not a simple matter of convention, it varied widely and was occasionally omitted. Nor was the committee seeking to win support merely by lavishing bouquets on Massachusetts towns. Its praise was intended to encourage and stimulate the same type of vigilant, active, political behavior that their pamphlet had sought. It was indeed flattering, but only because the towns' ideal of political virtue corresponded so exactly with that of the committee. All of the praise was directed to towns for fulfilling their duty by maintaining their knowledge of their rights, by expressing themselves in a demonstration of virtue, and by remaining true to their ancestors.

Praise for knowledge was typically given to small, relatively remote communities. After agreeing with Westborough's proceedings, the committee expressed its own encouragement by asserting that "the knowledge of the true Spirit of our Constitution, which has spread even to the remotest parts of the Province, must astonish those who represented us as ignorant, as savages." [14] Replying to a newly settled community, the committee reported its pleasure that "so thorough a sense of Liberty, civil & religious, [is] so early discovered in an Infant Body." [15] A small town in Middlesex was asked "to imagine the British Ministry upon the Perusal of the elegant Letter from the Town of Westford with the Votes accompanying it, and the many other productions from different Parts of the Province, with astonishment pointing out to each other upon Douglas's Map the several places where the Persons resided who were capable of such Performances." [16] Using the ministry as a foil, the committee's praise encouraged towns to develop their knowledge and maintain their vigilance.

Active participation in the opposition to infringements was also a frequent subject of praise. The committee expressed its confidence in Bolton, knowing it could "always rely upon their good sense, virtue, and patriotism, when a season of trial calls for their assistance." Going further, "we think the Proof they have given of their zealous Attach-

13. Boston committee to Chatham, Jan. 18, 1773, Letters and Proceedings received, photo 165.
14. Boston committee to Westborough, Jan. 19, 1773, Minute Book, V, 361.
15. Boston committee to Gardinerston, April 13, 1773, Letters and Proceedings received, photo 254.
16. Boston committee to Westford, Feb. 3, 1773, Minute Book, V, 370.

ment to their Country entitles them to universal Esteem." [17] The towns-people might be poor in the material things of this earth, but their political virtue was all that mattered: "Like freemen unbiased by the deceitful smiles and promises of the designing you chuse to remain the sole Lords of your own fortunes." Again and again the committee reaffirmed the belief that the poor but free man showed "a disposition infinitely superior to the wretches who would wish to inhabit palaces or govern Provinces in subjection to the will of others." [18] Here they not only reinforced the town's sentiment, they extended it by alluding to the character of unnamed governors whose ambition was wealth and power at the expense of liberty. Later on names would be supplied — Hutchinson and Oliver.

The committee's reply to Gorham revealed another significant aspect of the praise it dispensed. Gorham's proceedings, like a heroic epic, had sung the town's own praise in a transparent appeal for recognition. In reply the committee described a proposal which was circulating to compile and publish all of the town proceedings, so as to give "the present and future generations a connected view of the sentiments of the present inhabitants." This was needed because "the virtues of millions are utterly unknown, barely for want of opportunity to be drawn into light." [19] In the meantime the Boston committee itself provided the desired recognition for obscure, out-of-the-way communities.

In the newer or less prominent towns the committee could underline its message by praising the knowledge or public virtue of the inhabitants more or less directly, but in better established towns it used a more oblique appeal. The same functions could be served by glorifying the inhabitants' ancestors. The most elaborate, full-blown example of this type of flattery came in the letter composed for the town of Plymouth. Here the committee began by expressing its pleasure with the proceedings "of the Metropolis of the ancient Colony of Plymouth," and then went on to tender congratulations "on the Return of that great Anni-

17. Boston committee to Bolton, Feb. 2, 1773, Letters and Proceedings received, photo 93; also to Pepperell, Feb. 2, 1773, ibid., photo 616.

18. Boston committee to Pepperell, Feb. 2, 1773, Letters and Proceedings received, photo 616; also to Harpswell, April 6, 1773, ibid., photo 318.

19. Boston committee to Gorham, Feb. 5, 1773, ibid., photos 276–277. An elaborate satire on the plan and a critique of the pamphlet appeared in the Boston Weekly News-Letter, Dec. 17, 1772, 1:1–3. In Jan. 1773 Draper explained to his readers that he would not print more town proceedings because of space, and because of a plan to print them all together as a volume, Boston Weekly News-Letter, Jan. 21, 1773, 3:1.

versary, the landing of the first Settlers at Plymouth, & on the religious & respectful Manner" in which the town had celebrated it. Plymouth could "say without Vanity, . . . that a handful of persecuted brave People, then made way for the extensive settlement of New England." Moreover Britain should thank Plymouth for all of its continental possessions; for had "it not been for their Efforts, Virginia would have soon been abandoned," and the French, Dutch, and Spanish would have divided North America. The Plymouth proceedings, the committee said, encouraged all the province by demonstrating that the virtue of the first settlers endured.[20]

Apart from their various forms of flattery, the general aim of the committee's letters was to encourage and reassure the towns in their political activity. In almost all its letters the committee reported that the people of the province had shown on every side that they were anxious and distressed under the present administration. It assured towns that their sense of the constitution and their rights was shared by all of their countrymen. There was a "uniformity of sentiment, tho' express'd in variety of language" among all the towns which had spoken.[21] The committee encouraged towns to communicate their views at all times and exchange information. Where towns had made particular observations about the nature of government which the governor had denied, the committee frequently endorsed their statements. It assured Lexington that "freedom from every legislative on Earth, but that of this Province, is the general claim."[22] To another it asserted that those "intrusted with places of authority" should indeed be "amenable to the People."[23] And to a third it confirmed the belief that a representative who ignored his instructions in order to serve the governor should certainly "be refused the sufrage of his constituents at their next Election."[24] It was beyond dispute that the province charter was "the only rule for the government here."[25]

Sometimes the committee took advantage of the opportunity to communicate a new grievance. For several weeks, while the news of the special royal commission to inquire into the *Gaspee* incident was still fresh, explanations of it, or a copy of Dartmouth's letter to Rhode

20. Boston committee to Plymouth, Dec. 29, 1772, Letters and Proceedings received, photos 636–637.
21. Boston committee to Lexington, Jan. 18, 1773, *ibid.*, photo 400.
22. Boston committee to Lexington, Jan. 18, 1773, *ibid.*, photo 400.
23. Boston committee to Scarborough, Feb. 4, 1773, *ibid.*, photo 739.
24. Boston committee to Rutland, April ?, 1773, *ibid.*, photo 688.
25. Boston committee to Lexington, Jan. 18, 1773, *ibid.*, photo 400.

Island's Governor Joseph Wanton establishing its procedures were included, accompanied by suitable remarks. When news came that Virginia had chosen a committee of correspondence to join with the other colonies, that information was also communicated. Later, after the letters of Governor Hutchinson and Lieutenant Governor Oliver had been made public, the committee commented on the perfidy which it believed they revealed. Indeed throughout the long series of committee replies, general allusions to self-seeking domestic enemies who carried out the ministerial plan were stressed with greater regularity than the towns themselves had stressed them in their own proceedings.

The Boston committee's letters to the few towns that did express some reservation with the pamphlet or Boston's initiative, contained earnest, respectful explanations of the point in question. In an apology to Weymouth the committee assured the town that Boston's "intention was not to obtrude their opinions upon their fellow Countrymen," but rather to know the sentiments of the country and whether it "was perfectly reconciled to the Measures of the British Administration." [26] For several other towns the committee felt it useful to reassure them that Boston's efforts were not meant to reflect on the high esteem which they held for the House of Representatives; and the committee re-emphasized Boston's respect for civil authority as well as its devotion to peace and order.[27]

The Boston committee's individual responses to the towns, taken together, reveal a policy which was an extension of the pamphlet. Their confident letters stimulated the towns to continue to stand in a moral defense of their rights and gave the recognition of the provincial metropolis to every town which had spoken up. Generally laudatory, never argumentative, their letters virtually always reinforced a town's position. Moreover the committee's deliberate tone of self-effacement and its fraternal posture, which worked to eliminate distinctions among towns, were meant to elicit local confidence and to encourage town political engagement. Re-emphasizing the necessity of continued vigilance in every letter, it maintained a tone of moderation carefully deleting signs of enthusiastic overconfidence when they turned up in its draft replies.[28] The committee paid close attention to every sen-

26. Boston committee to Weymouth, April 13, 1773, Minute Book, V, 393–394.
27. See Boston committee to Medford, Feb. 9, 1773, Letters and Proceedings received, photo 512; to Sturbridge, Jan. ?, 1773, *ibid.*, photo 806; to Weymouth, April 13, 1773, Minute Book, V, 393–394.
28. Overconfidence was a particular fault of Thomas Young. See Boston committee

tence because it knew that equally close scrutiny would be given to its letters in the towns. The committee acted on the belief that its letters of reply would be instrumental in establishing a continuing relationship of confidence between Boston and the other Massachusetts towns.

II

Although neither the Boston pamphlet, nor indeed any of the Boston committee's letters, ever called on towns to establish committees of correspondence, many followed Boston's example. Agreeing that remonstrances were necessary, and that a union of the towns and communication among them could provide a means for redress, they set up local committees of correspondence. Marblehead was one of more than fifty towns which, "in imitation" of Boston, established a standing committee, to be "continued from Year to Year, so long as may be thought necessary." Its task was to discuss and communicate proposals for relief, and to lay them before the town meeting.[29] Newbury gave a similar charge to its committee, believing that by communication "the wisest & best measures may be pitched upon, united in, & prosecuted for the Removal of our Difficulties."[30] Often the committees were directed to apply to the selectmen for a town meeting "upon any emergency," so that the town might "consider of any intelligence of importance they may have received."[31] In every case the committees were regarded as subordinates of the town meetings, wholly answerable to them.

Owing to the lack of precedent, and to the absence of specific direction from Boston, there was some uncertainty concerning the precise role of the committees. A few towns, reacting to the emphasis on grievances in the Boston pamphlet, called their committee a "com-

to Gloucester, Feb. 2, 1773, Letters and Proceedings received, photo 268; to Salisbury, Jan. 12, 1773, *ibid.*, photo 719; to New Salem, April 6, 1773, *ibid.*, photo 570; to Dorchester, Jan. 7, 1773, *ibid.*, photo 207.

29. Marblehead, Dec. 8, 1772, Boston Committee of Correspondence, Minute Book, I, 11–14.

30. Newbury, Jan. 8, 1773, Letters and Proceedings received, photos 552–556. See similar charges by Plymouth, Nov. 26, 1772, Boston Committee of Correspondence, Minute Book, I, 7–8; Ipswich, Dec. 28, 1772, Letters and Proceedings received, photos 359–360; Winchendon, March 1, 1773, Boston Committee of Correspondence, Minute Book, VII, 575–576; Ashby, June 10, 1773, Letters and Proceedings received, photos 30–31.

31. Plymouth, Nov. 26, 1772, Boston Committee of Correspondence, Minute Book, I, 7–8; Cape Elizabeth, Dec. 28, 1772, Letters and Proceedings received, photos 136–137.

mittee of grievances," expecting them to discover and formulate complaints.[32] Others, impressed with the need for viligance, erected committees "in order to watch over our Liberties"; they would maintain a surveillance of their constituents' rights.[33] Some, perhaps most, of the towns which formed committees regarded them as a sign of virtue, proof that they had "Spirit Enough to Stand up in Defense of their Charter Rights & Privileges." [34] One town in Worcester County where the Boston pamphlet was for some reason never actually delivered showed itself so anxious to demonstrate its concern that it voted resolves, chose a committee of correspondence, and began a correspondence with Boston all on its own initiative.[35]

The people chosen to serve on the committees were, very much as Adams had planned for his corresponding societies of the Bill of Rights, "composed of the most respectable inhabitants." Selectmen, moderators, deacons, militia captains, physicians, and lawyers invariably served on committees, which included anywhere from three to ten members. Wherever possible men of property and "parts," the same men who regularly led town affairs, made up the local committees of correspondence.[36]

The pattern of local committee activities grew directly out of the towns' response to the Boston pamphlet. Virtually every town had, either before or after a public reading of the pamphlet, chosen a committee to consider it in detail and to report back to the town on what should be done. Usually these "report committees" prepared the resolves which the town voted. When they recommended that the town form a committee of correspondence, several members of the report committee were normally chosen to serve as the committee of correspondence. During 1773 the activities of these two types of committees were practically indistinguishable; their most significant difference being that the committees of correspondence were standing committees, while report committees were chosen to deal with only one affair.

The local committees of correspondence rarely met except to consider material received from the Boston committee, and if they kept

32. E.g., Marblehead, Dec. 8, 1772, Boston Committee of Correspondence, Minute Book, I, 11–14.
33. Dorchester, Jan. 4, 1773, Letters and Proceedings received, photo 206.
34. Cape Elizabeth, Dec. 28, 1772, *ibid.*, photos 136–137.
35. Harvard, March 4, 1773, Letters and Proceedings received, photos 323–324.
36. Petersham, April 3, 1773, *ibid.*, photo 628, said that "the Name of a Committee of Carrospondence Especially at this day Carries in it a Considerable Degree of Importance."

their own records none have come to light. As a result their conduct can only be sketched on the basis of regular town records, the occasional protest, and a few private letters. It appears that, as the town's experts on provincial politics and the constitution, they considered information relating to such questions, even preparing recommendations before presenting any news to the town meeting. Afterwards they would forward any relevant proceedings to the Boston committee together with their own brief, often perfunctory comments. In spite of their charge directing them to correspond and consult with any and all towns in the province, they rarely exchanged letters with any town but Boston, so communication was almost exclusively at the Boston committee's initiative, between Boston and the particular towns. The town committees of correspondence did not communicate with one another until the summer of 1774.

Recommendations of committees of correspondence, like those of report committees, were usually readily adopted in town meetings. Potential conflicts were apparently resolved in committee, so the committees effectively functioned to preserve town unity. Where divisions in the town were likely to be serious, the committees of correspondence, like the report committees, included members of contending sides. As a result, by the time the committee reported to the town divisions had been resolved or at least compromised, so committee recommendations could be presented without the hazards of dissenting minority reports and adopted with a minimum of opposition in the general town meeting.[37]

In several respects the committees of correspondence and report committees were microcosmic expressions of town political structure. Like the towns, they first read and considered the Boston material. Then, as joint authors, they prepared statements which eliminated diversity among themselves, and which, they recognized, should equally provide unity for the town. Sometimes using subcommittees as the town used committes, they erased individual responsibility even though one man might have prepared the basic text. The reports they presented to the town represented the whole committee as, after adoption, they would represent the whole town. Since their recommendations accurately reflected the wishes of the town meeting, and since the leadership

37. This was not always the case. In at least two towns, Barnstable and Roxbury, the report committees were divided; and in a third, Littleton, the town voted to act after its report committee had recommended that the town take no action.

of the committee and the town so often overlapped, the recommendations were usually adopted unanimously on the same day they were
offered. When the committee itself was united then the only criticisms
raised in the meeting were comparatively small, questions of tone and
appropriate word choice.[38] As a rule several readings, discussion, and explanation by the committee sufficed before promulgating the town
political stand, since the committee represented the town for which it
spoke.

The questions raised by the Boston pamphlet and formation of a
committee of correspondence could not always be resolved so easily,
and occasionally a public dispute followed. Since this pattern appeared
in so few towns, one hesitates to generalize in describing it. Instead,
examining a few examples may serve to illuminate the significance of
such divisions. In Petersham, a Worcester town of 1,200 inhabitants,
the town meeting of January 4, 1773, had enthusiastically endorsed
Boston's lead and had established a committee of correspondence. Some
time afterwards an anonymous protest against the town's proceedings
appeared in Draper's *Boston Weekly News-Letter*, asserting that many
of the inhabitants had not attended the meeting because they "considered the assembling to be without Law," and therefore they had not
seen "fit to turn out of the common Duties of Life to attend the Meeting." Apparently the protesters regarded their time as important as
their scruples respecting the "legality" of the meeting. The protest
went on to explain that "there are Numbers in almost every Town who
would delight to display their Activity upon such an Occasion"; and
in Petersham "*our's* have discovered their Ignorance and Presumption
in censuring the Parliament of Great-Britain." The protest did not dispute the substance of the town's constitutional statement, rather it
complained that no one in Petersham was "so fully acquainted with the
Power of Parliament or the Laws and Statutes, and their Foundation,
as to debate, much less to judge the Cause." The town, it was argued,
should have recognized its ignorance by keeping silent.

This protest does not appear to have been "planted" by the administration because it went on expressly to avow support for the right of
resistance and the belief that "those who exceed their authority may
be disobeyed." In fact the whole thrust of the protest was tentative;

38. In Woolwich, April 19, 1773, Boston Committee of Correspondence, Minute
Book, III, 240–243, the proceedings were criticized at the town meeting and opposed
(in vain) because they were said to contain "too much tortollogy."

its signers did not want to judge the question of infringements "until we have heard both sides of the case." And their only objection to the town's remarkable suggestion that Massachusetts call on some foreign Protestant power to intercede for redress was that it was wrong to rely on human efforts rather than trusting in God.[39] In this case the division in the town was conditional, comparatively mild, and apparently short-lived.

In Stoughton, a Suffolk town of 2,100 inhabitants, the protest, in this case sent in to the Boston committee, was entirely different. Signed by ninety-nine voters, it claimed that a "rump" town meeting had undone the work of the town and thereby silenced it. The full March 1 meeting had seconded the Boston pamphlet, voting to record its proceedings in the Town Book and to send a copy to the Boston committee. At the adjournment two weeks later, a "thin" meeting had voted to reconsider and dismiss the proceedings. The ninety-nine protesters wanted to put themselves on record that "it becomes" the "People Unitedly in all lawful Ways to defend their Rights."[40] For the protesters at least, the division seems to have been an ideological issue entirely. They wanted their beliefs publicly and permanently recorded and then they rested.

Conflict, however, sometimes had deeper, more persistent roots. In Barnstable, a town of nearly 3,000 inhabitants, the division was intense and protracted. From the beginning, the town's report committee was divided, and the argument dragged on over a period of months both in and out of the town meeting. When the town finally voted resolves in May it supported the House of Representatives wholeheartedly, but, by omission, not Boston. No committee of correspondence was formed.

Old divisions in Barnstable conditioned its response to the Boston committee. These had existed long before the pamphlet appeared and long after it was forgotten. On one side, favoring the Boston committee and hostile to Governor Hutchinson, was the Otis family and their connections; on the other, was Representative Edward Bacon and his allies. Bacon had attempted to thwart the Boston pamphlet in Barnstable by denouncing the morality and general impiety of its authors in the town meeting. Subsequently he disowned his statements at the Boston committee's request, but when the committee provided the Otises with

39. Petersham protest, n.d., in *Boston Weekly News-Letter*, May 13, 1773, 4:1.
40. Stoughton protest, March 31, 1773, Boston Committee of Correspondence, Minute Book, III, 238–240.

fifty copies of his retraction for distribution among townspeople, Bacon's allies claimed it was forged.[41] As a result of the delays and wrangling within the town, Barnstable did not act further. By a variety of maneuvers Bacon succeeded in keeping the town relatively "loyal" to the administration in 1773 and even as late as 1775.[42]

The conflict which occurred in Barnstable is especially revealing because it was so unusual. The town's leading citizens were already divided between friends and foes of the administration, so the Boston pamphlet provided another ground on which to battle. On the contrary most towns — practically all — began with no such division among local leaders, so report committees and committees of correspondence could establish unity where no substantial conflict already existed. In Barnstable, where the town was divided, the issues of political action raised by Boston exacerbated the existing conflict. But this case was almost unique; the other towns easily united behind their committees' statements, because their committees, composed of regular town leaders, represented united towns.

III

Before the Boston committee ever sent out the pamphlet or any of its letters, the towns of Massachusetts, large and small, old and new, shared a general respect for the capital town. If any city versus country conflict existed, or if Boston suffered the envy of lesser towns, these sentiments were not expressed to any significant degree. Boston was the foremost town in New England, and despite its occasional "mobs and riots" it held a recognized position of leadership. The Boston pamphlet and the communications of the committee of correspondence strengthened this position while developing a more particular, confidential relationship between Boston and the towns.

The nature of this new relationship varied from town to town. In the larger towns, and towns where commerce or geography brought townspeople into frequent contact with outside news, relations were friendly, businesslike. Such towns spoke to Boston as equals. Their inhabitants seemed pleased, but not excited, by Boston's kind words.

41. James Otis, Sr., to William Cooper, June 12, 1773, Letters and Proceedings received, photo 52.

42. One of Bacon's ruses was to read a pamphlet by Samuel Cooper, the New York Tory, to the town meeting claiming it was by the Boston Whig cleric Samuel Cooper. See Francis T. Bowles, "The Loyalty of Barnstable During the Revolution," Publications of the Colonial Society of Massachusetts, Transactions, XXV (1922–1924), 265–345.

Smaller, more isolated towns reacted with more enthusiasm, responding warmly to Boston's fraternal overtures. They had never expected to be treated as equals; some rose to the occasion, others hesitated to assume such a role.

Willbraham, a town of 1,100 people in Hampshire County, used "Scripture Language" to describe its feelings: "'I am young and ye are very old, wherefore I was afraid and durst not shew you mine opinion.'" They believed "'Days should speak and multitude of Years should teach wisdom.'" But they sensed their spirit rising as men, and after receiving Boston's pamphlet, they were ready to say, "'hearken unto me I also will show you mine Opinion.'" They did not care if others might say that such an infant town was "bold and impudent in meddling with the affair." They felt they had "a call to be very bold, and to stand for and maintain our Just Rights and Privileges especially at this so critical time."[43] Piersontown, a community of 600 inhabitants in Cumberland County, found it "very unexpected that a circular Letter . . . reached us, a few Individuals scattered in the Wilderness." They were sure "that this Respect shown us had its Rise from a Mistake, a Supposition that we were a Corporate Society." They explained that they were not yet a town, because they could not afford to pay the taxes. They would not pass formal resolves like a town, since it would be regarded as "assuming." Therefore they expressed informal support as "Members of the Community & Sharers in the Prosperity & Adversity of the Province." They would, they said, always stand fast and follow Boston's lead.[44] Medumcook, with less than 250 inhabitants, reacted in a similar vein, believing that they could not form a committee of correspondence since they were not incorporated. Instead, they sent their "Good wishes," explaining that they would follow Boston's planning and "Superior wisdom."[45] Such small communities often deferred to Boston, believing the filial relationship of children and father was more appropriate than the equality of brothers.

Some, however, were pleased to stand as Boston's equals. They adopted lengthy, elaborate, even pretentious resolves. They sent back fulsome praise of Boston's heroism. If, as a result of Boston's resistance the people of Boston should be driven from their "goodly heritages," several towns expressed their readiness to invite them "to share with us in our small supplys of the Necessarys of Life." And if tyranny

43. Wilbraham, April 20, 1773, Boston Committee of Correspondence, Minute Book, IV, 337–339.
44. Piersontown, July 8, 1773, Letters and Proceedings received, photos 599–600.
45. Medumcook, Sept. 1, 1773, *ibid.*, photo 516.

should still stalk them, they would all flee together into the inland wilderness. A few towns felt so encouraged by their correspondence with Boston that they became chatty, exchanging letters with the committee on their own initiative. Once more they justified themselves with Scripture: "For we read, that those that were faithful spake often, one to the other." [46]

Within local communities Boston's correspondence became extremely important. For in many of them the committee's letters provided their only reliable source of political intelligence. They furnished "Knowledge of those Facts, which many of us should not otherwise come at, which yet it is interesting to us to be made acquainted with." [47] Furthermore, the Boston committee, the interim spokesman for Massachusetts in the absence of a session of the General Court, provided assurance that the views of individual towns were part of the general unity. Always fearful of being isolated, town after town took satisfaction in learning from Boston that it was a full participant in the defense of American liberty. Many towns, especially frontier settlements, took special delight in the recognition bestowed by the committee "for their imperfect scribblings." [48] They hoped Boston would forgive their imperfect language and spelling, and that the Boston committee would correct them if their proceedings were printed. [49] Having little contact with other towns, they expressed "great satisfaction" when their own ideas "found so great acceptance from men of so great abilities and possessed with so many social virtues." [50] The Boston committee's circular letters and its individual replies had succeeded in promoting a relationship of trust and a sense of community between Boston and the other towns.

IV

Four months after the Boston town meeting had given the committee its first assignment, the pamphlet, it gave it a second. Boston had unanimously adopted a statement vindicating it from "the gross misrepresentations and groundless charges in his Excellency's message,"

46. Petersham, Jan. 4, 1773, Letters and Proceedings received, photo 623. Gorham was the most talkative town.

47. Royalston, May 26, 1773, *ibid.*, photos 685–686. Grammatical usage serves as a rough index of the degree of formal education.

48. Gorham, May 14, 1773, *ibid.*, photo 277.

49. Woolwich, April 19, 1773, Boston Committee of Correspondence, Minute Book, III, 240–243; Petersham, April 7, 1773, Letters and Proceedings received, photo 631.

50. Gorham, May 14, 1773, Letters and Proceedings received, photo 277.

respecting Boston's proceedings during October and November 1772. Now, on March 23, 1773, the town directed the committee to transmit printed copies of this vindication "to such towns and districts as they have or may correspond with."[51] The committee had not drawn the statement, and strictly speaking its only part in the affair was the routine task of sending the 2,000-word broadside out. Nevertheless the statement must be regarded as primarily a committee of correspondence effort.

Its authorship cannot be separated from the committee of correspondence. Of the seven Boston Whigs who as a committee prepared the statement, five, Joseph Warren the chairman, Benjamin Church, Joseph Greenleaf, James Otis, and Thomas Young, were members of the committee of correspondence.[52] Its substance, and the audience toward which it was directed, the Massachusetts towns, made it an integral part of the committee's other activity. It added the official, unanimous voice of the town of Boston to the committee's own support of local political action. Boston was not merely defending itself alone, it was vindicating all the active towns in the province.

The statement began with a rehearsal of the governor's aspersions against Boston, almost all of which applied equally to any other town that had discussed the judges' salaries or other constitutional questions. By placing the governor's remarks in juxtaposition with quotations from the Massachusetts charter, the statement "proved" that the Boston meeting had been legal in every respect, and that every town in Massachusetts was guaranteed the right to freely meet, discuss, and petition if it wished. The governor's objections, it was argued, spoke "the very language of tyranny." Instead of standing with his province, the governor was singled out as "a fellow citizen" who had made himself part of the plan to enslave it. His effort to discourage public consideration of the problems was motivated by "a design to keep the people in ignorance of their danger, that they may be the more easily and speedily enslaved."[53]

According to the vindication Boston had merely spread notice that

51. *Boston Town Records, 1770–1777*, Boston Record Commissioners, *Report*, XVIII (1887), 125; also broadside of March 30, 1773, "By Direction of the Committee of Correspondence for the Town of Boston, I now transmit to you an attested Copy of the Proceedings of said Town on the 8th Instant . . . ," Massachusetts Historical Society.

52. *Boston Town Records, 1770–1777*, p. 118. The remaining two who helped prepare the statement were Samuel Swift and Benjamin Kent.

53. Broadside of March 30, 1773, "By Direction of the Committee of Correspondence for the Town of Boston."

the last step in the *"iniquitous system"* was about to be completed. Many towns had applauded Boston's effort and "gentlemen of figure in other colonies" were also pleased by its measures. The governor had castigated Boston's constitutional sentiments, but they were precisely the same as those affirmed by the House of Representatives and many towns. Moreover Boston denied that it had invited towns to "adopt" its principles as the governor charged; it had merely requested a public exchange of views. It emphasized that the towns had "acted *their own* judgment and expressed *their own* principles." Closing the vindication in terms which were similar to the reply letters, Boston expressed its "unspeakable satisfaction, . . . that their [the towns'] sentiments so nearly accord with ours." No town could doubt the propriety of its activity when the House of Representatives itself had expressly declared that the principles advanced by the town of Boston were warranted by the constitution.[54]

The Boston statement, it was clear, was as much a vehicle of information and explanation, as it was argument. Functioning to reinforce the towns in the same way as the committee's reply letters, it justified all of the towns as it vindicated Boston. Moreover it succeeded in turning Boston's defense into a sharply pointed attack on Governor Hutchinson, who, it emphasized, was an active participant in the systematic plan of enslavement which was hastening toward completion.

On March 30 the committee directed its clerk to have three hundred copies of this Boston vindication printed. One would be sent to every town and district "as soon as possible."[55] But before sending them out the committee took a significant step on its own initiative. Reliable news had just arrived from Virginia that the House of Burgesses had voted a series of Resolves, initiating a system of intercolonial committees of correspondence and inviting all the assemblies on the continent to join to defend colonial rights. The committee of correspondence rapidly decided to include this information with the Boston statement together with an extract from a letter which Samuel Adams had received from Virginia.[56] Virginia's approval of the Boston pamphlet and its emula-

54. Broadside of March 30, 1773, "By Direction of the Committee of Correspondence for the Town of Boston."
54. *Ibid.*
55. Boston Committee of Correspondence, minutes, March 30, 1773, Minute Book, III, 213.
56. Boston Committee of Correspondence, minutes, April 9, 1773, *ibid.*, 215–216. The letter was probably from Richard Henry Lee to Samuel Adams, since the two maintained a regular correspondence and together sought to further a union of the colonies.

tion of the idea of committees of correspondence to promote a defensive union furnished a far more impressive justification for Boston and the towns than the Boston statement alone. In its covering letter the Boston committee characteristically focused attention back on the towns: "We congratulate you upon the Acquisition of such respectable Aid as the ancient and patriotic Province of *Virginia*, the earliest Resolvers against the detestable Stamp-Act." [57] Here was reassurance that not only the towns were united, but that the colonies were also on the way to union. The Virginia Resolves repudiated the governor's assertions that the other colonies were quiet and Massachusetts isolated. This news, together with the Boston vindication, gave further encouragement to political activity in the towns. [58]

Until this period, the spring of 1773, the institutional definition of the Boston Committee of Correspondence had remained reasonably clear. In spite of the overlapping associations and activities of its members, it was clearly a Boston town committee, like other standing committees. But as the scene of political battle in Massachusetts shifted from the towns back to the General Court, the Boston committee became in some respects affiliated with the assembly. The governor's reply to the committee had been delivered in the assembly, and the whole assembly controversy with the governor was in one sense an extension of the committee's argument with the administration. However, the critical factor in determining the ties of the committee with the General Court was its personnel, in particular Samuel Adams. Adams, the clerk of the House, was always in close communication with Thomas Cushing, the speaker, who attended meetings of the committee of correspondence, and who seems to have made the correspondence he received from the Massachusetts agent at Westminster, Benjamin Franklin, available to the committee. [59] As a result of these connections, and the obvious common interests of the committee and the House of Representatives, the committee co-ordinated its activity with that of the House.

The Boston committee's only formal contact with the House of Representatives had been in late February 1773. At that time, acting entirely on its own initiative, the committee, "considering the growing

57. Broadside of April 9, 1773, "The Committee of Correspondence of this Town have received the following Intelligence . . . ," Massachusetts Historical Society.
58. See Samuel Adams to Richard Henry Lee, April 10, 1773, *Writings of Samuel Adams*, III, 25.
59. Boston Committee of Correspondence, minutes, April 29, 1773, June 1, 1773, Minute Book, III, 216–218.

uneasiness of the People" in regard to the judges' stipends, decided to petition the House. Its petition, originally calling on the House to take steps for redress of all the grievances, was given unusually intense consideration in the committee on February 24 and 25, requiring three alternative drafts. When at last one was unanimously accepted by the committee, the petition concerned only the judges' salaries. Presumably the committee had decided that its petition must deal with that one point specifically — otherwise it would be merely a repetition of numerous instructions to representatives, only a diffuse plea for action. On February 26, Warren, Church, Dennie, Bradford, and Molineux presented the petition to the House.[60] Five days later the House acted, passing several resolutions upholding the assembly's exclusive right to pay the judges, and declaring that any justice who accepted such a salary "has it in his heart to promote the establishment of an arbitrary government in the province."[61] The House was warning the judges that they would be risking the displeasure of both the House and the people. This threat, it seemed to believe, might be sufficient to prevent them from accepting the stipends; at least it would give these royal appointees a suitable pretext to offer to the Crown if they did decide to refuse the salaries.

Whether these House resolves grew directly out of the committee petition remains uncertain. Throughout the month of February the House had been arguing the subject of the salaries with the governor; perhaps the petition of the Boston committee made little impact, or none at all. But whatever its effect in the House, the petition marked a significant step in the development of the committee. For this unusual measure, unusual for a town committee, was the Boston committee's first political maneuver taken on its own initiative, and its first effort to directly influence local representatives gathered in the House. Already the committee was expanding its sphere of activity, defining its own role in Massachusetts politics. During the course of

60. Boston Committee of Correspondence, minutes, Feb. 23–26, 1773, *ibid.*, 207–208. I have been unable to find any versions of this petition. According to Thomas Hutchinson the petition was an effort by the Boston "faction" to pressure the House which backfired. After presenting the petition, he said, they quickly retreated for fear of being charged with dictating to the assembly. This account is plausible, since the committee was anxious to prod the House on the issue of judges' salaries, but even more anxious to avoid being effectively stigmatized as dictator of the province. See Thomas Hutchinson, *The History of the Colony and Province of Massachusetts-Bay*, ed. Lawrence Shaw Mayo (Cambridge, Mass., 1936), III, 278–279.

61. Alden Bradford, ed., *Speeches of the Governors of Massachusetts, 1765–1775* (Boston, 1818), 396–398.

the next year the committee would initiate further steps associating it with both the assembly and the towns.

Printing and mailing the Virginia Resolves, the committee's next initiative, while immediately directed to the towns also influenced the House, since it obviously promoted the intercolonial committee of correspondence plan. Indeed, shortly after the assembly met late in May, the House did second Virginia by erecting an intercolonial committee of correspondence.[62] However it was a later step, the Boston committee's publication and distribution of Governor Hutchinson's and Lieutenant Governor Oliver's private letters to London officials, together with the House resolves on them, which set the committee in a new relationship to the House and the towns. For by sending the letters and the resolves out to the towns, the Boston committee temporarily became a kind of informal, self-constituted House committee of correspondence inside the province. The House itself had never created such a committee, nor would it, since the representatives might voluntarily inform their townsmen as far as was necessary. But the Boston committee actively brought the General Court proceedings into the town meetings, further promoting local involvement in provincial politics.

The letters of Hutchinson and Oliver, written to the administration in London during 1767, 1768, and 1769, had come into Benjamin Franklin's possession and he had sent them on to the speaker of the Massachusetts House, Thomas Cushing. The letters arrived sometime in May before the assembly met, and Cushing circulated them surreptitiously among some political associates. Samuel Adams believed they were so incriminating that "could they be made generally known, his [Hutchinson's] Friends must desert him." Franklin had requested that the letters be kept private, but their political utility proved irresistible and overruled his wishes. Adams remarked: "It is a pity when the most important Intelligence is communicated with such Restrictions, as that it serves rather to gratify the Curiosity of a few than to promote the public good."[63] His sentiment seems to have been shared by Cushing, who

62. May 28, 1773. See Massachusetts Historical Society, *Proceedings*, 2d Ser., IV (1887–1889), 82–90, for journal of Massachusetts Committee of Correspondence. Of the fifteen men on the Massachusetts committee, at least five were members of town committees, and one, Samuel Adams, was on the Boston committee.

63. Samuel Adams to Arthur Lee, May 17, 1773, *Writings of Samuel Adams*, III, 39–40. Samuel Cooper, in a letter to Benjamin Franklin of June 14, 1773, confirms that Hutchinson's letters were sent to Speaker Cushing and that he "managed" them. In *The Works of Benjamin Franklin*, ed. John Bigelow (New York, 1904), VI, 126–131.

laid the letters before the House which, after clearing the public from the gallery, voted that they be read aloud. Now news of the affair, together with various accounts of the contents of the "secret" letters spread rapidly through Boston and its environs, creating an uproar.[64] In the following days, during June, the House considered the letters, determined their authenticity, and ended by condemning them and their authors by a vote of 101 to 5.[65] They requested that the King remove both Hutchinson and Oliver from office forever.

The contents of the letters served to confirm everything that the Boston Whigs had been arguing for years. For Hutchinson, in describing the *Liberty* incident of 1768 and provincial politics, had insulted or impugned every political element in Massachusetts which was not firmly allied to the administration. Hancock and James Otis were mentioned personally, and disparaging remarks were used in describing the House and Council, the grand and petty juries, the Boston town meeting, the *Boston Gazette*, and indeed the whole populace. Hutchinson's main point was that Massachusetts lacked any internal authority. He advised basic reforms of its political and institutional structure in order to curtail popular influence. Reluctantly, he had even suggested that the charter be unilaterally altered.[66] A Crown civil list for the province, administration control of the selection of jurors, and the creation of "an Order of Patricians" to inhabit both the Council and other high offices of government were among his particular recommendations.[67]

All these specifics, and the disgust and disdain which Hutchinson expressed for people and institutions that from time to time opposed the administration, infuriated Massachusetts inhabitants. Hutchinson was aware of this potential at the time he had written the letters, so he had asked that his name be kept secret, even though he "wrote

64. See John Andrews to William Barrell, June 4, 1773, Massachusetts Historical Society, *Proceedings*, VIII (1864–1865), 323.

65. Samuel Adams to Arthur Lee, June 16, 1773, *Writings of Samuel Adams*, III, 40–41.

66. Thomas Hutchinson, *Copy of Letters Sent to Great-Britain, by his Excellency Thomas Hutchinson, the Hon. Andrew Oliver, and several other Persons, Born and Educated Among Us . . . In which (notwithstanding his Excellency's Declaration to the House, that the Tendency and Design of them was not to subvert the Constitution, but rather to preserve it entire) the judicious Reader will discover the fatal Source of the Confusion and Bloodshed in which this Province especially has been involved, and which threatened total Destruction to the Liberties of all America* (Boston, 1773), 30.

67. *Ibid.*, 22–23, 29, 31.

nothing but what in my conscience I think an American may upon just principles advance."[68] In fact the theoretical substance of the whole group of letters was identical with that of the speech of January 6, 1773, only here the consequences of the theory were elaborated.[69] In the letter of January 20, 1769, he had written:

I never think of the measures necessary for the peace and good order of the colonies without pain. There must be an abridgment of what are called English liberties. I relieve myself by considering that in a remove from the state of nature to the most perfect state of government there must be a great restraint of natural liberty. I doubt whether it is possible to project a system of government in which a colony 3000 miles distant from the parent state shall enjoy all the liberty of the parent state . . . I wish the good of the colony when I wish to see some further restraint of liberty rather than the connexion with the parent state should be broken; for I am sure such a breach must prove the ruin of the colony.[70]

Here, in the published letters, the governor himself exposed the consequences of the theory he had proposed in his effort to persuade the province on January 6, 1773.

Late in June 1773 the Boston committee voted to send the letters and the House resolves out to the towns. In its covering letter the committee expressed gratitude for the interest and approval of "so large a Majority of the Towns," and went on to present the letters as an extraordinary discovery by which God had "wonderfully interposed to bring to Light the Plot that had been laid for us by our malicious and insidious Enemies." The committee then quoted a House resolve indicting the governor as a subverter of "our constitutional liberty." The committee was confident that the letters would make the conspiracy and the crisis self-evident so it made its most direct appeal for unanimous action: "This Period calls for the strictest Concurrence in Sentiment and Action of every individual of this Province, and we may add, of THIS CONTINENT; all private Views should be annihilated, and the Good of the Whole should be the single Object of our Pursuit."[71] This appeal, stressing the necessity of elevating public over

68. *Ibid.*, 23–24. In several other letters he cautioned secrecy.
69. Thomas Hutchinson himself said that his speech contained identical sentiments. *Additions to Thomas Hutchinson's "History of Massachusetts-Bay,"* ed. Catherine B. Mayo (Worcester, Mass., 1949), 63.
70. Hutchinson, *Copy of Letters*, 16.
71. Boston Committee of Correspondence circular letter of June 22, 1773, broadside, "Sir, the Committee of Correspondence of the Town of *Boston*, conformable to that Duty which they have hitherto endeavoured to discharge with Fidelity, again

private values and implicating corrupted rulers whose private ambition had tempted them to forsake the public good, played on traditional themes profoundly implanted in the public mind.

The House resolves and the publication and distribution of Hutchinson's letters marked the climax of the Whig opposition effort to annihilate the governor politically. For Governor Hutchinson it was an irreversible defeat. Although he thought his letters contained "nothing more than might naturally be expected from a confidential correspondence," although he persistently maintained that "there is not one word in any of them exceptionable," they had "answered their [the faction's] purpose by prejudicing the people against me to that degree as to destroy that confidence which remained." [72] As a result he believed his political usefulness to the Crown had been ended, so he decided to request the ministry to honorably replace him. [73] He still believed that the House resolves, not the letters, were most damaging, and that if people had actually bothered to read the letters they would be convinced of his good intentions. [74] He still did not realize that his own fundamental political assumptions differed radically from those in the province.

For the Boston Committee of Correspondence, the letters furnished not only an excellent opportunity to continue and extend its original aims but also positive verification of its interpretation of the administration. Having earlier received proof from the towns that its own assumptions were shared, the committee now had only to offer the letters as evidence to the inhabitants; it could be confident that the letters would awaken them to the immediacy of the enslavement plan. The accompanying House resolves would provide an example of the way in which unity was being achieved. The towns would know how to join in.

Massachusetts had not achieved total consensus, but the votes of the assembly and the public declarations of the majority towns in the province had radically altered the climate of provincial politics. Towns

address you with a very fortunate important Discovery . . . ," Massachusetts Historical Society.

72. Hutchinson to Dartmouth, June 14, 1773, to Governor Tryon, July 6, 1773, to Hillsborough, June–July ?, 1773, Thomas Hutchinson Letter Books, Massachusetts Archives, XXVII, 495, 509–510, 506.

73. Hutchinson to Dartmouth, June 1–14, 1773, to Hillsborough, June–July ?, 1773, Hutchinson Letter Books, Mass. Arch., XXVII, 489–492, 506.

74. Hutchinson to Governor Tryon, July 6, 1773, Hutchinson Letter Books, Mass. Arch., XXVII, 509–510.

no longer lived in isolated ignorance of their neighbors' beliefs, uncertain of the acceptability of their own political credo. Now their ideas had been confirmed and reinforced by the Boston committee and by the proceedings of scores of towns published in the press. Confirmation had even come from beyond the province, a thrilling experience for many towns: "our hearts even leap for joy upon Reading the Resolves of the Patriotick House of Burgesses in Virginia." The towns and the colonies were, they believed, realizing their strength at last; for the "fair Prospect of a Union of the Colonies, if once effected will Chase away all fears of slavery." They hoped that "every Colony will most cheerfully embrace this lucky opportunity to Cultivate the Strictest union, by choosing Committees of Correspondence." Some expected that representatives of the colonies would now meet together to consult on united action.[75] Through their own exertions the colonies had brought the prospect of relief into sight.

If their united protests could not produce a full restoration of their rights and liberties, many had come to believe "that the Colonies united as one man, will make their most Solemn appeal to Heaven, in the sense of Mr. Lock, and drive tyranny from these Northern Climes."[76] The Boston committee had made no allusions to redress by military means, but such references had begun to appear in the towns' statements. Britain could indeed send "armed Vessels & Soldiers" to take their rights "by force." But Britain should be warned: "so may an armed Robber take from an unarmed Traveller all the Money he has with him, but, if the Robber is found out it may Prove fatall to him." If Britain used force, one town warned, "The Soldiers might Come off like those that were Defeated a few Years ago in General Braddock's fight, be Cut in Pieces & Destroyed."[77] Such talk was unusual, but it appeared with sufficient frequency to indicate a mood of crisis and of confidence.

One town committee of correspondence believed that the ultimate crisis had already arrived. Parliament, it said, had destroyed Massachusetts' charter, therefore no "Door is open by Divine Providence for our Escape but for the People of this Province to Resume their old Charter and Chuse all our officers." This, the town said, was the only way to avoid tyranny "without mobs or Riots." Since those holding com-

75. Cambridge, May 3, 1773, Letters and Proceedings received, photo 123; Gorham, May 14, 1773, *ibid.*, photo 278; Cambridge, May 3, 1773, *ibid.*, photo 123.
76. Cambridge, May 3, 1773, *ibid.*, photo 123.
77. Bellingham, May 19, 1773, *ibid.*, photos 58–59.

missions from the Crown could no longer be trusted, "it must be done by the Common People."[78] This town was unique in its suggestions during the spring of 1773, but its confidence in popular political action supported by united sentiments was widespread. Indeed it was the general character of this belief which had led, virtually without controversy, to the formation of local committees of correspondence and to the broad examination of constitutional issues in the towns. Moreover the Boston committee, taking advantage of the townspeople's sense of duty and desire for recognition, had brought them to commit themselves publicly to political action in support of their beliefs.

Consequently, by the summer of 1773 the Boston Committee of Correspondence had emerged as an important force in Massachusetts politics. Its pamphlet together with its correspondence with the towns, and the publicity it had given the Virginia Resolves, the House resolves, and the governor's letters, all demonstrated that it could awaken the power of the local political units by engaging them in provincial politics. Ready to seize initiatives, the committee had shown a willingness to act both for the town of Boston and perhaps even for the House of Representatives. Its tendency to blur institutional boundaries by enlarging its own sphere should not be taken for usurpation by the committee, as both sides, Whig and Tory, frequently blurred institutional lines since the same leaders were employing all the political resources available to them. The Boston Committee of Correspondence was not supplanting existing institutions, it was creating a new role for itself — a role based on a new standard of widespread local participation in general political affairs. The traditional balance, in which the governor and the two chambers of the General Court ruled provincial issues while towns ruled their own local affairs, was being decisively challenged; and the chief catalyst and co-ordinator of this process was the Boston Committee of Correspondence.

78. Petersham, April 3, 1773, Letters and Proceedings received, photos 628–631.

7

Massachusetts Opposes the Tea Act: The Boston Committee and the Towns

With the passage of the Tea Act in May 1773, Parliament established the framework for what was to become a decisive test of will between England and the colonies. The act, initiated on behalf of the East India Company, was drawn to accommodate both the company's need to dispose of surplus tea and the political aims of the ministry headed by Lord North. It permitted the company to export tea directly to the colonies and also provided it with allowances to repay the customs duties which would be collected in America. The company and its factors were thus enabled to sell their tea at prices lower than other merchants, while the existing duty on tea would be maintained as a matter of principle.[1] Consequently the issues raised by the act were the familiar ones that had been contested after the passage of the Townshend duties six years earlier. But now, owing in part to the activity of the Boston Committee of Correspondence, the context for resistance had so changed that instead of ebbing away as it had in 1770, resistance would now become rebellion.

In Massachusetts the test between Britain and the colonies occurred at two distinct, though contiguous, levels: in Boston, the center of com-

---

1. Benjamin W. Labaree, *The Boston Tea Party* (New York, 1964), 66-74; Danby Pickering, ed., *The Statutes at Large from Magna Charta to the End of the Thirteenth Parliament of Great Britain, Anno 1773* (Cambridge, Eng., 1773), XXX, 74-77.

merce and administration; and in the province at large, the other towns and districts in which 95 percent of the population lived. Boston, where the tea was to be landed and the duty paid, stood in the front line together with Atlantic ports in other colonies. As Whigs saw it, their opposition would be totally undermined if tea entered the capital according to the terms of the act. It was in Boston, therefore, that active resistance was imperative, and Boston Whigs met in private clubs, in the town meeting, and in the Boston Committee of Correspondence to organize it. In the province the situation was somewhat different. There was less cause for immediate action because the tea was being shipped only to Boston. Nevertheless Whigs believed the attitude of the towns would be crucial to the success of resistance. Boston needed support; it could not stand alone.

Therefore the Boston committee was again called upon to communicate with the towns, advising them of circumstances at Boston. Now local reactions often went beyond Boston's own stated position, and demonstrated that the year-old committee of correspondence had already achieved substantial success in arousing political self-consciousness and involvement at the local level. For town responses were not confined simply to the Tea Act, but overflowed into general constitutional discussion. In some towns this new issue became an occasion to further extend the re-examination of political beliefs originally begun in answer to the Boston pamphlet. Moreover as time went on it became apparent that such re-examinations were tending in a single direction — republicanism. Radical assumptions about the nature of government were becoming increasingly explicit at the local level.

Consequently the opposition to the Tea Act served as both a symptom of alterations in the character of provincial politics and as an impetus toward further change. Massachusetts, it had been demonstrated, no longer called for so much guidance and solicitude as the Boston committee had previously supplied, so in the wake of the Tea Party the interests of the committee shifted beyond the province to colonial union. It now assumed responsibility for co-ordinating Boston's resistance with that of other colonies, effectively superceding the Massachusetts Committee of Correspondence which had been appointed by the House. It became the province's quasi-official body for planning and organizing resistance to the ministry. Political circumstances were reshaping both the committee's role and the roles of the towns in Massachusetts and imperial politics.

I

After sending out Hutchinson's letters in late June 1773, the Boston committee spent a quiet summer. Since agriculture dominated the countryside in summer, curtailing town meetings, the time was inappropriate for large-scale correspondence. Moreover the assembly had acted decisively, petitioning for the removal of Governor Hutchinson in the same way as it had asked to be relieved of Governor Bernard after his letters had been published four years earlier. Now Massachusetts was waiting to see whether the King, the ministry, and Parliament would redress their grievances. People were hopeful; they expected some form of relief.[2] The Boston committee and the Massachusetts Committee of Correspondence anticipated important news from England, perhaps news of a favorable shift of power in Parliament, possibly an alteration in the international diplomatic balance, or a renewal of European warfare, which would make England dependent on her colonies.[3] At present the committee believed it was best to postpone action.

As the summer ended the Boston committee, now chaired by Samuel Adams, renewed its efforts, again focusing attention on the judges' salaries.[4] For the moment it appeared that the resistance of the previous winter and spring had been moderately successful; all of the justices except Chief Justice Peter Oliver had so far been paid exclusively by the province. But victory remained uncertain since the administration continued to assert its right and intention to pay all the judges. Only one, Edmund Trowbridge, had declared publicly that he would never accept a Crown stipend under any circumstances. Continued public outcry might bring more judges to stand with Trowbridge and thereby seal the victory.

In Suffolk County, the grand jury, influenced if not led by Boston Whigs, had initiated a new method of opposition to the stipends. When the superior court convened, the jurors presented it with a "Memorial" defending their own "Independence" and requesting that, in view of the popular anxiety, the court make an explicit, public declaration of

2. E.g., Thomas Cushing to Benjamin Franklin, Dec. 10, 1773, *The Works of Benjamin Franklin*, ed. John Bigelow (New York, 1904), VI, 250–253.
3. Massachusetts Committee of Correspondence Journal, Massachusetts Historical Society, *Proceedings*, 2d Ser., IV (1887–1889), 82–90; Josiah Quincy to George Clymer, August ?, 1773, *Memoir of Josiah Quincy junior*, ed. Elizabeth S. Quincy (Boston, 1874), 119–120.
4. Samuel Adams was chairman on Sept. 7, 1773. Whether he served as chairman previously is not clear from the records.

its views respecting Crown stipends. The Boston committee hoped that the grand juries of the other counties would similarly challenge the intentions of the judges. Since the court would next meet in Worcester, the committee prepared an account of the activities of the Suffolk grand jury and sent it on to the Worcester committee of correspondence, while it also had the Suffolk "Memorial" printed in the newspapers where it could be consulted in detail. In the meantime, the Boston committee suggested that it would "be serving the Cause if every County would take similar Measures." Careful not to insist, the committee relied on the Worcester committee's "Discretion & good Judgment to take such methods as shall be most proper." [5]

At the same time the Boston committee was eager to maintain the general state of vigilance which had developed in the province. When the news arrived that no redress for Massachusetts was being contemplated in England, the committee voted to direct Joseph Greenleaf to prepare an article for the newspapers "relative to the Parliaments rising without taking proper notice of our petitions." [6] This unusual expedient, almost unique as a specifically directed act of the committee, or indeed any town committee, became the prelude for a broad effort to keep the towns on the alert by means of another circular letter.

The committee voted in early September that Joseph Warren "prepare a circular letter from this Committee for the several towns in the Province; and also for the other Colonies." Here the committee was anticipating a role beyond Massachusetts. When Warren quickly reported a draft the committee accepted it, voting that it be printed and sent immediately to the local committees of correspondence. For the moment no further mention was made of a circular letter for the other colonies, although the committee did decide that each of its members should take several of the circulars printed for the towns and "transmit them to their Friends in the other Governments." [7] Whether they were to send them as friends or on behalf of the committee is not certain; in either case it is clear that the committee was looking beyond provincial politics.

5. Boston Committee of Correspondence to Worcester Committee of Correspondence, Sept. 11, 1773, *The Writings of Samuel Adams*, ed. Harry A. Cushing (New York, 1904–1908), III, 51–52; also Boston Committee of Correspondence, minutes, Sept. 7, 1773, Minute Book, V, 402–403, New York Public Library, photostats at Massachusetts Historical Society.

6. Boston Committee of Correspondence, minutes, Sept. 7, 1773, Minute Book, III, 226–227.

7. *Ibid.*; also *ibid.*, Sept. 10, 1773, 227–228.

Individually some of its members had been actively promoting colonial unity for years. In the spring of the year one of its members, Josiah Quincy, had taken a tour of the southern colonies for reasons of health and had used the opportunity to cultivate acquaintance with Whig political leaders northward from the Carolinas through Virginia, Pennsylvania, and New York. Afterwards he had written to a new Pennsylvania acquaintance, George Clymer, observing that "a mutual exchange of sentiments will give us, as men, a knowledge of each other; that knowledge naturally creates esteem, and that esteem will, in the end, cement us as colonists." Quincy was convinced "we must think *alike*, before we shall form a union." Now his associates on the Boston committee had apparently adopted colonial unity as one of their active, if not most immediate goals.[8]

The primary target of the new circular, however, remained Massachusetts. Its precise contents and the question of which towns, specifically, should receive it seem to have raised second thoughts among some members of the committee. For on September 25, four days after the circular was printed, they reconsidered the whole measure, reading the letter over paragraph by paragraph before once more deciding to send it out.[9] Afterwards the committee determined that it should be sent not only to those committees in touch with Boston, but also to any other towns which members of the committee thought might benefit from it.

This circular of September 21, 1773, was a general call to remain firm and vigilant in opposition to the administration. No violations of rights or particular grievances were mentioned. Instead the committee chose to explain the consequences of Massachusetts' political stance in the context of current English politics. First, they said, the colonists held a position of strength. The existing union within the province and "the Confederacy into which they [our enemies] expect the whole Continent of America, will soon be drawn, for the Recovery of their violated RIGHTS" had alarmed the English administration to such a degree that it was industriously attempting to persuade Massachusetts

8. Josiah Quincy to George Clymer, Aug. ?, 1773, *Memoir of Josiah Quincy junior*, 119-120; Samuel Adams (?) as "Observation," *Boston Gazette*, Sept. 27, 1773, 2:2, called for an American congress to draw a bill of rights and send one ambassador to reside at Westminster.

9. The vote was 12 in favor, 1 opposed. Samuel Adams was either absent or opposed the measure. Minutes at this meeting were kept by John Bradford, who listed the names of those who voted in favor. Boston Committee of Correspondence, minutes, Sept. 25, 1773, Minute Book, III, 228-229.

and the other colonies that if they would only yield their claims of rights, redress would be "readily granted." According to the committee the absurdity of such a contention had been conclusively demonstrated at the time of the nonimportation directed against the Townshend duties. At that time the administration, by meeting the colonists half-way had succeeded in dividing and confusing them, and then it was able to ignore their complaints with impunity.[10] This, the committee urged, must not be permitted to happen again.

The administration, the committee went on, was particularly anxious to silence the united opposition of the colonies because, after violating the East India Company Charter in the recent session of Parliament, it feared that the East India Company, the City of London, and the "other great Corporations" might combine with the colonies in opposition at the forthcoming election for Commons. With this new election approaching, the colonies should stand firm. Otherwise by appearing to acquiesce in the ministry's policy, the English friends of American liberty would be undermined, and the colonies themselves would be aiding in the election of a House of Commons "determined to subvert the Liberties of America."

The committee closed with a justification of its letter which aimed at further stimulating a vigilant union of the towns with Boston. They disclaimed any wish "to agitate the minds of our Brethren with groundless Apprehensions." Rather they meant to "excite in them that Watchfulness which alone will be a Guard against a false Security." They begged "that the Eye of Jealousy may be still attentively fixed on the Movements of our Enemies, in Britain and America." The towns, they were confident, would "always communicate to us any Discoveries or just Suspicions of their sinister Designs." Together all would encourage the "Unity and Harmony in Councils" which was necessary if they and posterity were to be preserved from "*Tyranny & Bondage.*"[11] This call, suggesting no immediate action, assumed that the towns were acquainted with provincial politics and that they understood both their rights and the general character of the constitution. Its whole emphasis was toward encouraging the towns to comprehend the larger significance in imperial politics of their own opposition, and to appreciate the

10. The same argument is found in Samuel Adams to Joseph Hawley, Oct. 4, 1773, *Writings of Samuel Adams*, III, 52–58.

11. Broadside circular of Sept. 21, 1773, "Gentlemen, The State of publick Affairs undoubtedly still demands the greatest Wisdom, Vigilance and Fortitude . . . ," Massachusetts Historical Society.

value, the necessity, of union with the other colonies. The latter point was already widely recognized, though not with the same urgency.

II

One reason why the Boston Committee of Correspondence dropped its plan to prepare a special circular to send beyond the province, was that the Massachusetts Committee of Correspondence, in which Samuel Adams was active, was planning a circular letter of its own. This letter, when it was finally approved and sent out on October 21, 1773, four weeks after the Boston circular, resembled it in several important ways.[12] Drafted by Samuel Adams and James Warren of Plymouth, it was an ardent appeal for unity in defending the rights of every colony. It particularly stressed the strategic value of united exertions for obtaining redress. Specifically, it recommended joint agreement on the precise colonial rights to be defended, so that in case of a European war the colonies, like the House of Commons in former periods, could jointly refuse to furnish aid to the administration until colonial rights had been explicitly guaranteed. Though it covered more ground than the Boston circular, in a similar way it furnished a practical analysis of the impact of colonial behavior on English politics.

This circular was probably the final act of the Massachusetts Committee of Correspondence before it lapsed into months of inactivity.[13] Its message closed by calling attention to "a fresh Instance of the temper & Design of the British Ministry; and that is in allowing the East India Company, with a view of pacifying them, to ship their Teas to America." This, it warned, would destroy colonial trade while increasing Britain's unconstitutional revenue. Here was one more reason for united colonial resistance.[14] Ironically, it was the resistance to the Tea Act which would extend the activities of the Boston committee until it became the de facto committee of correspondence for Massachusetts, operating beyond its borders as well as within the province.

News of the consequences of the Tea Act had only just arrived in Boston when Adams and James Warren drafted the Massachusetts circular.[15] In New York and Philadelphia public protests had already

12. *Writings of Samuel Adams*, III, 62–68.
13. See Massachusetts Committee of Correspondence Journal, Mass. Hist. Soc., *Proceedings*, 2d Ser., IV, 85–90.
14. Massachusetts Committee of Correspondence circular letter, Oct. 21, 1773, *Writings of Samuel Adams*, III, 62–68.
15. Benjamin W. Labaree, in *Boston Tea Party* (New York, 1964), 106, says

begun. At Boston the North End Caucus, meeting on October 23, quietly began the series of protests that would culminate in the tea's destruction, voting to "oppose the vending any Tea, sent by the East India Company to any part of the Continent, with our lives and fortunes." Recognizing the possibility of a need for emergency resistance, the caucus chose a committee "to correspond with any Committee chosen in any part of the town, on this occasion; and call this body together at any time they think necessary." None of the members of this intramural committee of correspondence were part of the Boston committee.[16]

When the North End Caucus met again on November 2 it sent committees to wait on both the Boston Committee of Correspondence and John Hancock, requesting that they attend the caucus' meeting. Now the caucus resolved that the East India tea absolutely "shall not be landed." They went on to prepare a public resolution "to be read to the tea consignees to-morrow 12 O'clock, noon, at Liberty Tree." The resolution called for their resignation as consignees of East India Company tea; and if they failed to give "satisfaction" they were threatened with the "just resentment" of the North End Caucus and whoever else had gathered at the Liberty Tree. The authors of the resolution, Thomas Young, Benjamin Church, and Joseph Warren, were members of both the Boston committee and the North End Caucus, and the action they had in mind probably paralleled the demonstration against the stamp master of August 14, 1765.[17]

In spite of the caucus' invitation, it seems unlikely that the Boston committee, as such, attended the meeting at the Green Dragon Tavern or took any part in the planning or execution of the November 3 activi-

---

that a few people in Boston knew about shipments of tea under the Tea Act in late September and that public opposition began in mid-October. The evidence I have seen strongly suggests the news came later. The first report of the East India tea shipment appeared in the *Boston Gazette* on October 11, and full news was not printed until October 18. On October 13 Samuel Adams wrote a long letter to Joseph Hawley on colonial politics, but made no mention of the Tea Act. His first written notice of it is in the Massachusetts Committee of Correspondence draft circular of October 21. The first press attacks on the Tea Act did not appear until October 14 in the *Massachusetts Spy*. Apart from the press, public opposition did not begin in Boston until early November, and Hutchinson only took notice of it on November 11 when he first learned that the tea shipment was on the way. Thus it appears that full news did not arrive until mid-October.

16. North End Caucus, minutes, Oct. 23, 1773, in Elbridge H. Goss, *The Life of Colonel Paul Revere* (Boston, 1891), II, 641. The North End committee included Paul Revere, Abiel Ruddock, and John Lowell.

17. North End Caucus, minutes, Nov. 2, 1773, *ibid.*, 641–643.

ties. It did meet on November 2, but at the selectmen's chamber, its normal meeting place.[18] The invitation committee from the North End may have joined it there and discussed the following day's demonstration, but there is no evidence that this was the case. Throughout this six week period of resistance to the Tea Act in Boston it is often difficult to designate precise responsibility for events, since the same individuals frequently took a leading part in various capacities. Individual members of the Boston committee, Young, Church, Warren, Molineux, Dennie, Adams, were prominent as members of the North End Caucus, as members of the Boston town meeting, and as representatives of the massive gathering known as the "Meeting of the People," in addition to being active in the committee of correspondence. In each case they participated with various other political leaders, and their authority was different. Therefore, in order to describe and analyze the role of the Boston Committee of Correspondence, which did itself assume a critical position of leadership when the tea arrived in the last days of November, it is necessary to distinguish as carefully as possible between the actions of the Boston committee as constituted by the Boston town meeting, and the various activities of its members in other bodies. Otherwise, the committee may be seen as the author of nearly every event in Boston or, conversely, the North End Caucus may be assigned responsibility for all of the activities of the Boston Committee of Correspondence. The wisest course appears to be to attribute to the committee only those acts which surviving evidence definitely assigns to it, even though its complicity may have been broader.

At the gathering at the Liberty Tree on November 3, the tea consignees did not give satisfaction by resigning their positions. The meeting ended in a tumult at the house where the consignees were consulting among themselves, but they remained firm. Two days later Boston met to consider its own stance in relation to the Tea Act.

The town met in response to a petition which pointed to the Tea Act's "threat" to colonial trade and its "unconstitutional" taxing provisions. Hancock was elected moderator, and after a lengthy discussion of the "nature and tendency" of the act, the question was raised whether anyone could show that "the introduction of Tea in the manner projected would not be detrimental to the Interest of the People in general

18. Boston Committee of Correspondence, minutes, Nov. 2, 1773, Minute Book, III, 230. Benjamin W. Labaree says that the Boston Committee of Correspondence planned these events with the North End Caucus (*Boston Tea Party*, 109).

as well as to the Mercantile & Trading part of the Colonies." As no one had anything favorable to say of the Tea Act, the meeting went on to express its views by unanimously adopting verbatim the Philadelphia Resolves, which reasserted the colonists' right to taxation by consent and their right to independent legislatures, while promising implacable opposition to both the Tea Act and its supporters.[19]

Then, repeating the approach begun by the North End Caucus, the town sent committees, including members of the committee of correspondence, to tell the consignees that the town requested their resignation. After making several delays the consignees refused to resign, explaining that they were not yet sufficiently informed of their obligations to judge their proper course. The town meeting voted its unanimous dissatisfaction with these replies.[20] At the same time Boston resolved that it would not only oppose the importation and sale of the East India Company tea, it would oppose the importation of all duited tea. This resolve warned the merchants that Boston would henceforth expect every merchant to adhere once more to the old nonimportation agreement with respect to tea. The meeting closed with an order to the committee of correspondence "to transmit the Transactions of this Meeting to every Town in the Province." [21] As had been true at the time of the March town meeting, the committee of correspondence was merely given the routine task of sending out a circular.

The committee, however, took the opportunity to prepare its own circular to accompany the town's proceedings as a covering letter. Warren, Appleton, and Young were chosen as a subcommittee to prepare the draft, but after a week had passed and the committee was still not satisfied with their version, Adams was added to the subcommittee.[22] The next day a ship arrived in Boston with reliable news that the East India tea was certain to arrive within the next two weeks. Two days later Warren, Appleton, Young, and Adams reported back to the committee; they had resolved the question of the contents of the circular by substituting a dramatic new proposal. The Boston committee would meet with the committees of correspondence of several neighboring towns, and together, in joint committee, they would adopt a circular

19. *Boston Town Records, 1770–1777*, Boston Record Commissioners, *Reports,* XVIII (1887), 142–143.
20. This effort was repeated with identical results at the town meeting of Nov. 18, 1773.
21. *Boston Town Records, 1770–1777*, p. 146.
22. Boston Committee of Correspondence, minutes, Nov. 9 and Nov. 16, 1773, Minute Book, III, 230–231.

letter to the towns of Massachusetts. The joint authorship of this letter would broaden its appeal, prevent Boston from appearing overaggressive, and it would encourage towns by its example of united determination to resist the Tea Act. Therefore the Boston committee invited its counterparts from Roxbury, Dorchester, Brookline, and Cambridge to meet with it at Faneuil Hall on the afternoon of November 22.[23]

When the five committees convened they immediately decided to act "Jointly, at the present Meeting." They then voted "to use their joint influence to prevent the Landing and Sale of the Tea expected from the East India Company." To facilitate united, effective resistance, they chose a subcommittee to advise the other towns in the province of their own sense of "the evil tendency of the late Ministerial maneuver," and "to impress upon their minds the absolute necessity of making an immediate & effectual opposition to this detestable measure." Adams, Warren, and Church were chosen to draft the letter together with William Hyslop of Brookline and Captain Thomas Gardner, the Cambridge representative.[24]

The next afternoon the draft letter was unanimously accepted. It carried a strong moral and practical appeal for resistance to the Tea Act, opening with a call to remain true to "the happy constitution which our fathers framed and for many years supported with such wisdom and fortitude as rendered them the admiration of the age in which they lived, and must make their memory glorious in all future times." The implication was that the present generation could win similar esteem by supporting the constitution with the same vigorous determination. In the past several years their enemies had launched various attacks on colonial liberties, some open, others devious; now the Tea Act threatened. "We know," the joint committee said, "that great dependence is placed upon this masterpiece of policy for accomplishing the purpose of enslaving us." This was to be the critical test.

From their perspective American resistance was doubly important because of the existing internal pressures of English politics. For the Tea Act, the circular explained, was an ingenious scheme both to reinforce the revenue acts and to mollify the powerful East India Company since its petition for the total repeal of the tea duty had just been rebuffed. The company needed to sell its tea; if the colonists refused to buy it subject to duty under the Tea Act, then the company

23. *Ibid.*, Nov. 19, 1773, 232.
24. *Ibid.*, Nov. 22, 1773, VI, 452–453.

would be forced to rejoin the colonies in pressing for repeal of the duty.[25] The joint committee was, it said, "convinced" that the administration would then be forced to comply. Thus the colonists could remove one burden, and this "crafty" plan to take American property by arbitrary power would be frustrated.

The alternative, as the circular described it, was total slavery and corruption. When this tax was accepted, others ever more grievous would surely follow — "to support the extravagance and vices of wretches whose vileness ought to banish them from the society of men." Virtue would be wholly engulfed, and vice would reign triumphant. The dutied tea was "more to be dreaded than plague or pestilence, for these can only destroy our mortal bodies," but the tea, by enslaving them would inevitably destroy their virtue, dooming them and their posterity to eternal damnation. The letter closed with the request that its readers "impress upon the minds of your friends, neighbours, and fellow townsmen, the necessity of exerting themselves in a most zealous and determined manner, to save the present and future generations from temporal and (we think we may with seriousness say) eternal destruction." Here the moral necessity of resistance was stressed more directly and more passionately than in any of the earlier circulars. Evidently the Boston committee had recognized Massachusetts' special responsiveness to a moral appeal.

The joint committee left its circular with the Boston committee to transmit to the towns. But before sending it out, the committee added its own postscript which nearly equaled the original letter in length. This addition, comparatively free of emotional rhetoric, furnished "some particulars" which the joint committee had "not fully treated." Specifically, it pointed out that men in Boston and the other colonial capitals had computed a potential drain of 1.6 million dollars in specie from the colonies as a consequence of the tea duty. Farmers would need no prompting to appreciate the drastic consequences of the resulting scarcity of cash. The committee also predicted that when the consignees' monopoly was established, they would raise to exorbitant levels the price of the tea to which colonists were addicted. Boston, as the towns would see by its enclosed proceedings, had taken every measure to obtain the consignees' resignation. The committee finished by posing

25. This interpretation had come from Benjamin Franklin's letters to Thomas Cushing — for example, March 9, 1773, June 4, 1773, Sept. 12, 1773, *Works of Benjamin Franklin*, VI, 88–89, 125–126, 201–202.

the alternatives once more: should they "sit down quiet under this, . . . as good natured slaves, or rise and resist . . . as becomes wise freemen." As in the original circular of November 1772, they requested the advice of the towns and expressions of their sentiments.[26]

Before the Boston committee could have the joint circular printed and sent out, it was diverted by more immediate business. On Sunday, November 28, the *Dartmouth* under Captain Hall arrived in the harbor with part of the East India Company tea. In the emergency the committee met, though it was the sabbath, to avert the disaster of the landing and sale of the tea. Assuming for itself executive authority, it sent a three man subcommittee "to wait on Mr. [Francis] Rotch, Owner of Capt. Hall's ship, . . . and to desire him to defer entring or Reporting his vessel untill Tuesday."[27] Rotch agreed to delay the ship's entry and assured the committee that the entire shipment remained intact in the hold of his ship, that none of it had been previously landed on Cape Cod as had been reported.

Having been assured of two days' delay, the committee resolved to use the time to mobilize whatever further public pressure might be brought in order to prevent the landing and payment of the duty on the tea. The means chosen was another joint meeting of the committees of correspondence that had drawn the circular. This time, however, it would be an open, public meeting. The letter that Samuel Adams drafted to the four other committees inviting them to Faneuil Hall at 9:00 A.M. on Monday the 29th, did not mention a public meeting. It did urge that they warn their towns to "be in readiness to exert themselves in the most resolute manner to assist this Town in their efforts for saving this oppressed Country." The committee members were encouraged to bring their friends. Later they would find that public notices had also invited everyone in Boston and the surrounding towns to attend.

The "Meeting of the People of Boston, and the neighbouring Towns," was in many ways a larger repetition of Boston's earlier meetings dealing with the tea. Quickly adjourning to the Old South Meeting House to accommodate the several thousand participants, the meeting, with ad-

26. Broadside circular, Nov. 23, 1773, "In consequence of a conference with the committees of correspondence for the towns in the vicinity of Boston, November 23, 1773, and with their advice the following letter is addressed . . . ," Massachusetts Historical Society.

27. Boston Committee of Correspondence, minutes, Nov. 28, 1773, Minute Book, VI, 457–459.

journments, covered two days. In the course of it the resolution to have the tea returned to England, like Boston's resolve, was unanimously voted three times. The effort to order the consignees to resign was again repeated with similar delays and identical results. But in the minds of Boston Whigs this "Meeting of the People" differed from a town meeting in crucial ways. A town meeting, possessing a formal corporate status, was bound by law whereas a meeting of the people was bound only by its sovereign judgments. The town of Boston was, of course, legally responsible for any infractions the town meeting might commit; whereas the self-constituted meeting of the people was beyond the reach of the law and might therefore act with greater freedom in resisting the Tea Act, in the manner of the Stamp Act resistance.[28] Perhaps it was this precedent which led to the meeting's first achievement — extracting promises from Rotch and Captain Hall as well as the owners of the other tea ships that they would not permit the tea to be landed and that instead they would seek to have it returned to England. To enforce its prohibition on landing the tea the meeting established regular watches of volunteers to guard the ships and warn the countryside if any attempt should be made to land the tea. Then this informal meeting directed the Boston Committee of Correspondence, a standing town committee, to see that every vessel arriving with any tea on board was assigned such a watch.

Here the Meeting of the People made a real departure. For the town meeting of November 5 had only resolved that it would "expect" no further importations of duties tea. The Meeting, however, while it was enforcing the ban on landing the East India Company tea went on to extend it to include all tea, resolving that anyone who "hereafter" imported it was "an Enemy to his Country." In effect, it charged the Boston committee with guarding against the landing of any more duties tea, resurrecting the ban of 1769–1770. In closing, the Meeting voted that its resolves dealing with all tea importation should be printed and sent both to England and to all of the Massachusetts seaports. Copies of the entire proceedings were to be transmitted to New York and Philadelphia. A separate committee of leading citizens, not the Boston Committee of Correspondence, was assigned this task.[29]

28. Pauline R. Maier, "From Resistance to Revolution: American Radicals and the Development of Intercolonial Opposition to Britain, 1765–1776," Ph.D. diss., Harvard University, 1968, ch. 2.
29. Committee: Samuel Adams, John Hancock, William Phillips, John Rowe, Jonathan Williams (moderator of the Meeting of the People).

Two days later the Boston committee finally sent its circulars out to the towns. By now its enclosures included the proceedings of the Boston town meeting of November 5 and 18 in the form of a fifteen-page pamphlet, the joint committee's circular letter with the Boston committee's postscript, and in addition copies of the entire proceedings of the Meeting of the People. Together, these documents made several points. First, they exposed the "evil tendencies" of the Tea Act. Equally important, they provided an exemplary description of active, untiring, united resistance by the townspeople of Boston and the neighboring towns. The Philadelphia Resolves showed once more that the political beliefs of Massachusetts were shared in the other colonies. The proceedings of the Meeting of the People illustrated how popular resistance might be organized effectively. Moreover the "regularity" and order with which all of the resistance was conducted, entirely free of "riots and tumults," vindicated Boston's propriety, making its resistance seem entirely reasonable. The governor proclaimed the whole affair "unlawful," but the Boston committee, printing his proclamation in a prominent part of the proceedings, knew that most towns would sanction the resistance since it had stopped short of violent coercion.

III

From this time, early December 1773, the attention of the Boston committee, despite its involvement in the local resistance to the Tea Act, gradually shifted beyond the province. Massachusetts, it judged, needed no further stimulation. Coordinating the motions of Boston and Massachusetts with the resistance in other colonies and developing the union among all the colonies were becoming its primary goals. After the destruction of the tea these efforts would assume critical importance.

The most immediate task, however, continued. The tea must not be landed. The committee, now following the direction of the Meeting of the People rather than the Boston town meeting, continued its surveillance of arriving ships. When the two remaining ships arrived bearing the tea, the committee arranged with their captains to have them conveniently tied up near the first ship so that one watch could cover all three.[30] To Rotch and the other owners it gave specific direc-

30. Boston Committee of Correspondence, minutes, Dec. 3, 5, 7, 1773, Minute Book, VI, 460–461, 477–478.

tions as to what steps to take to satisfy the public. The directions were characteristic of the tactics of Boston Whigs; they made sure that every possible procedure, however futile, was attempted in order to have the tea returned to England.

Yet the impasse remained. The committee quieted doubts about events in New York—it had been said that the East India tea was being sold there—by having Young and Warren publish a true account explaining that the New York consignees had expressly renounced their responsibility for the tea.[31] But in Boston the consignees, supported by the governor, stood firm. In spite of the Meeting of the People which the committee arranged for December 13 to focus public pressure—and which adjourned to the 14th and then the 16th, the final day before the tea had to be taken ashore—the consignees and the governor would not permit the ships to return the tea to England because, as Hutchinson later explained, such permission would violate a Massachusetts statute and lead to violation of an act of Parliament prohibiting the return of tea to England once it had been exported.[32] Therefore, in the face of the governor's inflexibility, "patriots" destroyed the tea by dumping it in the harbor.

Specific accountability for the destruction of the tea, deliberately concealed at the time, remains uncertain. Benjamin W. Labaree in *The Boston Tea Party* assigns "final responsibility" to the Boston Committee of Correspondence.[33] His evidence is conjectural. There is no evidence that the committee did more than arrange the Meeting of the People and provide for the volunteer watches to prevent the tea's landing. Nevertheless the Boston committee cannot be dissociated from the event. Nearly a dozen of its members had some part in the proceedings surrounding the Tea Party, making speeches, offering resolves, serving on committees. Its members were among the leaders and planners of the entire Boston opposition. As a result they cannot have been ignorant of what was being planned. Moreover since the committee was in charge of the watches guarding the ships, the destruction of the tea could not have been effectively carried out without at least its tacit consent. Therefore the Boston committee must be assigned some share of the responsibility for the Tea Party, though the actual direction and execution were probably carried out by the North End Caucus and

31. Boston Committee of Correspondence, minutes, Dec. 8, 1773, Minute Book, VI, 461–462.
32. *Ibid.*, Dec. 10, 1773, 462–463; Labaree, *Boston Tea Party*, 147.
33. Labaree, *Boston Tea Party*, 142.

several other private associations like the Lebanon and Long Room clubs in Boston.[34]

On the day after the Tea Party the Boston committee, apparently aware that it might be called to account for popular resistance and the tea's destruction, appointed Church, Young, and Warren "to draw up a Narrative of the Proceedings of this Committee from the first of their appointment in order to be ready to lay before the Town, when called upon for that purpose."[35] Unfortunately the narrative, if it was ever written, has not survived. In any case the committee immediately turned its attention to communicating news of the tea's disposal to contacts in New York and Philadelphia. Adams prepared a brief letter explaining that "the moment it was known out of Doors that Mr. Roatch could not obtain a Pass for his Ship by the Castle, a number of People huzzad in the Street, and in a very little time every ounce of the Tea . . . were immersed in the Bay, without the least injury to private property."[36] This news, the committee believed, would reassure the cities to the south of Boston's firmness and reinforce the resistance in the other ports.[37]

The Boston committee's communication with New York and Philadelphia was of very recent origin. It had begun less than two weeks earlier with a letter to Alexander McDougal and Isaac Sears in New York and Thomas Mifflin and George Clymer in Philadelphia, requesting them to use their "influence with your Fellow Citizens at any future Meeting to appoint a similar Committee of Correspondence" to Boston's. This, the committee had urged, would facilitate a swift, reliable exchange of intelligence on public affairs.[38] At the same time the

34. Among the private organizations involved in the Tea Party Labaree lists: Long Room Club, Grand Lodge of Masons, Hancock's Corps of Cadets, Lebanon Club, and North End Caucus (*ibid.*, 142–143). By Grand Lodge of Masons he probably means St. Andrew's lodge. All of these clubs included mariners and artisans as members. For a detailed contemporary description of the public meetings in which members of the committee were prominent see L. F. S. Upton, ed., "Proceedings of Ye Body Respecting the Tea," *William and Mary Quarterly*, 3d Ser., XXII (1965), 287–300, esp. 300.

35. Boston Committee of Correspondence, minutes, Dec. 17, 1773, Minute Book, VI, 464–469.

36. Boston committee to Philadelphia and New York, Dec. 17, 1773, Minute Book, VI, 468–469.

37. Whigs in New York and Philadelphia had doubted the firmness of Boston. William Palfrey to [Samuel Adams?], Phila., Saturday, Dec. ?, 1773, Palfrey Family Papers, II, b, 92, Houghton Library, Harvard University.

38. Boston committee to New York and Philadelphia, Dec. 6, 1773, Minute Book, VI, 470–471. The letter was delivered by William Palfrey, John Hancock's associate (Palfrey Family Papers, II, b, 92).

committee had written to acquaintances in Portsmouth, New Hampshire, and Bristol, Newport, and Providence in Rhode Island. The message was almost identical: committees of correspondence would permit an exchange of political advice and enable the port towns to co-operate "in the glorious purpose of rescuing the present and future Generations from ignominious and debasing Thraldom." [39] The Boston committee was anxious that the resistance of all of the port towns should be co-ordinated so that the ministry would not be given an opening through which it could divide and conquer the colonial opposition. In the coming months this effort would draw more and more of the committee's attention.

Once the Boston committee had begun informing the world outside Massachusetts of Boston's successful resistance to the introduction of East India Company tea, it could turn to matters of local security which for a short time seemed pressing. During the week after the Tea Party, reports had spread in Boston that those responsible for it would be arrested and sent to England for trial. To counter this supposed threat someone in Boston suggested a mutual protection association. Those entering it would pledge to resist the detention or transportation from Boston of anyone who was being punished for his actions on behalf of liberty. This plan was offered to the Boston committee which apparently regarded the threat as genuine and the means proposed to combat it as useful. It redrafted the plan, replacing the association with a simple private "agreement." There would be no organization; instead individuals would simply pledge support. But as the impotence of the royal government to apprehend patriots became more and more apparent as each day went by, the agreement became unnecessary and it was set aside. [40]

This weakness of the royal government stemmed from the general, practically unanimous public approval of the resistance to the tea in

---

39. Boston committee to individuals in New Hampshire and Rhode Island, Dec. 5, 1773, Minute Book, VI, 471–472.

40. The above interpretation, which differs significantly from that of Labaree (*Tea Party*, 149–150), is based on two documents found among the committee's general correspondence at the New York Public Library. One, the proposal for an association to defend persons arrested for destroying the tea, exists as a rough draft titled "Association to Bear Harmless." The other is a record of a vote of December 24 on the same subject. Labaree concluded that the members of the committee entered and signed such an association, apparently mistaking William Cooper's list of members voting for the proposal for a list of signatures. Labaree argues their implication in the Tea Party on the basis of this supposed joint pledge. But the list is entirely in the hand of the clerk, Cooper, and begins with the words "Voted by."

Boston. Bostonians were elated by the success of their actions, believing that their order and regularity together with their repeated, persistent effort to send back the tea had placed the onus of its destruction on the governor. For them the Tea Party was a magnificent political demonstration because nothing but the tea had been touched. Boston could not be charged with riot or attacks on private property. Whigs believed that Boston had escaped the trap and stymied both the governor and ministry. Its firmness and its success testified to its virtue.

The Boston committee, in spite of the unauthorized, revolutionary steps it had taken, was not called upon to justify or even explain its activities. Clearly, during the weeks of resistance it had become much more than an organ of correspondence. Yet the committee's spontaneous assumption of powers normally exercised by the selectmen and town meeting was underwritten by the tacit support of nearly everyone in Boston. In the emergency the town's reluctance to act as a corporate body, resulting from a desire to escape culpability in case of violence, had left a vacuum which was filled by the Meeting of the People, the Boston committee, and private associations. In these circumstances the Boston Committee of Correspondence shifted its attention toward Boston's immediate problems away from its earlier long-range goals in the Massachusetts countryside. This pragmatic reaction was to be reinforced by town responses to the Tea Act and the Tea Party, responses which made it apparent that the long-range goals of active local involvement in provincial and imperial political issues were being realized.

IV

During the winter of 1773–1774 the proceedings of scores of towns demonstrated that the activity initiated by the Boston Committee of Correspondence the preceding autumn had established the context for local responses to the Tea Act. Now, although the Boston committee had not made any direct appeal to the towns to correspond, more than eighty towns, twenty of which had never before communicated with Boston, sent their resolves endorsing resistance. At least a dozen now formed local committees of correspondence. Specific references to the Tea Party itself were rare, as in the letters from the other colonies. Even though two towns did explicitly justify the tea's destruction as a legitimate, last-resort means of resistance provoked by the royal officials, they were balanced by two others which publicly condemned it, and by a third which showed its displeasure by ignoring Boston's recent circulars and by disbanding the committee of correspondence it had earlier established.[41] Generally, however, there was no need to take any special notice of the Tea Party since neither the Boston committee nor the town of Boston was regarded as responsible for it.

One index of local support for and involvement in resistance may be seen in the various types of tea boycotts which towns entered. These boycotts, voted in town meetings, pledged that no tea whatsoever would be used in the town. If anyone chose to violate the ban, they were threatened with the town's displeasure and stigmatized in advance as enemies to American rights. In some cases towns even pledged that they would boycott anyone who used or dealt in tea and anyone who countenanced such behavior. Frequently the selectmen were directed to withhold licenses from any inn or tavernkeeper who dispensed tea. Such boycotts, entirely prohibiting the use and sale of all tea, went well beyond Boston's mere prohibition on its further importation.

In Charlestown, one of the first towns to adopt a tea boycott, a committee of inspection was formed to enforce its terms. The town directed this committee to purchase at cost all the tea owned by residents, down to the smallest quantity, and voted that "the *Tea* so collected, be destroyed, by Fire on Friday next at Noon Day in the Market Place." Furthermore the town instructed its committee of correspondence to meet with the Boston committee in order to urge Boston to adopt parallel measures.[42] Similar initiative, and a particular hostility to the tea itself as a symbol of oriental luxury and intoxication, was characteristic of virtually all of the more than twenty-five towns which unilaterally adopted tea boycotts without reservation. Two towns, Hull, a Suffolk community of two hundred, and Grafton, a Worcester town of nine hundred inhabitants, outstripped the others by pledging not only a boycott of tea but of all duties goods. The boycotts, entered unilaterally, were not really practical political maneuvers intended to coerce Britain; rather, they were concrete acts of public virtue as it was understood in Massachusetts.[43]

41. In favor of the Tea Party: Watertown, Jan. 3, 1773, Boston Committee of Correspondence, Minute Book, VI, 530–533; Montague, Jan. 20, 1774, Letters and Proceedings received, photos 536–537. Against the Tea Party: Freetown, Jan. 25, 1774, *Boston Weekly News-Letter*, Feb. 10, 1774, 1:1–2; Marshfield, Jan. 31, 1774, *ibid.*, Feb. 3, 1774, 2:1. Littleton disbanded its committee of correspondence on Jan. 8, 1774, *ibid.*, Jan. 13, 1774, 3:1.

42. Charlestown, Dec. 28, 1773, Letters and Proceedings received, photos 152–154.

43. Hull, March 28, 1774, *ibid.*, photos 355–356; Grafton, Jan. 25, 1774, *ibid.*,

Nevertheless some historians have argued that the towns were the dupes of Boston merchants and the pawns of Boston radicals.[44] Cheaper tea, they say, was the towns' real interest, not resistance to "illusory" political demons. According to this view, the towns must have misunderstood the Tea Act to have acted as they did; they must have been misled by the merchants, whose tea profits were threatened, in league with the radicals, whose continuing interest was conflict between Britain and the colonies. This explanation of the towns' behavior, consistent according to its own premises, is contradicted by nearly every aspect of local responses to the Tea Act. The towns not only outpaced Boston's leadership, to the distress of the merchants whose stocks they boycotted; their proceedings often explicitly demonstrated that they thoroughly understood the Tea Act.

In several towns, however, it is true that the Boston committee's circulars misled the townspeople, at least in part. An Essex town of eight hundred people boycotted the tea because, as the Boston committee's postcript to the joint committee circular had suggested, it believed that tea purchases "would be extreamly impoverishing to the American Colonys, even if there was no duty imposed on it." With the duty, the town felt the tea "had a much greater tendency to impoverish and inslave us." Nevertheless the town said it would lift the boycott as soon as the duty was repealed. Thus economic and constitutional principle reinforced each other, but it was the latter which was decisive.[45] A Middlesex community of five hundred imposed a tea boycott until the duty was removed, believing this "to be the most Effectual means, within the Compass of our power, to prevent our becoming Subject to this & other *Impending* Taxes."[46] Apparently the specter of possible taxes described by the circulars became impending taxes in the understanding of this particular community. Such errors, however, were exceptional. All but a few of the towns, if they responded at all, attacked the contents of the Tea Act specifically. As they saw it, its overt purposes were sufficiently threatening; the towns

photos 295–296. Edmund S. Morgan emphasizes this moralistic element in the resistance in his "The Puritan Ethic and the American Revolution," *William and Mary Quarterly*, 3d Ser., XXIV (1967), 3–43.

44. Notably Arthur M. Schlesinger, *The Colonial Merchants and the American Revolution, 1763–1776* (New York, 1957), first published in 1918.

45. Topsfield, Feb. 3, 1774, Boston Committee of Correspondence, Minute Book, VII, 631–633.

46. Bedford, March 8, 1774, Letters and Proceedings received, photo 55, italics added.

had no need to depend on any special pleas formulated by the Boston committee.

The "professed purpose in the acts laying Impositions on the Americans" was the very infringement the towns had so recently remonstrated against — "support of government & administration." [47] The Tea Act, it was said, was intended to raise a revenue to salary colonial officials. The towns recognized this as a blatant attempt to fix both the principle and the practice of an officialdom supported independently of the people they served by a revenue raised from that same people without their consent. Some towns repeated their earlier sentiments on this point, others believed it too obvious for serious discussion.

The second stated purpose of the act, the provision permitting the East India Company to sell its teas in the colonies at a reduced duty to be collected in the colonies, was also harmful in their opinion. It gave a practical monopoly on tea sales to the East India Company and its consignees. Here they saw "the most glaring Partiality in making one and the same Act to operate for the Ease and Convenience of a *Few* of the most opulent Subjects in Britain on the one hand, and for the oppression of *Millions* of Freeborn and most loyal Inhabitants of America on the other . . . we lose all patience when we consider that the industrious Americans are to be stripped of their honest earnings to gratify the humours of Lawless & ambitious Men." [48] Towns reasoned that if a monopoly could be established on one product, it might be extended to others. Monopolies, they had read, were the practice during "the unhappy Reigns of the Stuart family." People believed that the act, by its stated aims, "strikes at the Sinnews of our mercantile Interest." [49]

If the overt aims of the Tea Act were outrageous, then the secret purpose of the act, the establishment of full colonial submission to the principle of parliamentary taxation, was even more alarming. "Some indeed would gladly make us believe, that the Act of the British Parliament imposeing Duties on Tea, . . . is not of the nature of a Tax; but is only a commercial Act" — but this view they found incredible. "Is not this an affront to common Sense, — when the Purposes to which the Money thus taken from us, is applied, to be taken into view, viz.

47. Hull, March 28, 1774, Letters and Proceedings received, photos 355–356.
48. Brookline, Dec. 1, 1773, *ibid.*, photo 117, first part; Newburyport, Dec. 21, 1773, *ibid.*, photos 563–564, second part.
49. Pelham, Nov. 16, 1773, *ibid.*, photo 605; Framingham, Jan. 25, 1774, *ibid.*, photos 249–250.

The Support of Government, the Administration of Justice," and military defense?[50] Having witnessed the ministry's previous efforts to tax the colonies and to gain control over their officials' salaries, towns frequently interpreted the reduction in the tea duty as a lure to "ensnare" them into yielding the points they had long been contesting.[51] They believed the scheme was particularly crafty because it was built around cheaper tea, a near-staple commodity to which they had grown addicted. After pointing to the "true" nature of the act, they sometimes took pleasure in heaping it with scorn: "We look upon the stratagem [as] too low, the snare too obvious, & the bait too chaffy for old birds."[52]

But though they might cover it with rhetorical scorn, many towns agreed with Boston that it posed a serious threat to the entire structure of their rights and their constitution. An arbitrary tax on a staple could be disastrous: "From such beginnings of Oppressions on the properties of the French did that ill fated & worse pated Lewis XIII by the Cruel Craft of a Reichlieu . . . utterly Sap the very foundations both of Civil and Religious Liberty, and Establish arbitrary power in that (now) kingdom of slaves."[53] Two towns where Scotch-Irish emigrants had settled believed that the Tea Act was part of an English plan to enslave the colonies just as it had already subjected Ireland. One wrote: "It plainly appears to us that it is the design of this present administration to serve us as they have our brethren in Ireland; first to raise a revenue from us sufficient to support a standing army, as well as place men and pensioners, and then laugh at our calamities and glut themselves on our spoil (many of us in this town being eye witnesses of those cruel & remorseless enemies)."[54] For these towns the dangers to the constitution were especially immediate. They were grateful to the Boston committee for "Shewing us our Greivances, and giving such timely notice." They prayed Boston would "stand as firm as the mountains in America."[55]

If the townspeople had been blind followers of Boston merchants

50. Great Barrington, Jan. 25, 1774, *Boston Weekly News-Letter*, Feb. 10, 1774, 2:2.

51. E.g., Piersontown, Feb. 10, 1774, Letters and Proceedings received, photos 603–604; Brookline, Dec. 1, 1773, *ibid.*, photos 117–118.

52. Chatham, Nov. 12, 1773, *ibid.*, photo 169.

53. Pelham, Nov. 16, 1773, *ibid.*, photo 604.

54. Colrain, Jan. 31, 1774, *ibid.*, photos 179–180; Pelham, Nov. 16, 1773, *ibid.*, photos 604–607.

55. Pelham, Nov. 16, 1773, *ibid.*, photo 607; Colrain, Jan. 31, 1774, *ibid.*, photo 180.

and Boston radicals, one would not expect the issue of the Tea Act to have aroused searching constitutional discussion. Yet like the question of judges' salaries it prompted careful examination, resulting in a further elaboration of local constitutional views. As before, the character of discussion was various, and its quality uneven, but in the aggregate it revealed more fully the radical series of expectations about government which were emerging in Massachusetts. People did not recognize them as radical, they seemed to believe their assumptions were almost self-evident; but in England they would have been swiftly denounced as "republican."

"Balance" everyone on both sides of the Atlantic had agreed was the critical element in the British constitution since the Revolution of 1688. It protected liberty. In England, however, when people spoke of balance they normally meant the equilibrium between King, Lords, and Commons, an institutional balance reflecting the pattern of the social order. Massachusetts towns, though they were not aware of it, had developed different conceptions of the balance vital to the constitution. The central tension they perceived was not among the social orders but between the governors and the governed. The balance they craved was between the people and their servants, wielding power and dignified by authority. At best, "the Ruler & the Ruled, when acting in their proper Spheres, are under the Dictates of this glorious Directory, the Advantage of the whole."[56] At worst, the governors became tyrants enslaving those from whom they derived their power.

To protect themselves from this contingency, the towns had already insisted that public officials were or ought to be servants of the people, and that they should be dependent on the people for their support. This device of popular control of official salaries, unknown in England, was intended to curb officials' natural, dangerous thirst for excessive power. Now, in arguing against parliamentary taxation, it was suggested that popular representation in the legislature was itself another check on official usurpation by appointed rulers. Moreover, as an additional "Counterbalance" it was urged that legislators ought to be personally subject to the laws they voted.[57] Clearly the danger that the

56. Framingham, Jan. 25, 1774, *ibid.*, photos 249–250. These generalizations and those which follow are based on over-all impressions derived from local statements. On the question of balance, Richard Buel, Jr., "Democracy and the American Revolution: A Frame of Reference," *William and Mary Quarterly*, 3d Ser., XXI (1964), 165–190, presents a similar view, see esp. 168–176.
57. Bolton, March 21, 1774, Letters and Proceedings received, photos 90–91.

towns feared came from self-seeking governors, not a turbulent people, the bogeyman of English political thought.

In Britain, legislation was recognized as the combined act of the three branches, the three orders of society uniting in Parliament. In Massachusetts, the towns explained, "the Subjects Frame the Laws, and Majesty by its Consent, puts the Sanction upon them." People mistakenly believed that this was just like Britain.[58] In their view the problem in Massachusetts was that one of the branches of the legislature, the governor, refused to unite with the other branches, the House and the Council which had already formed a "happy Union."[59] Ideally the three branches, all servants of the people and responsible to them, would unite to promote the interests of the people over whom they governed. This scarcely articulated republicanism described the status quo as it was conceived by the Massachusetts towns.

In the reconsideration of constitutional principles engendered by the Tea Act several towns recognized the necessity for reform within the province. At least two towns protested that since they were not represented in the General Court they should not be taxed by it. One recommended that, therefore, all districts should be exempted.[60] On another plane, a few towns recognized that liberty in Massachusetts was contradicted daily by the existence of Negro slavery. Medfield, a Suffolk town of eight hundred, had already instructed its representative to seek the abolition of the slave trade in January 1773, even before the Negroes' circular letter was sent to the towns.[61] This circular, which was sent to the representatives by a committee of four slaves, may have been drafted with the assistance of Samuel Adams or John Pickering, Jr., a Salem representative who, with Adams, had recently urged anti-slavery legislation. The circular itself had drawn a parallel between the plight of the Africans and that of the colonists and called for an emancipation and emigration program for slaves. Now, almost a year later, Medfield, which was boycotting tea, issued an ardent call for an end to slavery itself. They declared:

58. *Ibid.*; Braintree, March 11, 1774, *ibid.*, photos 100–101. Braintree said that the people make all the laws by their representatives.

59. Acton, March 7, 1774, *ibid.*, photos 19–20.

60. East Hoosuck, March 2, 1774, *Boston Weekly News-Letter*, April 15, 1774, 1:1; Piersontown, Feb. 10, 1774, Letters and Proceedings received, photos 603–604.

61. Medfield, Jan. 13, 1773, *ibid.*, photo 506. The broadside circular of April 20, 1773, "Sir, The efforts made by the legislative of this province in their last sessions to free themselves from slavery, gave us, who are in that deplorable state, a high degree of satisfaction . . . ," was signed by a committee of slaves headed by Peter Bestes. It is at the Massachusetts Historical Society.

. . . it incumbent upon us to bear testimony against that Iniquetous practis of enslaving the affricans — it appears at first view Greatly absurd for us to plead for Liberty and yet patronize the most Cruel Servetude and Bondaze — the poor affricans when taken from all that is dear to them in their native soil have not the least shadow of Liberty Remaining they have nothing they can Claim as their own their time is Entirely Devoted to the service of their absolute Lords — their Bodys are at their Disposal to be bartered and Traded from man to man as the senceles Beasts their Children (if any they have) are born in a state of abject servitude than which nothing can be more repugnant to Liberty for which we so universally Contend — we wish to maintain Constitutional Liberty our selves and cant endure the thoughts of its being with held from the same flesh and Blood for no other reason that we can Conceive of but because the God of nature has been pleased to tinge their skin with a Diferent Couler from our own if we would look for Liberty our selves we conceive we ought not to continue to enslave others but immediately set about some effectual method to prevent it for the Future.

In a similar vein, Gorham concluded its letter to the Boston committee "by wishing every kind of Happiness & Prosperity to the Friends of our Country White or Black." [62] In some towns the implications of libertarian theory were clearly overflowing conventional limits.[63]

One town, rebutting the governor's charge of advocating an *imperium in imperio*, blithely explained the federal principle while it corrected his Excellency on the nature of the imperial relationship. As they saw it, "there may be Imperium *Preter* Imperium, *A Government besides, and distinct from another,* if said Governments respect different places and Constitutions; although one and the same Branch be at the head of both Constitutions." [64] Englishmen would have been startled by such a formulation. But in Massachusetts the observation that two governments with separate jurisdictions might be united in a single royal branch at the top passed unnoticed. It was simply an explicit statement of a common provincial assumption.

The local proceedings, extremely various in their emphasis, demonstrated that the towns, far from following Boston blindly, used the Tea Act, like the judges' salaries, as a point of departure for formulating their own conceptions of government. These ideas, never previously set

62. Medfield, Dec. 19, 1773, Letters and Proceedings received, photos 508–509; Gorham, Jan. 17, 1774, *ibid.*, photo 282.
63. This is a specific example of the general case regarding the impact of constitutional discussion on chattel slavery, as argued by Bernard Bailyn, *The Ideological Origins of the American Revolution* (Cambridge, Mass., 1967), 232–246. See also Winthrop D. Jordan, *White Over Black: American Attitudes Toward the Negro, 1550–1812* (Chapel Hill, N.C., 1968), ch. 7.
64. Bolton, March 21, 1774, Letters and Proceedings received, photos 90–91.

down because they had never before been challenged, were expressed in the language of conventional English political thought because that was the only political language people had ever heard. Indeed the inhabitants themselves hoped and believed their ideas were conventional, and that the great mass of Englishmen "at home" shared their beliefs. In fact, however, the routine habits of government in the towns and congregations of Massachusetts had produced radically different expectations concerning the nature of government.

Self-governing corporations, ruled by their constituents and responsible to them, exercising definite, practically exclusive fragments of government power, comprised the major part of their experience with government.[65] Thus, though specific arguments may sometimes have been drawn from the Boston press, their basic assumptions were derived from this experience. The town, the congregation, the province, each exercised its own power, including legislation, within definite limits. The General Court was "supreme" in the province, but it was not omnicompetent. Town officers, without exception, were dependent on the town and every representative was dependent on his constituents. The function of annual elections was to check officeholders, not normally to rotate them in office. Deacons like selectmen were answerable to their congregation, and the minister himself was responsible to and dependent on the congregation that had called him to serve.[66]

Once entrusted with authority, officials properly commanded respect and obedience. But it was here, apparently, that tension developed. For the structural problem of Massachusetts government was not balancing the conflicting interests of social or economic orders; few such conflicts existed. Instead the crucial problem for their quasi-republican society was establishing respect and obedience for officials and at the same time curbing their potential tendency to abuse their power. In the towns and congregations the dilemma was not serious because it was circum-

65. For the fullest description and analysis of the interplay between attitudes, expectations, and structure in local government see Michael W. Zuckerman, "The Massachusetts Town in the Eighteenth Century." Ph.D. diss., Harvard University, 1967. This and the following comments, which locate the town as the key unit of authority, are based on my own reading of local government in the 1760's and 1770's, as well as Zuckerman's dissertation, Clifford K. Shipton's "The Locus of Authority in Colonial Massachusetts," in George A. Billias, ed., *Law and Authority in Colonial America* (Barre, Mass., 1965), 136–148, and Buel, "Democracy and the American Revolution," 168–176.

66. This was a lively topic in the early 1770's. See Alan Dawley, "The Political Theory of Church Government: Ministerial Dismissions of the 1770's," seminar paper, Harvard University, 1966.

vented by the personal characteristics of the officers; their wealth, learning, moral character, and family commanded a respect and often a deference which they carried with them into office. Royal government in Massachusetts, however, was organized on different principles. Both authority and the right to respect and obedience were inherent in the office itself; while the responsibility of officials was directed upward toward superiors in the England-based hierarchy, not downward toward the people whom they immediately "served" as rulers. One consequence of this arrangement, which was "perverse" and in need of reform from the Massachusetts viewpoint, was a serious conflict between "rulers and ruled."

As a result, the conventional "balance" of English politics, between King, Lords, and Commons in Parliament assembled, was irrelevant to Massachusetts townspeople when they thought about balance in government. Balance was certainly important, but it was the equilibrium furnished by popular checks on official abuses of power which mattered most. At the local level this was seldom a problem, although towns occasionally warned their representatives that they would turn them out of office if they ignored the wishes of their constituents. The critical area was the sphere covered by royal officials. Here "abuses" seemed to have grown common, and in view of the officials' presumed motives, personal wealth and power, and the real and suspected motives of the English government, checks on the power of officials became vitally important. Without such checks officials would naturally abuse their power, ultimately becoming tyrants. Since the Tea Act pointed specifically in this direction it was especially provocative.

The tendency of these opinions, applying the assumptions of local government in Massachusetts to the entire imperial structure, was clearly radical. Law established by representatives of the people and executed by officials answerable to and controlled by the public comprised the essence of republicanism. Yet the willingness of Massachusetts communities to publicly affirm such beliefs did not, in their own view, stamp them as radical. Within their own perspective these principles were conventional even though they had not, in most cases, been previously articulated in such an explicit manner. Their expression now, in response to the Tea Act, marked a further stage in a continuing process of revelation, a revelation of republican assumptions in Massachusetts stimulated but hardly controlled by the Boston Committee of Correspondence. Indeed by early 1774 it was becoming apparent that, with the Boston committee shifting its attention beyond the province, its role in the countryside was being reduced. Meanwhile a fundamental radicalism of ideology, not tactics, was emerging in the towns, a radicalism which rivaled that of Boston.

8

Resistance:

The Search for Unity

As a consequence of the Tea Party, Boston and the province were placed in a politically exposed position. Boston became the focal point for English reaction to the entire colonial opposition to the Tea Act. Indeed the main thrust of the parliamentary response in early 1774 was aimed at Massachusetts. Boston was the target of the Port Act, which directed the closing of the harbor until payment was made for the destroyed tea. In addition a reform of provincial government was decreed in the Massachusetts Government Act and the Administration of Justice Act, both of which were intended to strengthen the royal administration in the province. As members of Parliament understood it, the purpose was both to punish lawlessness and reassert parliamentary authority effectively by making an example of Boston and Massachusetts. The lesson of parliamentary supremacy, they believed, would extend to all disobedient colonies.

Whigs in Massachusetts understood these aims, but in addition they saw an even more sinister object in the English program. Here, they believed, was a strategy intended to divide and conquer colonial opposition. The people of Massachusetts would be forced to submit to parliamentary taxation and required to accept the destruction of their charter. They would be permanently enslaved, while other colonies were left alone. Later, Whigs believed, the other colonies would be attacked one by one. In light of these fears, united resistance to English authority became the central goal of both the Boston Committee of Correspondence and the awakened towns of Massachusetts.

The goal of united resistance, however, was not easily or immediately achieved. Resistance, after all, meant action, and action meant making policy choices. Political choices inevitably opened the way to division and internal conflict — among the colonies, among the towns, and within individual towns, whether large or small, commercial or agricultural, whether Boston or Brimfield. Therefore to create and maintain unified resistance was a continuous challenge to Massachusetts Whigs.

The Boston Committee of Correspondence itself had turned to promoting intercolonial unity right after the Tea Party. Pleased with the resistance displayed by Boston, and confident that Boston would be sustained by the countryside, it had seen fit to turn its attention beyond the province. Owing to the changed circumstances of provincial politics, intense concentration on the towns had become superfluous. Instead, even before Parliament adopted coercive measures, the Boston committee began a new project, sponsoring a plan for an independent colonial post office. The committee moved even further when news arrived of the Port Act and the two reform acts. It decided unilaterally that an immediate nonconsumption agreement, a Solemn League and Covenant, would be the most effective means of resistance. But the political cost of such a strategy, immediately applied, was substantial. It threatened the unity of the capital town, prompting a direct attack on the Boston committee in the town meeting. Elsewhere, in the province at large, the Solemn League and Covenant was overwhelmingly rejected because it was judged hasty and divisive, threatening to the very unity which was believed necessary for successful resistance. Again and again towns would endorse the principles of nonconsumption while setting aside the specific Solemn League and Covenant. Their primary concern in resisting Britain was unity — unity within the town and union among the colonies. Resistance on any other terms was too hazardous.

In light of the values which permeated community life in the Massachusetts towns it is not surprising that unity was the pre-eminent local concern in choosing a path of resistance. Community values and experience had always provided much of the framework for local political interpretation and action. Now, when the tactics of the Boston Committee of Correspondence diverged from local political judgments, towns hastened to affirm their own views publicly. Local views and strategies for resistance, however radical in theory, were usually based upon the hope of achieving substantial consensus. These were the values that were emerging as rules to guide revolutionary action by mid-1774; and so the movement for resistance in Massachusetts became inextricably bound to a drive for unity achieved through consent.

I

As the new year 1774 began the general colonial resistance to the Tea Act permitted the Boston committee to establish contact with similar committees as far south as Charleston, South Carolina. To the north, Portsmouth had immediately responded to the committee's invitation by choosing a committee of correspondence in town meeting, and by passing resolves condemning the Tea Act and its constitutional implications.[1] Similar steps were taken in Rhode Island by both Providence and Newport. From New York, prior to the Tea Party, Alexander McDougall had written that its "patriots" would "use their utmost endeavors to adopt your measures." The committee's own realization of the value of communication and united action was shared everywhere, so its invitation to correspond was eagerly accepted.[2]

Knowledge of the tea's destruction was rarely acknowledged in letters from other colonies. Usually the praise for Boston's firm resolution circumspectly omitted specific reference to the tea's actual fate, although the Philadelphia "friends of liberty" did mention it, saying they were sure it had been "Justified by a strong Necessity" caused by "inveterate Enemies . . . who seek their own Advantage in compelling you to any measures of Violence" tending to separate England and the colonies.[3] The Boston committee itself never apologized for the Tea Party, and it never returned to the subject after announcing the fact in its original letters to New York and Philadelphia.

Resistance of any sort was scarcely mentioned in the committee's letters to towns outside Massachusetts. Union and the exchange of information necessary to achieve it was the first priority and the main

1. Portsmouth Committee of Correspondence to Boston committee, Dec. 16, 1773, Boston Committee of Correspondence, Minute Book, VII, 546–549, New York Public Library, photostats at Massachusetts Historical Society.
2. Newport Committee of Correspondence to Boston committee, Jan. 13, 1774, ibid., VI, 541–543, VII, 558; Alexander McDougall to Boston committee, Dec. 13, 1773, ibid., VI, 472–473.
3. Philadelphia to Boston committee, Dec. 25, 1773, ibid., 487–488.

theme of each letter. Counseling Charleston, South Carolina, the committee urged internal harmony as well as unity among the colonies, warning that "if your divisions don't give way upon this occasion, Carolina will be a dreadful support of that truth, 'that by uniting we stood and by dividing we fell.'" In a letter to George Wyllis, an important figure in the provincial government of Connecticut who also served Hartford as town clerk, the committee suggested not only a committee of correspondence to unite Connecticut with the other three New England colonies, but also local statements by the towns individually, after the pattern of Massachusetts. Such statements, it said, would help testify to "a union of the whole People throughout the Colonies." In the committee's view, the recognized union of sentiment achieved by the majority of Massachusetts towns should be a model for every colony.[4]

A mechanism which could help establish colonial union on a durable basis was suggested to the committee in March by William Goddard, a printer from Philadelphia and Baltimore.[5] Goddard was promoting an independent postal system for the colonies. It could provide secure privacy for communications between the colonies, and it would cut off the revenue which the existing post office raised for the ministry. Goddard arrived in Boston carrying a vigorous recommendation for the plan from the New York Committee of Correspondence and an assurance from Newport that it would join if the plan was generally adopted.[6]

The idea was new to the Boston committee. The post office established by Parliament, they agreed, was "certainly unconstitutional." Indeed its fees were just as unconstitutional as the tea duty, though the revenue was smaller. They had "never meant to countenance it or submit to its regulations as any way binding upon us." Rather, they had merely acquiesced in it "only as a convenient appointment." The committee confessed that it had not been "sufficiently attentive to its consequences"; and immediately set out to rectify its own oversight. Goddard was invited to meet with the committee while it considered his proposal.[7]

4. Boston committee to Charleston, S.C., Jan. 20, 1774, *ibid.*, IX, 719–720; Boston committee to George Wyllis, Jan. 18, 1774, *ibid.*, 717–718.

5. See Ward L. Miner, *William Goddard, Newspaperman* (Durham, N.C., 1962).

6. New York Committee of Correspondence to Boston committee, Feb. 28, 1774, Boston Committee of Correspondence, Minute Book, IX, 742–746; Newport Committee of Correspondence to Boston committee, March 10, 1774, *ibid.*, 746–747.

7. Boston committee to New York Committee of Correspondence, March 24,

The first step, they decided, was to familiarize the public with the novel idea of replacing the "unconstitutional" post with a colonial system. Joseph Greenleaf, Church, and Young were directed to "prepare a piece for the Spy in order to shew the utility of the proposal for Provincial Post Riders." [8] At the next committee meeting Goddard presented letters and proposals for the post office in more detail. Initially it would need financial support, so the committee prepared a tentative "preamble" for a voluntary subscription list and sent a subcommittee "to wait on the principal gentlemen in the Mercantile department to obtain their opinion and approbation." These merchants liked the idea, but suggested that more Boston merchants be consulted. [9] The committee agreed since it believed wide support was "the best way by far to originate a continental company who can by their Committees regulate the whole matter and bid defiance to all the force of the opposite interest let them attack in what form they please." [10]

But since the post office was contingent on support from all the colonies, it would be a mistake to decide immediately upon a particular plan. Instead Boston would promise New York its support, while soliciting the aid of the ports to the north. The Boston committee left it to the New York committee to establish a specific post office arrangement because of its central location. [11] In the meantime the committee assigned John Pitts, a merchant who had frequently met with it since the arrival of the East India Company tea, to present the subscription paper "to the Gentlemen of the Town for their signing." Samuel Adams prepared the letter for the committees of correspondence in the northern ports, Marblehead, Salem, Newburyport and Portsmouth. [12]

This letter, outlining the plan, persuasively covered the arguments

1774, *ibid.*, IX, 737–739; Boston Committee of Correspondence, minutes, March 15, 1774, *ibid.*, IX, 732–733.

8. Boston Committee of Correspondence, minutes, March 15, 1774, *ibid.*, IX, 732–733. The New York Committee suggested this in its letter of Feb. 28, 1774, *ibid.*, IX, 743–746. In the *Massachusetts Spy* of March 17, 1774, a brief article urged the creation of a post office and letters from New York supporting the plan were quoted extensively.

9. Boston Committee of Correspondence, minutes, March 17, 1774, Minute Book, IX, 733.

10. Thomas Young to John Lamb, March 18, 1774, John Lamb Papers, I, 40, New-York Historical Society; Boston Committee of Correspondence, minutes, March 17, 1774, Minute Book, IX, 733.

11. Boston Committee of Correspondence, minutes, March 22, 1774, Minute Book, IX, 733–734, 734–741; Boston committee to New York Committee of Correspondence, March 24, 1774, Minute Book, IX, 737–739.

12. Boston Committee of Correspondence, minutes, March 24, 1774, Minute Book, IX, 334–341.

in its favor. The first point was the necessity of unhindered private communication, especially important since "not only private Letters of Friendship and Commerce but *publick Intelligence* is conveyed from Colony to Colony." Without free communication and mutual counsel, the union was doomed. Moreover the post office was founded on an act of Parliament so the revenue it raised was "equally as obnoxious as any other revenue Act."[13] The only serious question was whether or not the alternative of a colonial post office was practicable.

The Boston committee asked other committees to give the matter careful consideration. They should try to "collect" the "Sentiments of the Gentlemen of your Town & more particularly the Merchants and Traders." Information on their sentiments should be sent back to Boston with Goddard as soon as possible; and they might also send their views on to New York and Philadelphia. New York, the committee explained, had initiated the project and was anxious to know New England's view. Boston, the committee assured them, would support the measure.

Nearly a month later, in the latter part of April 1774, Goddard returned to Boston with the northern ports' replies. Marblehead, troubled with an outbreak of smallpox and a sharp division over the efficacy of a hospital, made no reply, but the other three towns embraced the plan warmly. Portsmouth, like Boston, was raising a subscription.[14] The Boston committee, encouraged by this response began once again to develop a specific plan which was printed on April 30. It directed that subscribers in each colony appoint seven-man committees charged with regulating postal rates and selecting postmasters wherever necessary. To supervise the entire operation an American "Post-Master General" would be elected by the votes of all the provincial committees. The post office would be a semipublic, nonprofit organization ruled by voluntary local committees composed primarily of merchants.[15]

As the Boston Committee of Correspondence envisioned it, the post office project furnished an ideal example of joint colonial action and an excellent opportunity to develop the cherished defensive union among

13. Boston committee to Salem, Marblehead, Newburyport, Portsmouth Committees of Correspondence, March 24, 1774, Minute Book, IX, 734–736. In this context the removal of Benjamin Franklin as postmaster was regarded as particularly significant.

14. Portsmouth Committee of Correspondence to Boston committee, April 11, 1774, *ibid.*, VIII, 689–690.

15. Boston Committee of Correspondence, minutes, April 21, 26, 27, May 3, 1774, *ibid.*, IX, 752–753; Thomas Young letters of March 18, and May 13, 1774, John Lamb Papers, I, 40, 46; Miner, *William Goddard*, 126–127.

the colonies. The committee's enthusiasm for the project and its labors in its behalf was much less an attempt to resist a revenue producing act of Parliament than it was part of the committee's over-all effort to see a reliable union established among the colonies.[16] Resistance, after all, had already become a generalized colonial phenomenon by the spring of 1774; the union needed to make it effective was the vital remaining goal.

But though the primary direction of Boston committee activity had become intercolonial, it remained active in Boston and Massachusetts. It still saw to it that town proceedings were printed when they arrived in Boston, and it continued to return its encouragement to the towns which had sent them in. Surveillance over the entry of tea into Boston, originally assigned by the Meeting of the People, remained the committee's responsibility, and when a small quantity of tea was landed on Cape Cod the committee encouraged an uncertain Wellfleet to make sure that it was not sold.[17] When a shipment of tea arrived in Boston harbor early in March the committee followed the pattern it had set in December. After first consulting with the captain and owner of the ship to make certain the tea was not surreptitiously landed, it called the committees of the neighboring towns in for a joint meeting. But before they could meet to plan further measures an unexpected "little tea party" disposed of the problem. This second tea party plainly surprised the committee.[18]

During these months public support for the committee remained firm in Boston.[19] No one made any public move to oppose its activities, and its efforts in behalf of the post office and colonial union were given explicit support. The newly expanded scope of committee activity, embracing Boston, the province, and all the colonies, received the town's tacit approval. The Boston committee, buoyed by colonial unity and the

16. On Boston committee enthusiasm for post office, see Paul Revere to John Lamb, March 28, 1774, John Lamb Papers, I, 42–43; Samuel Adams to James Warren, March 31, 1774, *The Writings of Samuel Adams*, ed. Harry A. Cushing (New York, 1904–1908), III, 92–94. Samuel Adams saw a close connection between establishing the post office and a union of the colonies. See also Miner, *William Goddard*, 118–127.

17. Boston committee to Wellfleet Committee of Correspondence, March 24, 1774, Minute Book, IX, 740–741.

18. Boston Committee of Correspondence, minutes, March 7, 8, 1774, *ibid.*, IX, 726–728.

19. Samuel Adams was chosen moderator at the March 5, 1774, town meeting, and Oliver Wendell and John Pitts were chosen selectmen on March 14, 1774, *Boston Town Records, 1770–1777*, Boston Record Commissioners, *Report*, XVIII (1887), 148, 151.

evidence that the province was "wonderfully enlightened and animated," had suddenly emerged as the leader of Massachusetts opposition to Parliament.[20]

Yet the circumstances of the Boston committee's leadership were precarious. Opposition in Massachusetts did not depend on the Boston committee. Its influence derived more from its capacity to reflect common views than from any ability to direct them, and so when it overstepped the limits of consensus in its Solemn League and Covenant, it inadvertently undermined the sources of its own power. The Boston Committee of Correspondence remained strong in Boston, but its influence in the province declined. It was not in Boston, but in the towns of Massachusetts that the terms of resistance would be defined.

II

In early May news arrived of the passage of the Port Act. Excepting the entry of food and fuel, the port of Boston was to be closed until such time as "full satisfaction" was given to the East India Company and the customs officers for the losses they had sustained in December and January. Either the inhabitants of Boston must pay, or payment must be made on their behalf. Blockade or restitution, these were its terms.[21]

The Boston committee's first actions followed closely the tactics it had chosen against the Tea Act. The committee invited committees from neighboring towns to a joint meeting. In the meantime it directed Adams, Joseph Greenleaf, and Warren to draft a circular to the ports outside the province, and another subcommittee to draft a circular for the Massachusetts towns. Immediately, the committee had moved to make certain that Boston would not be isolated in the misery threatened by the act.[22]

Only hours before the joint committee meeting began, the Boston committee received a report from the speaker of the Rhode Island House of Representatives, John Bowler. He informed the committee that the Rhode Island assembly had received word from every government on the continent, except Nova Scotia, that they were ready to

20. Samuel Adams to Benjamin Franklin, Boston, March 31, 1774, *Writings of Samuel Adams*, III, 88.
21. Danby Pickering, ed. *The Statutes at Large . . .* (Cambridge, Eng., 1773), XXX, 336–341.
22. Boston Committee of Correspondence, minutes, May 7, 1774, Minute Book, IX, 753–754.

join in measures for "preserving the Liberties and promoting the Union of the American Colonies."[23] This news gave the committee reason to believe that all the colonies might indeed unite in defense of Boston. The crisis at Boston, they realized, might stimulate colonial union.

The joint committee that convened on May 12 was composed of committees of correspondence from eight towns apart from Boston. Three of the committees, Newton, Lynn, and Lexington, had never attended before. The others, from Charlestown, Cambridge, Brookline, Roxbury, and Dorchester, had all met with the Boston committee at least once in the past. After electing Samuel Adams as chairman, their first business was choosing a subcommittee to consider their sense of the Port Act. Members from Charlestown, Lynn, and Cambridge joined with Warren in preparing a statement which was unanimously adopted. It exclaimed that the "Art Injustice and cruelty" of the act was beyond words; it was "aimed seemingly at the Town of Boston but through them at all America." The act "accused tried and condemned" Boston without a hearing, and by singling it out for punishment "endeavoured to dissolve that Union between the Colonies on which their safety solely depends." The joint committee emphasized that the act was only superficially an attack on Boston and Massachusetts. Actually it was part of a strategy to divide the colonies and conquer them individually, so it threatened every colony. Without argument or explanation it asserted that colonial union was the sole defense for the colonies, implying that there was no reason to expect any protection from England.[24]

Circular letters to ports in other colonies and to the Massachusetts towns had already been prepared by the Boston committee, and these were unanimously approved by the joint committee. The letter which was sent to port towns and several committees of correspondence in other colonies, outlined the provisions of the Port Act, but stressed the argument that the act attacked every colony. The ministry sought to divide, but "ALL should be united in opposition to this violation of the Liberties of ALL." "You," they assured the others, "will be called upon to surrender your Rights, if ever they should succeed in their Attempts to suppress the Spirit of Liberty here." The remedy they suggested "to defeat the design" was a total suspension of trade with Great Britain.[25]

23. Boston Committee of Correspondence, minutes, May 12, 1774, Minute Book, IX, 754.
24. Ibid., May 12, 1774, 755–757.
25. Joint committee to Rhode Island, Philadelphia, New York [city], New Jersey, Connecticut, Portsmouth, May 13, 1774, Minute Book, X, 810–811.

The circular to the towns spent more time describing the evils Boston would suffer as a result of the act. But it too made the same point: the cause of Boston, it said, was "interesting to *all* America." In view of the general defense of liberty previously begun, surely Boston would not "be left to struggle *alone*." Again they called for a suspension of trade, though this time indirectly. In a two sentence postscript the circular denied the charge "that the patriotic Col. Barre had become our Enemy." In fact he had said: "*America is stamped upon every Loom and Anvil in Great-Britain!*" To remove any possibility that the point might be lost they translated his metaphor, saying, "In plain English, let America discontinue its Trade, and the British Manufacturer must *emigrate* or *starve.*" The joint committee's hint at a boycott could not easily be overlooked.[26]

The day after the joint committee met the Boston town meeting convened. It gathered at the request of the Boston committee, and its purpose was to consider the Port Act. Samuel Adams was chosen moderator, and the first business was a public reading of the act, after which a committee was chosen to consider proposals "relative to our Conduct on the present Exigency." Five of the eleven men chosen to serve on this committee, Adams, Warren, Quincy, Molineux, and Appleton, were members of the committee of correspondence.[27] In the meantime the town sent a committee of five to Salem and Marblehead to consult with those ports to see what measures they would take, and whether they would follow Newburyport by suspending their trade with Britain. Three of the members of this committee, the chairman Wendell, Pitts, and Dennie, were also members of the Boston committee.

The support which the committee of correspondence possessed was demonstrated not only in the conspicuous roles assigned to its members, but also in the specific actions of the meeting. It voted that the Boston committee communicate news of the Port Act to all the colonies and all the towns, encouraging a suspension of trade. Since the committee was already at work on these tasks, the votes in the town meeting had the effect of ratifying the committee's own decisions. But there

26. Joint committee broadside circular, May 12, 1774, "Gentlemen, By the last advices from London we learn that an Act has been passed by the British Parliament for blocking up the Harbour of Boston, with a Fleet of Ships of War . . . ," Massachusetts Historical Society.

27. Adams was supported by the North End Caucus, among others, which voted he be moderator at its meeting of May 9, 1774. Elbridge H. Goss, *The Life of Colonel Paul Revere* (Boston, 1891), II, 644; *Boston Town Records, 1770–1777*, p. 173.

was one difference between the plans of the town meeting and the Boston Committee of Correspondence. The town was recommending a boycott only in the event that all the colonies would "come into a joint Resolution." Immediate entry into a boycott covenant, however exemplary, was not Boston's wish. Suspending trade was a political lever against Britain which could only be effective if it was undertaken by all the colonies. Boston was anxious to see it operate so it requested "every Gentleman, who has Friends & Correspondents in the other Sea Port Towns & the Colonies," to "strongly" recommend a suspension of trade to these friends and correspondents. In addition the Rhode Islanders present at the meeting were specifically "desired" to use their influence so that Rhode Island would second the measure.[28] But Boston did not seek to demonstrate its militance or virtue by entering such a boycott unilaterally.

As soon as the town meeting adjourned, the Boston committee sent Paul Revere out with the letters already prepared by the joint committee. These circulars were accompanied by copies of Boston's proceedings and a brief covering letter assuring the other ports that Boston's present morale was good. In effect, the town meeting had endorsed the measures the committee had begun. So far the committee had not taken any steps which were not generally popular with Boston.

On May 20, however, the committee started a project which ultimately divided the merchants of Boston. It began to press for a merchants' agreement to countermand their orders for fall imports. Warren drew a preamble, and Appleton, Wendell, Pitts, Bradford, and Davis, all members personally concerned in trade, were directed to present it to the merchants of Boston, seeking their names as signers.[29] This measure achieved partial success, but a significant number of merchants who were not closely allied with the governor had serious doubts. In the first place the time was already late to countermand fall orders. Moreover they had already committed their capital and would, they felt, suffer losses without effecting any substantial damage to English commerce. In addition, they reasoned, their imports were needed now more than ever since the province faced a winter with its main port closed. The committee, these men believed, was overzealous and its proposal imprudent.[30]

28. *Boston Town Records, 1770–1777*, p. 174.

29. Boston Committee of Correspondence, minutes, May 20, 1774, Minute Book, IX, 759. Arthur M. Schlesinger, *The Colonial Merchants and the American Revolution* (New York, 1957), 315 cites a different measure.

30. Taken from John Andrews' letters to William Barrell, especially Boston,

But the committee followed a wholly different line of reasoning, one tied completely to the understanding of English politics which its London correspondents, mainly Benjamin Franklin and Arthur Lee, had taught it. Britain, they believed, must be immediately convinced that the measures of the ministry and Parliament would not, as was supposed, divide and weaken colonial resistance. Instead, the colonies should demonstrate that, if anything, their resistance was now firmer and more united than ever before. If this could be done, or at least made to seem likely, the opposition in England, America's friends, might succeed in overturning the punitive acts.

At the moment, however, there seemed no possibility that the colonies would quickly enter an agreement to suspend their trade. It would take months, and it would require additional months before England began to feel the pinch. By that time Boston would not only have suffered grievously, it might even capitulate. If, however, Boston and Massachusetts could take swift, decisive action, showing that they would never yield and that coercion was fruitless, the result might be different. They could stir the other colonies to emulate their example, and they would remove any lingering doubts that Boston might break the ranks of resistance and yield as it had in the nonimportation in 1770. The ministry would be thrown off balance by the colonial challenge, perhaps, they hoped, fatally.

To achieve this goal the committee believed that Boston, especially its merchants, and the province, already aroused, needed to be galvanized into united, active, commercial resistance. But the merchants continued reluctant. The best they would do was to pledge that they would suspend trade at whatever time the colonial ports generally agreed on a suspension. Some of them, a prominent minority, publicly addressed their respects to retiring Governor Hutchinson and warmly greeted the incoming Governor Thomas Gage. As a result in an effort to pressure merchants into adopting nonimportation the Boston committee became devoted to the idea of nonconsumption. It would echo loudly in English politics as evidence of Massachusetts resistance, and at the same time it would virtually compel merchants to suspend their trade immediately. The tea boycott and some recent letters from country towns, as well as the experience of 1769–1770 convinced the com-

---

July 22, 1774, Massachusetts Historical Society, *Proceedings*, 1st Ser., VIII (Boston, 1864–1865), 330–332, and the rebuttals printed in the *Boston Weekly News-Letter* during June 1774.

mittee it could rely on the province. They decided it was "the yeomanry whose Virtue must finally save this Country." [31]

On May 30 the town meeting convened once more. The committee which had been chosen two weeks earlier to consider what the town should do in the extremity still had no recommendations it wished to report, so the meeting was adjourned once more to June 17. But before the meeting broke up the town voted that this committee on "Ways & Means" prepare an agreement "to be carried to each Family in the Town, . . . not to purchase any Articles of British Manufactures, that can be obtained among Ourselves, & that they will purchase Nothing of, but totally desert those who shall Counter-work the Salutary Measures of the Town." The committee of correspondence was directed to "communicate the Non Consumption Agreement aforesaid" to the other Massachusetts towns.[32] The Boston town meeting was ready to endorse only this limited form of nonconsumption.

Three days later news arrived of the two acts reforming Massachusetts government and the administration of justice in the province. The first act provided for a radical centralization of power in the hands of the Crown and its agent, the governor. Henceforth the Council would be appointed by the Crown, in place of annual election by the House. Moreover the governor would now have exclusive power to appoint and dismiss all judicial and administrative officers without consulting the Council; and the county sheriffs would be placed in charge of summoning juries, a power which had traditionally rested with the towns. The power to call town meetings, previously vested in local selectmen, was abrogated and instead towns were limited to a single, annual election meeting. Permission for additional meetings would have to be obtained from the governor. In effect the act was closing many of the legitimate channels of opposition.

The Administration of Justice Act was much narrower in scope. But its purposes were complementary in that it empowered the governor to remove the trial of any magistrate or official outside the province, if they were placed under indictment for murder owing to their efforts to suppress riot or enforce revenue laws. Taken together, the two acts effectively revised the Massachusetts Charter of 1692, providing the

---

31. Samuel Adams to Charles Thomson, May 30, 1774, *Writings of Samuel Adams*, III, 122-125, italics removed; also Samuel Adams to Silas Deane, May 31, 1774, *ibid.*, 125-127; Thomas Young to John Lamb, June 19, 1774, John Lamb Papers, I, 49.

32. *Boston Town Records, 1770-1777*, p. 176.

governor with as much control as Bernard and Hutchinson had sought, and far more than that possessed by any other colonial governor. It is no wonder then that when these two bills "vacating the Charter of this Province in its most essential Articles" were read aloud in the Boston committee meeting, they "excited a Just indignation." [33] These "reform bills" served as either a pretext or a catalyst for the committee's decision to discard the limited nonconsumption agreement which had been voted by Boston and which it had been charged with distributing to the province. In its place the committee set about drafting "a Solemn League and Covenant, respecting the disuse of British Manufactures." [34] This covenant was to provoke an all-out challenge to the Boston committee in the Boston town meeting, and it would ultimately prove to be a tactical blunder. In its effort to outflank Boston merchants the committee apparently misjudged the nature of provincial radicalism. Like the Boston committee, the towns shared a radicalism grounded on republican principles, but in addition they were devoted to a prudence in tactics which was aimed at achieving united resistance.

The name of the covenant was taken from the Scotch movement to reform the Anglican church during the 1640's. The committee believed the analogy would be understood by townspeople who had already begun to see themselves as reformers of a corrupted Britain. The covenant's preamble offered "suspension of all commercial intercourse with the island of Great Britain" as the only alternative to "the horrors of slavery" or "the carnage and desolation of a civil war." The purpose of the nonconsumption rather than a nonimportation covenant was clearly stated. It would force an immediate cessation of trade with Britain and demonstrate Massachusetts unity in resistance. It was recognized that its signers would not be importers themselves or persons likely to have commercial intercourse with Britain, but their covenant would mean "less temptation to others to continue in the said, now dangerous commerce." The signers, by eliminating themselves as a market for British imports, would compel merchants to cease their imports. In fact the whole direction of the covenant was toward multiplying the impact of each signer's boycott so that the pecuniary interest in dealing in "contraband" goods would be erased.

The terms of the covenant were far more rigorous than the non-

33. Pickering, ed., *Statutes at Large*, XXX, 381–390, 367–371; Boston Committee of Correspondence, minutes, June 2, 1774, Minute Book, IX, 763–764.

34. Boston Committee of Correspondence, minutes, June 2, 1774, Minute Book, IX, 763–764.

consumption agreement of the Boston town meeting. Where the town had only prohibited the purchase of British goods which could be had otherwise, the covenant proscribed every British import and called for a secondary boycott of everyone who continued to import or purchase British products. To insure that no one would "impose upon us by any pretence whatever," the covenant required that no goods be purchased from persons who had not signed the covenant or who could not otherwise certify that their goods had been imported prior to the covenant's effective date, August 31, 1774. In addition anyone who refused to sign the covenant when it was offered to him was to be boycotted and his name published "to the world." [35] In contrast, the town meeting agreement had merely called for a boycott of a vague category of persons, those who were working against Boston's measures. Finally, the town agreement made no commitments as to its duration, simply affirming that it was to last until further notice. But the covenant declared that it would continue indefinitely, until all Massachusetts liberties were fully restored.

The Boston committee accompanied this covenant with a lengthy letter explaining that at last the ultimate "stroke" which the committee had foreseen and foretold had finally come. "Tyranny," they said, had "usurped the place of reason and justice," eradicating civil liberty and placing religious liberty in immediate doubt. The Port Act was itself "replete with injustice and cruelty," but if anyone still believed that Boston alone was to be subjected they must now be awakened by the two bills introduced in Parliament giving "still more glaring evidence of a fixed plan of the British administration to bring the whole continent into the most humiliating bondage."

The Massachusetts charter, they said, was being snatched away. The previously elective Council was to be placed completely under royal control, and the judiciary made utterly dependent on the governor. Trials would be movable to any county, and juries would no longer be selected by the freeholders. Moreover since the governor would be able to move the trials of royal officials to other colonies or to England in the case of murder, officials were being licensed to "murder and destroy" in Massachusetts. It was equally outrageous that the freedom of town meetings to meet as they saw fit was being circumscribed. As the com-

35. From circular broadside of June 8, 1774, "Gentlemen, The evils which we have long foreseen are now come upon this town and province, the long meditated stroke is now given to the civil liberty of this country . . . ," Massachusetts Historical Society.

mittee viewed it, the balance in the provincial government was being annihilated, and the power of the freeholders in the systems of justice and local government was being annulled.

The only escape other than civil war was "by affecting the trade and interest of Great Britain, so deeply as shall induce her to withdraw her oppressive hand." Nonimportation, the committee was sure, would succeed because people all over Massachusetts had given "almost universal" assurance "of their readiness to adopt such measures as may be likely to save our country." To facilitate the agreement the committee had "drawn up a form of a covenant to be subscribed by all adult persons of both sexes." It was being sent immediately to every town in the province so that "we might not give our enemies time to counteract us." The committee expressed the wish that it be subscribed as rapidly as possible.[36]

This covenant with the covering circular was sent out on June 8. The inhabitants of Boston do not seem to have been immediately aware of its existence, but in several days it became generally known and public opposition to both the covenant and the committee developed. The Boston committee had opened the way for division. From neighboring towns members of local committees of correspondence inquired whether it was necessary to follow the form of the covenant exactly. They asked whether changes might be properly made. The Boston committee, anxious that the effort be in no way jeopardized, quickly sent out a circular assuring towns that it did not in any case "mean to dictate," and that only the spirit of the covenant was essential. At the same time the committee continued to urge that a nonconsumption agreement with a secondary boycott taking effect on August 31 was the only way to ensure "the salvation of North-America."[37] Any later cut-off date would permit large-scale autumn imports which would be lucrative for Britain.

The divisiveness of the covenant was immediately apparent in the reactions of Boston merchants who were not closely tied to the Whig cause. They were shocked and dismayed. The town meeting had not approved the covenant and the August 31 deadline would, they be-

36. From circular broadside of June 8, 1774, "Gentlemen, The evils which we have long foreseen."
37. From circular broadside of June 10, 1774, "Boston, June 10, 1774. Gentlemen, Whereas several of our brethren members of the committees of correspondence in the neighbouring towns, have since our letter of the 8th instant applied to us . . . ," Massachusetts Historical Society.

lieved, ruin Massachusetts individually before the other colonies could unite for assistance. In addition a false report persisted that the covenant also prohibited the purchase of goods which merchants already held in stock. As a result merchants and even a number of tradesmen tended to believe that their purses were being thrown into a useless front-line of defense.[38]

Several merchants, friends of the administration, believed the best course was to privately subscribe sufficient money to pay for the tea, thereby freeing Boston from the commercial blockade. Others, though not friendly to the administration, agreed that this was the best practical solution. Together they pressed this plan forward, and together they were anxious to restrain if not destroy the committee of correspondence. By mid-June the Boston committee felt that "the Party who are for paying for the Tea and by that making a way for every Compliance are too formidable." With the town meeting set to convene again on June 17, the committee anticipated "a warm Engagement." Warren wrote Adams, busy at the assembly meeting at Salem, that his attendance at this adjournment would be vital.[39] However confident the committee had been when it created the covenant, by mid-June its members recognized they were in for a battle.

When the town met, Samuel Adams, the moderator, was still absent. James Bowdoin, a wealthy merchant and leader of the Whigs in the governor's Council, was chosen moderator pro tem but when he could not be found at home, John Rowe, another wealthy merchant, was chosen instead. Rowe claimed he was prevented by "Business" from attending, so finally the lawyer John Adams was selected.[40] Boston Whigs had succeeded in gaining a sympathetic replacement for Samuel Adams.

The first business of the meeting was a report from the "Ways & Means " committee which had failed to report on May 30. Joseph Warren spoke for the committee because its chairman Thomas Cushing was busy at Salem. He explained that they had decided not to make

38. John Andrews to William Barrell, June 12, 1774, Massachusetts Historical Society, *Proceedings*, VIII (Boston, 1864–1865), 329–330; "X" in *Boston Weekly News-Letter*, June 16, 1774, 2:1–2; June 23, 1774, 2:1–2.

39. Joseph Warren to Samuel Adams, June 15, 1774, Samuel Adams Papers, New York Public Library.

40. In his diary Rowe recorded that he "was much engaged & therefore did not accept." June 17, 1774, *Letters and Diary of John Rowe, Boston Merchant, 1759–1762, 1764–1779*, ed. Annie Rowe Cunningham (Boston, 1903), 275.

any hasty recommendations but to wait "till they had heard from the other Governments" before making a report. The meeting then entered once more into "serious Debates" as to what should be done. The outcome was a victory for the Boston committee. For it was voted, "with only one Dissentient":

> That the Committee of Correspondence be enjoined forthwith to write to all the other Colonies, acquainting them that we are not idle, that we are deliberating upon the Steps to be taken on the present Exigencies of our public Affairs; that our Brethren the landed Interest of the Province, with an unexampled Spirit and Unanimity, are entring into a Non-Consumption agreement; And that we are waiting with anxious Expectation for the Result of a Continental Congress; whose Meeting we impatiently desire, & in whose Wisdom & firmness we can Confide, & in whose Determinations we shall chearfully acquiesce.[41]

This vote, although silent on the specific question of the covenant, gave tacit endorsement to the committee's ventures. So even though the meeting of June 17 was not a direct test of the Boston committee, the results suggested that the committee retained a substantial base of supporters in Boston who were ready to unite behind its leadership.

In the afternoon the town requested the Boston committee to lay before it the replies it had received from the other colonies and the Massachusetts ports. The support contained in these letters prompted a vote that Boston's thanks be sent "to our Brethren on the Continent." The committee was then explicitly vindicated by a unanimous vote of thanks to the committee of correspondence for "their Faithfulness, in the Discharge of their Trust," and a vote "that they be desired to continue their Vigilance & Activity in that Service." The meeting closed with an instruction to the Overseers of the Poor and the committee of "Ways & Means" to administer the donations which had begun to arrive for the use of Boston's poor. The clerk was directed to publish the proceedings.[42]

The committee itself publicized its vindication by sending copies of these proceedings to all the towns. Boston's votes would encourage each town to act if it had not already; and the directions to the Overseers of the Poor would furnish an oblique hint that Boston was anxiously seeking material support. From the Boston committee's viewpoint the votes of June 17 could hardly have been better had they been

41. *Boston Town Records, 1770–1777*, p. 176.
42. *Ibid.*, 177.

REVOLUTIONARY POLITICS IN MASSACHUSETTS

written and adopted within the committee itself. Perhaps they were; in any case the committee had not suffered by Samuel Adams' absence.

In spite of the one-sided outcome of the June 17 meeting, opposition to the committee persisted. At the next adjournment, June 27, opponents turned out in force, having carefully prepared their arguments in advance. The committee, however, could be confident. Thomas Young, one who sometimes tended toward overconfidence, reported:

> The Tories among us are becoming desperate. The expected Congress and undoubted effects of it drive them to desperation! . . . all their forces are to be set in array aganst us tomorrow . . . Some Lawyers it is said are to man their artillery who are not remembered to have ever attended a town meeting in their lives. We may have a trial but we are prepared for the Combat.[43]

The battle, which lasted two days, was indeed a trial, a trial of the Boston Committee of Correspondence.

Jonathan Williams, the merchant who had served as moderator for the Meeting of the People on November 28 and 30, 1773, has left the sharpest description of the opening round of the battle. In a letter to John Adams, moderator pro tem of the meeting which immediately preceded the great contest, Williams wrote:

> Yesterday a town meeting was held in the Morning at the Hall, but it being a very warm day, & many People just idle enough to attend, the Room was much crouded; Those People at the farther End of the Room were continually crying out "a little louder," & the Speakers finding themselves fatigued by heat, & obliged to exert themselves to be heard, Thought best to adjourn, & a Motion was made for an adjournment to the Old South, which after a faint opposition was carried. J. Quincy moved to adjourn to one o'clock & then observed, in his flourishing way, that Some might think this would interfear with their Dinners, but he thought the present alarming state was of too great importance, to think of dinners, however they cou'd not be perswaded to adjourn notwithstanding the importance of the day. — at three in the Afternoon there was a very respectable Meeting there was nigh as many torys I believe as Wigs, Lechmere, Irving, the Amorys Greens Hubards & all that sett attended, Amory had a long speech in writing in which he concluded with a Motion to remove Censure & annihilate the Committee of Correspondence, this was seconded by many Voices & all as cou'd a debate for the whole Afternoon & is not yet finish'd, the Meeting stands adjourned to nine this Morning — There was a liberal flow of Sentiments & much Severity from the Tories upon the Committee without any ill treatment, Mr. Francis Green was hiss'd for discenting to a motion for

43. Thomas Young to John Lamb, June 26, 1774, John Lamb Papers, I, 50.

reading some public Letters but they were silenced; — I am told there was several other Speeches in Writing; . . . there is very little Business to be done every body seems engaged in the Politicks of the Day — the Bells are now ringing for the meeting and a very full one is expected.

Williams was in doubt concerning the outcome.[44]

The meeting had begun with Samuel Adams in the chair. The first business had been a reading of the committee's correspondence, both letters sent and received prior to the covenant. This move, apparently intended as a defense for the committee, expended considerable time and presented the activities of the committee in a rather ordinary, businesslike light. Most people felt there was nothing very exciting contained in the letters. But before William Cooper, clerk of both the town and the committee, could drown the opposition by repeating the conventional rhetoric of dozens of letters, a motion was carried that the meeting come to the point by reading the covenant, its covering letter, and whatever other letters might be "particularly" called for. Then John Amory made his motion of "Censure," moving also that the committee be "annihilated."

Before debate began Adams, as a member of the committee, moved that he be temporarily replaced as moderator, and another Whig, Thomas Cushing, was chosen to serve pro tem. Then the debate proceeded as Williams had described. On behalf of the committee Adams, Warren, Molineux, Quincy, Young, and Benjamin Kent spoke; all except Kent were committee members.[45] In opposition were the province treasurer Harrison Gray, the merchants Thomas Gray, Samuel Eliot, Samuel Barrett, Edward Payne, Francis Greene, and Ezekiel Goldthwait, and the lawyer John Amory. Eliot gave a long speech, "deliver'd in so masterly a stile and manner as to gain the plaudits of perhaps the largest assembly ever conven'd here, by an almost universal clap . . . He related his own particular case." He had a large quantity of goods on order which he could not stop and which must arrive after August 31. The covenant would ruin him and serve no purpose since imports would continue in the other colonies. Others, sharing Eliot's situation, felt the same way.[46] But the critical points were whether or not

44. Jonathan Williams to John Adams, June 28, 1774, John Adams Papers, Massachusetts Historical Society.

45. June 27, 1774, in Rowe, *Letters and Diary*, 276. Benjamin Kent, a member of the North End Caucus.

46. John Andrews to William Barrell, July 22, 1774, Mass. Hist. Soc., *Proceedings*, VIII, 330–332.

the committee had exceeded its power, and if it had, could it be justified?[47] When it grew dark the meeting adjourned.

The next day, June 28, the doubt which Williams carried with him to the meeting was decisively removed when, "after long Debates" the censure and annihilation motion was beaten "by a great Majority."[48] It was replaced by a motion that "the Town bear open Testimony that they are abundantly satisfied of the upright Intentions, and much approve the honest Zeal of the Committee of Correspondence & desire that they would persevere with their usual Activity & Firmness, continuing stedfast in the Way of well Doing." The confidence vote passed "by a *Vast Majority*." An unfriendly observer estimated the division at four to one in the committee's favor.[49] The Boston committee had more than survived its test.

In resisting the Port Act, like the Tea Act six months earlier, the committee of correspondence had plunged into the center of town politics. According to its own assessment of political circumstances the Solemn League and Covenant was a necessity. But unlike the committee's judgment during the tea resistance, this plan for resistance ran directly contrary to the Boston mercantile interest and the merchants' political analysis. The result, a direct challenge in the Boston town meeting, the committee's "home territory," brought a timely vote of confidence to the committee, but it could not bring Boston to endorse the Solemn League and Covenant. Instead, the town meeting stood firm on its original position. Boston would not unite in the program of resistance which the committee advocated.

The limited significance of the committee's victory is underlined by the fact that the opposition was vocal and powerful in spite of the committee's wide voting margin. There were many in Boston who considered themselves Whigs, merchants especially, who privately expressed serious misgivings about the committee's disobedience to the town meeting in promoting its own nonconsumption plan.[50] Hancock's merchant associate William Palfrey, who was a 1766 Son of Liberty with a long record of support for Boston Whigs and subsequently served

47. June 28, 1774, in Rowe, *Letters and Diary*, 276–277.
48. *Boston Town Records, 1770–1777*, p. 178.
49. June 28, 1774, in Rowe, *Letters and Diary*, 276–277.
50. *Ibid.*; John Andrews to William Barrell, July 22, 1774, Mass. Hist. Soc., *Proceedings*, VIII, 330–332. The Boston Committee of Correspondence itself admitted that most merchants importing goods from England opposed the covenant. Boston committee to Colrain Committee of Correspondence, July 18, 1774, Letters and Proceedings received, photo 184.

as paymaster of the Continental army, expressed his reprehension for the committee's action in a letter to James Warren, an intimate political associate of Samuel Adams.[51] The committee's wide victory seems in part to have resulted from the excess zeal of the governor's friends. For the motion to censure and abolish the committee, a sharp counterthrust, was a far more extreme measure than many could support. Merchants would have preferred a simple order to the committee "to suspend the Covenant till the Congress shall meet."[52] But this more moderate tactic would have served the administration's interest no better than the covenant, since it would have provided a basis for united resistance.

In the end the test revealed the limits of the Boston committee's capacity for political leadership. The committee enjoyed its role as a leader only so long as the measures it initiated were grounded on a broad consensus and opposed by only a small group of the governor's associates. Its leadership was always a fragile instrument, resting on continuous public consent rather than any formal, institutionalized authority. In June 1774 Boston was prepared to resist Parliament, and it was ready to vindicate the Boston Committee of Correspondence as part of this resistance, but Boston would also veto the committee's covenant. In July it would become apparent that provincial reactions, though not always identical in their impulse, led to the same conclusions regarding political tactics. As a result Boston and the towns of Massachusetts succeeded in establishing union in resistance.

III

Massachusetts towns reacted to the Boston Port Act with surprise and indignation. People saw no justice in the punishment of an entire town and colony for the lawless actions of a few of its inhabitants. Since regular criminal procedures were available to punish the offenders, they believed the act was both excessive and inappropriate. It could only be intended to compel payment of the tea duty, and so the townspeople recognized it as another attempt to enforce subjection to Parliament. When the towns learned from the Boston committee that bills to alter the entire Massachusetts charter were being introduced in Parliament, any lingering doubts about the basic motives of the

51. James Warren to William Palfrey, Plymouth, July 4, 1774, photocopy at Massachusetts Historical Society, Photostat Collection.
52. John Andrews to William Barrell, Boston, July 22, 1774, Massachusetts Historical Society, *Proceedings*, VIII, 330–332.

present ministry and Parliament disappeared. As they understood events, these bills confirmed everything the Boston committee had been saying about a fixed plan to enslave Massachusetts.

Support for Boston poured in from all over the province. More than eighty towns, a dozen of which had earlier remained silent, sent moral and material encouragement in the form of grain, livestock, and cash. Many of the towns that had "for a long time been inactive, in a more public way," apologized, assuring Boston that among themselves they had "all along seen a determin'd Spirit of opposition." Boston, towns agreed, was "suffering in the Common Cause of Liberty & America." [53]

But though the towns responded to the Boston committee's circulars by expressing overwhelming support for the capital during the crisis, they did not embrace the Solemn League and Covenant with equal warmth. They endorsed the idea of nonconsumption agreements; some had called for nonimportation as soon as they received the committee's circular announcing the Port Act.[54] But they opposed, sometimes explicitly and sometimes by implication, the Boston committee covenant. They tended to agree with the merchants that it was premature, and more important, they believed it was divisive. Of the 260 towns and districts in Massachusetts, only 7 entered the Solemn League and Covenant, and even 2 of these expressed significant misgivings.[55]

The popularity of the principle of nonconsumption was based primarily on the belief that it would inevitably lead to success. In addition, however, the idea appealed to the towns' desire to demonstrate their virtue. Nonconsumption meant "a proper Discouragement of foreign Luxuries," and some believed it had become everyone's duty "to refrain from the Luxeries and Superfluities of life and to the utmost of our Power, to incorage our own Manufacters." Nonconsumption, especially of luxuries, was a moral test of self-denial. For at least one town it was also regarded as desirable as a means of stopping the drain "of all our Circulating Cash." Thus nonconsumption was a multiple remedy for Massachusetts' ills, political, moral, and economic.[56]

53. Haverhill, Aug. 4, 1774, Letters and Proceedings received, photos 339–342.
54. Gloucester, Lunenburgh, Rochester, Newburyport, Pembroke, Harvard, North Yarmouth.
55. The following probably used the Boston covenant: Athol, Billerica, Brimfield, Gorham, Lincoln, Montague, Murrayfield. Arthur M. Schlesinger, *Colonial Merchants*, 323–324, ignored the distinction between the popularity of nonconsumption and the unpopularity of the Boston covenant. His discussion suggests that the towns followed the Boston "radicals" in nonconsumption like everything else. He also represented towns as entering the covenant in part out of hostility to merchants. I have found no evidence of such behavior.
56. Braintree, May 16, 1774, *Boston Weekly News-Letter*, June 2, 1774, 2:1;

Yet although half the towns returning their encouragement to Boston specifically endorsed the idea of nonconsumption, they generally refrained from adopting the Solemn League because they were skeptical of the effects of several of its provisions. First, its deadline, August 31, came too soon. It did not give the countryside sufficient time to prepare for a boycott, and it unfairly penalized "patriotic" merchants without damaging Britain. Therefore when Berkshire County and the town of Worcester circulated covenants similar to Boston's they delayed the effective date until October 1. Nevertheless the towns did not generally adopt any covenant, not Boston's, Berkshire's, or Worcester's — although contrary rumors circulated among Boston merchants.[57]

A second reason towns held back was suggested by the Marblehead committee when it explained to the Boston committee why it delayed. Boston itself, it said, had not entered the covenant. They were sure "that if the plan is Entered into at Boston, all Difficultys will subside here."[58] Marblehead was addressing itself particularly to the situation of seaport towns wholly dependent on trade, as it believed inland towns could enter covenants with relative ease being largely self-sufficient. Yet inland towns, accustomed to following the metropolis, also perceived that the Boston committee was recommending a covenant that Boston itself had not entered.[59] Boston's example gave them no encouragement to join in the measure.

A more fundamental, more widely expressed reason for withholding support from any particular covenant, or entering one, came from the belief that it was advisable to wait for the Continental Congress. Boycotts preceding a general colonial boycott could not be very effective and might threaten the creation of the colonial union which towns believed essential. Charlemont, a town of 500 people in Hampshire, explained that they had not signed the covenant because "it would answer no valuable purpose for the Inhabitants of this Infant Settlement to Sign unless the people in general should adopt the plan but on the other hand might be attended with Inconvenience." Moreover it was "generally reported in these parts that but very few towns fall

Reading, July 11, 1774, Letters and Proceedings received, photo 654; Hopkinton, July 14, 1774, *ibid.*, photo 351. See also Edmund S. Morgan, "The Puritan Ethic and the American Revolution," *William and Mary Quarterly*, 3d Ser., XXIV (1967), 3–43, esp. 12–18.

57. See John Andrews to William Barrell, July 22, 1774, Mass. Hist. Soc., *Proceedings*, VIII, 330–332.

58. Marblehead, June 18, 1774, Letters and Proceedings received, photos 455–456; Marblehead, June 23, 1774, *ibid.*, photos 461–462.

59. Manchester, Aug. 22, 1774, *ibid.*, photo 439.

in with the proposals—it is likewise supposed by some that the Signing the Covenent is interfering with the Committees of the Several Colonies appointed for a General Congress." They were anxious to do all they could, but an immediate boycott seemed to them a vain act at the moment.[60]

Granville District, also in Hampshire, describing its sentiments fully, showed a reaction which seems to have been common, though it was not often expressed so clearly. They said that "although we approve of the sentiments and spirit of their [the Boston committee's] Covenant . . . yet we are of the Opinion the same is rather Premature and too precipitate." A boycott, "of the utmost importance to the British American Colonies" demanded serious consideration. Their fear, a common one, was that the covenant would "breed a discord among the Inhabitants, and that a Discord of Sentiment may be destructive of the good effect proposed." Therefore Granville, like nearly a score of others, explicitly chose "to defer the subscribing thereto but to wait the Determination of the American Congress." Like the others, their affirmative act of resistance was to "promise and pledge our Faith that whatever dutiful and Constitutional determinations and Resolutions shall be agreed upon and published by them [Congress] as a General rule of Observance of all the Colonies we will subscribe to."[61] As they saw it the commitment to unity was as vital as their pledge of resistance.

Some towns entered covenants in spite of the threat to their internal harmony; but they often modified the form of the covenant to suit their situation. Billerica, a Middlesex town of 1,500 inhabitants whose fervid proceedings pointedly recalled "the unlimited Prerogative, contended for by those arbitrary & misguided Princes, *Charles* the First & *James* the Second, for which the One lost his Life, & the Other his Kingdom," was one of the few which entered the Boston covenant. But the town pledged to adhere to it only as long as the Continental Congress saw fit, and it wholly excluded any method of ostracizing offenders against the agreement.[62] An example of the kind of tension a covenant could produce was described in one of the Brimfield committee's letters to Boston. Brimfield, a Hampshire community with a population just over 1,000, was reluctant to threaten its internal harmony. Its committee of correspondence explained that:

---

60. Charlemont, July 9, 1774, Letters and Proceedings received, photos 141–142.
61. Granville, Aug. 3, 1774, *ibid.*, photos 301–302.
62. Billerica, June 6, 1774, *ibid.*, photo 83–86.

We should have sent you a copy of the Covenant at large and a List of the few That as yet have not signed it, But under Expectation of our Uniting to a Man and the great Reluctance we have in holding up to the world a Brother a Fellow towns Man, as an Enemy to his Country till we have the best evidence of his Vileness, has determined us not to publish their Names at present.

Town unity was still their wish: "We would still think we are all of one Mind in the grand american Struggle for Liberty; but if any should long continue to oppose, by their Fruits we shall know them, you may depend on having Their Names in our next." The Brimfield committee never sent in a list of names; apparently its hopes for a unity more or less voluntarily achieved were realized.[63] In a number of towns — a small but significant number — unity was not so easy to achieve.

Divisions normally occurred in larger, more complex communities: port towns or the seats of county government. Virtually none of the more than two hundred smaller communities of 500 to 1,000 inhabitants experienced any sort of visible division. Moreover, conflicts were exclusively confined to towns where previous political alignments, such as Governor Hutchinson's friendship and patronage, or particular economic interest, as in the case of importing merchants, had created a basis for division. In towns where these circumstances existed, the political questions raised in the spring and summer of 1774 easily led to public disputes. Conflicts, often lasting for months, were always resolved in favor of overwhelming popular majorities which sought to compel harmonious behavior if not uniform beliefs among all the inhabitants. In the few towns where people who had addressed support for Governors Hutchinson and Gage refused to "recant" their sentiments, division was unusually bitter, and it was ended only by the departure of those who refused to accede to the popular will.

In Marblehead, the town's division over an issue wholly extraneous to the imperial dispute overturned the local committee of correspondence, giving the "friends of government" a temporary victory. This case was unique. Elbridge Gerry, Colonel Azor Orne, and John Glover, three members of the committee of correspondence, had built a small-pox hospital in 1773 to curb an outbreak of the contagion. The town had given its reluctant consent, but when the disease continued to spread, and when several patients died after being inoculated, the

63. Brimfield, Aug. 5, 1774, *ibid.*, photos 106–107; Brimfield, Town Records, No. 1, 243–255, Town Hall, Brimfield, Mass.

hospital was closed. In January 1774 the hospital was burned down by angry townspeople. When persons arrested for setting the fire were forcibly set free, Gerry and Orne, among others, called for military protection from their townsmen, whom they angrily described as the "savage mobility." [64]

The members of the Marblehead committee of correspondence were so outraged by their neighbors' behavior that they resigned their office. In a letter to the Boston committee they explained that they would have continued to serve "had not the late prevalent Disorders have put an End in this place to all Order & Distinction; & rendered publick Offices of every Degree obnoxious to the Controul of a savage Mobility." But they were unwilling to serve the town in the future "without material Alteration in the Conduct of the Inhabitants." [65] The smallpox hospital had so deeply divided the town that its supporters, by coincidence the committee of correspondence, had become an unpopular target. However the town did not itself remove them from office or abolish the committee; its members resigned.

Two months later reactions to the Port Act substantially reunited Marblehead, although a lesser division was created when some merchants publicly addressed their support to the governor. But now the town created a new committee of correspondence, including two members who had earlier resigned; however the three who had been proprietors of the hospital were left out. [66] As the new committee was constituted, it enjoyed the public support essential to its role as spokesman for Marblehead resistance.

In Plymouth, the Port Act and the alternatives of paying for the tea or resisting by means of a covenant served to inflame and magnify an existing division between allies of Governor Hutchinson and friends of the Boston Whigs. But even though the covenant issue had quickly divided the town, James Warren at first believed that Governor Gage's proclamation forbidding such covenants would bring people to sign it, if only as an expression of their right. [67] Indeed one town, Marlborough,

64. Samuel E. Morison, "Elbridge Gerry, Gentleman-Democrat," *New England Quarterly*, II (1929), 6–33, esp. 12–13. See also the forthcoming study of Gerry by George Athan Billias.
65. Marblehead Committee of Correspondence to Boston committee, March 22, 1774, Letters and Proceedings received, photos 441–442.
66. Marblehead, May 24, 1774, *Boston Gazette*, May 30, 1774, 2:1. It is also possible that they declined to serve.
67. James Warren to Samuel Adams, July 1, 1774, *Warren-Adams Letters, Being Chiefly a Correspondence among John Adams, Samuel Adams, and James*

had replied to the proclamation by burning the governor in effigy with his proclamation.[68] Yet Plymouth was more restrained; ten days later Warren reported that only a hundred of his townsmen, far less than a majority, had signed the Boston covenant.[69]

In the beginning, Warren informed the Boston committee, "Little Ned Winslow (one of my Cousins) with a few other Insignificant Tories appeared at the meeting and played their Game by holding up the Terrors of certain Expectation of your defeat"; but the Boston committee's victory on June 28 had silenced that approach. In Warren's view a more serious threat to the covenant was being posed by those who regarded it as a potential source of permanent division in the town. It was these "Wolves in Sheeps Cloathing who do the mischeif, principally by persuading people that great difficulties will Ensue by breaking up of Intercourse with non-Signers." Warren said he would try to keep this provision in the covenant in spite of the anxieties it generated. He was also hard-pressed because people wanted to know whether the covenant had been entered at Marblehead, Salem, and Newburyport. For that matter, he wished the committee would "mention Boston and tell me what you do with the Covenant there." [70] Plymouth had already divided, and without a substantial dose of encouragement from outside, Warren did not see how Plymouth could be united behind the covenant. In the end, in spite of Warren's effort and the hundred signers, Plymouth never joined a covenant. The division the covenant created was unwelcome, and the townspeople refused to exacerbate it or make it permanent by adopting a covenant prior to the meeting of the Continental Congress.

In Worcester the division that appeared over the covenant in June 1774, occurred as the climax of a profound alteration in town politics which had been in the making for several months. The battle, which ended in the demise of a traditional group of leaders, illustrated the readiness of townspeople to overthrow a recognized leadership group which was unwilling to lead along the path they wished to follow. Instead the town followed its committee of correspondence and a new

---

Warren, Massachusetts Historical Society, *Collections*, LXXII–LXXIII (Boston, 1917–1925), II, 405.

68. July 8, 1774, Ann Hulton, *Letters of a Loyalist Lady, 1767–1776* (Cambridge, Mass., 1927), 74.

69. James Warren to Samuel Adams, July 10, 1774, *Warren-Adams Letters*, II, 405–406.

70. *Ibid.*

local group, the American Political Society.[71] As a result Worcester became more radical than Boston. It entered a covenant which included a stringent secondary boycott, and even had this covenant printed and sent to every town in the county.[72] By the summer of 1774, the unity of Worcester had been shattered and it joined Boston in leading Massachusetts' resistance.

But Worcester's traditional leaders, the Chandlers, the Paines, and the Putnams, all closely associated with Governor Hutchinson, struck back.[73] They challenged the town's political course, calling for a meeting to reconsider Worcester's defiance of the administration. Their counterattack brought on a battle in the town meeting of June 20 which closely paralleled the conflict over the Boston committee a week later at the capital. Colonel James Putnam, a distinguished lawyer and attorney general of the province, led this move to withdraw the covenant and dismiss the committee of correspondence. But although the debate was long and heated, Putnam and his friends lost. The town voted that its proceedings and its covenant stand, and that the committee of correspondence continue its service. Yet the town's division did not end there. Putnam and his followers issued a heated protest. Their words, published in the press and entered in the Worcester town book by the clerk, who was himself one of the forty-three protesters, reveal the mixture of issues at stake in the divided town.[74]

The protesters argued that the town's recent behavior was hazardous, since it had already been "proved" that such conduct was "extremely prejudicial to the province." However, internal disorder was even more dangerous than external punishment. "Disorder and confusion," "licentiousness and distraction," was their reiterated fear and complaint. Events, they found, were scarcely comprehensible. They saw "so many,

71. The town had 1,900 inhabitants in 1774. The American Political Society was formed late in December 1773, to defend the "liberty and property" of Worcester residents. It began with thirty members, and by June 1774 had about fifty, including members of the committee of correspondence and the town representative. Like the North End Caucus in Boston, it met regularly at a tavern and concerned itself principally with town politics. It dissolved itself in June 1776. The fullest treatment of its activities may be found in William E. Lincoln, History of Worcester (Worcester, 1837), 76–82.

72. Donald E. Johnson, "Worcester in the War for Independence," Ph.D. diss., Clark University, 1953, p. 39.

73. Lillian E. Newfield, "Worcester on the Eve of the Revolution," master's thesis, Clark University, 1941, discusses the offices and kinship relations of the "leading" families of Worcester in the early 1770's. Lincoln, Worcester, includes a list of principal town officers.

74. Lincoln, Worcester, 86–88.

who we used to esteem sober peaceable men, so far deceived, deluded, and led astray, by the artful, crafty, and insidious practices of some evil-minded, and ill-disposed persons." These schemers, "falsly stiling themselves the friends of liberty; some of them neglecting their own proper business and occupation in which they ought to be employed for the support of their families; [were] spending their time in discoursing of matters they do not understand; raising and propagating falshoods and calumnies of those men they look up to with envy, and on whose fall and ruin they wish to rise." Their intention, the protesters declared, was "to reduce all things to a state of tumult, disorder, and confusion."

These "evil" persons who led so many townspeople "aside by strange opinions," were concentrated in the committee of correspondence whose "dark and pernicious proceedings" the town had refused to review, much less condemn. It was the protesters' opinion that all committees of correspondence, "creatures of modern invention," constituted a "public grievance." They had been "contrived by a junto, to serve particular designs and purposes of their own," and they possessed no legal foundation. These committees were the propagators of the divisive covenants which were "tending directly to sedition, civil war, and rebellion." To the protesters the committees symbolized or perhaps embodied the "evil genius" at work in their town and their province.[75]

This reaction to events was virtually identical to that of Thomas Hutchinson and Peter Oliver, who were witnesses of developments in Boston and all over the province. The emphasis on disorder, on the irregularity of popular activity, and on the evil leadership of the people, especially the committees of correspondence, was all the same. It was a natural reaction for a group of social and political leaders who, after enjoying the favor and esteem of the public for years, suddenly found themselves displaced for no reason which they could understand. From their viewpoint the active popular resistance to Britain was both impractical and immoral. But they could not convince majorities. As a result in Worcester, Northampton, and Springfield, where a few such leaders had long enjoyed the local influence that accompanied popular esteem, the summer of 1774 came as a shock. They could still rally a few supporters but, with the exception of Edward Bacon in Barnstable, never enough to maintain their influence. Frequently unwilling to join

75. Printed in Lincoln, *Worcester*, 87–88; it appeared at the time in both the *Boston Weekly News-Letter* of June 30, 1774, and the *Boston Gazette* of July 4, 1774.

the majority, they often departed their homes rather than live among hostile neighbors who frequently found public ways of expressing their contempt.[76]

But most towns, it should be emphasized, were united. They experienced no such conflicts or alterations in leadership as did Worcester. Their regular leaders, like the rest of the inhabitants, normally shared the Whig view, however local activity might vary. This diversity among towns on particular actions never became a basis for major division because the general aims and expectations of the towns were so similar as to be nearly identical. Variations were expected when 260 towns were making individual determinations; people were accustomed to modes of political activity which anticipated a certain diversity within a general frame of consensus.

Actually, the Boston Committee of Correspondence had not been far wrong in its assessment of local opinion; the countryside did embrace the idea of resistance enthusiastically, and many towns actually entered some kind of boycott covenant. But they rejected the Boston committee's own covenant because, with its early deadline and stiff secondary boycott, it was divisive. The committee had erred in its zeal to start a nonimportation movement immediately. The fact that mercantile interests were weak in the countryside did not mean that towns would indiscriminately embrace any boycott covenant. Their own unity carried a higher priority than an immediate boycott and, moreover, by mid-1774 they were generally conscious of the fundamental necessity of co-ordinating their own resistance with that of other colonies. Since the Solemn League and Covenant seemed to threaten these goals they quietly laid it aside.

The experience illustrated several characteristic elements in the pattern of Massachusetts politics during the Revolutionary era. First, it showed that although Boston leaders could arouse and stimulate local political activity they could neither direct nor dominate it. The highways of influence ran two ways, both out from Boston and in to it. During the first year of the Boston committee's existence political initiatives and the terms of resistance had largely been drawn from Boston

76. When a leader in Shutesbury, Rev. Abraham Hill, "obstinately" maintained his Tory views he was briefly impounded by his townsmen and fed on herrings thrown into jail by the public, according to Robert J. Taylor, *Western Massachusetts in the Revolution* (Providence, 1954), 69. Israel Williams of Hatfield and his son suffered the indignity of being smoked overnight in a smokehouse when they held firm to their views.

with other towns either following or standing aside. But now, as the crisis of authority deepened, this pattern was shifting to the towns, the fundamental political units. During the summer of 1774 most towns were operating in a state of alarm, and it was their activism which determined the nature of resistance in Massachusetts.

9

The Revolution

in Provincial Politics

During the second half of 1774 the organization and structure of Massachusetts politics were drastically reordered. Royal administration collapsed, and authority devolved exclusively upon representative bodies formed at the local, county, and provincial levels. While this process developed, conceptions of authority which had earlier been only partially operative became dominant as Massachusetts embarked on a program of general resistance. As was apparent in the representative character of the dozens of meetings, committees, conventions, and congresses, the necessity of consensus was dictating both the forms and the substance of the revolutionary movement.

In the summer of 1774 the county convention briefly emerged as the primary organ for coordinating and directing provincial political activity. Although the towns were the primary units of authority and although their decisions alone were binding and enforceable on the inhabitants, town leaders recognized the need for broader consultation and planning. In the absence of a provincial assembly, their response was the creation of ad hoc county conventions. These meetings of town-elected deputies never possessed any legal or coercive authority. Their powers were merely advisory; they were instruments for achieving unified, cooperative action without jeopardizing local initiative or control.

By the end of the summer, towns in nine counties had called conventions: Berkshire and Hampshire in the west; Worcester in central Massachusetts; Bristol, Essex, Middlesex, Plymouth, and Suffolk in the east; and Cumberland in Maine. The only counties in which conventions had not been called were those where the resistance movement was weak: Barnstable on Cape Cod; and two Maine counties, Lincoln and York.[1] In the rest of the province, towns succeeded in concerting their efforts by means of the conventions, without any prompting or suggestions from the Boston Committee of Correspondence. Clearly, the functions of leadership and coordination which the committee had previously served in Massachusetts were now being fulfilled at the local and county levels. The role of the Boston committee in provincial politics had become superfluous.

These developments occurred at the same time that the demands made on members of the committee by Boston's internal political needs reached their peak. In the summer of 1774 the besieged town faced several interlocking problems. First, it had to make provision for the hundreds of families that were threatened with poverty and starvation by the blockade. At the same time it had to maintain social order and political discipline, both as conditions of resistance and in order to retain the sympathy and support of other colonies. If Boston could not provide for its unemployed and keep order, then it would have to yield. Under these circumstances the Boston committee could hardly concentrate its attention on the province.

This crisis, moreover, was prolonged and the committee's involvement in Boston affairs continued through the autumn. During these months the Provincial and Continental Congresses took charge of managing resistance, so there would be no further need for the Boston committee in that regard. By January 1775 its role had become so circumscribed as to make all but its title unrecognizable, and its key members were either absorbed in the activities of the congresses or departed from Boston. The Boston town meeting continued to maintain a committee of correspondence, but henceforth it would operate within the confines of Boston, charged with local administrative duties and shorn of any role in provincial or continental affairs.

From the perspective of its founders these developments gave cause

1. William E. Lincoln, ed., *The Journals of Each Provincial Congress, of Massachusetts in 1774 and 1775, . . . with an Appendix containing the Proceedings of the County Conventions . . . and other Documents, Illustrative of the Early History of the American Revolution* (Boston, 1838), lii–lv. Note that conventions were unnecessary in Dukes and Nantucket counties because they were so small.

for satisfaction, not anguish. In their brief, two-year careers on the committee its members had never developed any profound institutional loyalty to the committee as such. The very idea would have been alien to them. Their commitment was not to any quasi-formal institution, but to a larger political cause. From their viewpoint the committee was a useful instrument, an expedient which they readily abandoned when the need disappeared. Instead of exchanging melancholy lamentations or bending their efforts to shore up the committee, they were indifferent to its demise. If anything, they gloried in the realization that it had indeed become superfluous. By the autumn of 1774 they believed that provincial politics had actually been transformed, and that the lethargy of nonparticipation had been supplanted by a local activism which promised commitment to Whig ideals.

The most important element in this process, which at once gratified the committee and rendered it insignificant, was the explosion of local political activity in the summer of 1774. Through it, initiative in the resistance movement rapidly passed from Boston to the countryside. It was here, in the towns and counties, that the Boston Committee of Correspondence saw the political stimulation it had been providing ripen into a revolutionary consensus.

I

The independence of the towns in responding to the Boston committee's covenant, and the initiatives displayed by various county conventions were not isolated, chance occurrences. During the summer of 1774, acting under the impetus of the Port and Massachusetts Government Acts, towns that had previously displayed their zeal only in response to the initiatives of the Boston committee began to originate their own methods of resisting the "unconstitutional" innovations. Local leadership appeared at the county level in the form of conventions of towns, organizing and directing political action. This development, wholly illegal according to English standards, was accepted throughout Massachusetts as both desirable and proper. All over Massachusetts local leaders recognized that resistance must be immediately organized entirely free of the governor's authority and influence. Their spontaneous response was based on the assumption that the people acting in town meetings literally possessed sovereign power.

This revolutionary assumption of authority outside the bounds of the traditional structure began in Berkshire County, a region where previously there had been relatively little participation in the politics of opposition. In early July sixty "deputies of the several towns" met at Stockbridge "to consult and advise what was necessary and prudent to be done."[2] Their unanimous resolutions combining a declaration of rights with a nonconsumption covenant and a pledge to maintain constitutional local government, set a pattern which other counties subsequently followed. One month later Worcester, the second county to convene, expanded the role of the county convention even further. Together these first two conventions demonstrated the breadth and depth of the provincial desire to repel invasions against the constitutional rights of Massachusetts.

The conventions, all of them, followed the model of town meetings from their organization and conduct to the substance of their proceedings. Moderators were elected, committees and subcommittees were chosen to report, and then, after deliberation, the conventions voted resolves. Unlike the towns, however, their resolves were merely advisory, not binding.

The Berkshire declaration of rights was characteristic of views held everywhere in the province. Particular emphasis was given to the equality of colonists with Englishmen, equal rights, including specifically the granting of property only by consent, the right to trial by a jury of local peers, and the corporate rights of political bodies such as Boston and Massachusetts whose liberties could not be unilaterally abolished by Parliament. The Berkshire nonconsumption covenant, also entitled a "solemn league and covenant," was similar to the Boston Committee of Correspondence covenant though it was to take effect later (October 1) and expressly pledged that its signers would follow whatever future directions the general Continental Congress might give respecting a boycott. Unlike the Boston committee covenant, it included no pledge of an indefinite boycott until redress was granted. Yet as a nonconsumption agreement enforced with a secondary boycott against nonsigners, it rested on the same radical principles as that of the Boston committee.[3]

Where it differed fundamentally from the committee covenant was in the broader area of local government. For the Boston committee had concerned itself primarily with nonconsumption, the secondary boycott, and to a lesser degree the encouragement of domestic industry. Town

2. Lincoln, ed., *Journals of Each Provincial Congress*, 652.
3. *Ibid.*, 652–653.

affairs and the issue of order had never been mentioned. In contrast the Berkshire covenant, after outlining nonconsumption, devoted equal consideration to the maintenance of order and unity among the inhabitants. Its signers pledged not only a boycott of British goods, they also promised to maintain internal peace and harmony. By the force of consent, the authority of the people would maintain order.

These pledges illustrate the common fear that tumults and disputes might accompany resistance to Britain in the present crisis. Signers were required to bind themselves to "observe the most strict obedience to all constitutional laws, and authority." Moreover they agreed to "at all times, exert ourselves to the utmost for the discouragement of all licentiousness, and suppression of all mobs and riots." All existing government in the county was to be maintained, the convention declared, by public self-restraint sworn in the covenant.[4]

This ideal sought by the convention for Berkshire was a general aspiration throughout the province, and it was embodied in the Berkshire oath, that "we will all exert ourselves, as far as in us lies, in promoting love, peace, and unanimity among each other; and for that end we engage to avoid all unnecessary lawsuits." Here it was expected that the same self-restraint that would prevent riotous behavior would also generate unity, a harmony that would eliminate all "unnecessary" conflict.[5] The Boston committee, now immediately absorbed in imperial politics and intercolonial union, had overlooked this problem of internal unity. But for the Berkshire convention it was a pressing issue of intense concern. The proposed solution, harmony by mutual consent, to be enforced by the sanction of public approval, was characteristic of county conventions oriented toward town affairs.[6] In England the suggestion of government by popular self-restraint would have been seen as ludicrous, a prescription for anarchy; but in Berkshire County and elsewhere in Massachusetts it was generally assumed and expected that it could function effectively. In large measure government by a combination of self-restraint and public sanction had been everyday practice for generations.

The closing resolves of the Berkshire convention, calling for donations to the town of Boston and for a day of fasting and prayer, reflected

4. Lincoln, ed., *Journals of Each Provincial Congress*, 653–654.
5. *Ibid.*, 654.
6. In addition to Berkshire, the following counties are known to have passed similar resolutions: Cumberland, Hampshire, Plymouth, Suffolk, and Worcester. *Ibid.*, 659, 629, 625, 605, 627.

the profound sense of moral duty embodied in the resistance movement throughout the province. Donations to Boston did not merely represent solidarity and sustenance, but also charity — there was a moral obligation implicit in the call. The resolution for a fast day was more than a call on the Lord for insight and wisdom in the present calamity, it was also a symbol of Christian repentance and devotion which they and their ancestors had always invoked at critical times. That such a call should be routinely included in an otherwise radical series of political resolves was typical of the provincial outlook which intertwined traditional values and concepts with revolutionary action.

The later Worcester convention differed from that of Berkshire primarily in the extended, detailed leadership it offered the county, culminating in advice on military preparation and the direction of a major political demonstration. Its resolves were similar to those of Berkshire and dozens of towns, containing both a pledge of allegiance to the King and an exposition of "American" rights including the assertion "that we have, within ourselves, the exclusive right of originating each and every law respecting ourselves." Though the convention did not draft a covenant, it recommended nonconsumption agreements as the best way to influence Britain, pointing out that in addition it would "greatly prevent extravagance, save our money, encourage our own manufactures, and reform our manners." [7] From the provincial perspective, nonconsumption was the universal panacea — political, economic, and moral.

The convention went on, however, to recommend even more immediate resistance, condemning all justices who publicly supported Governor Gage and urging every town to adopt measures which would thwart enforcement of the Massachusetts Government Acts. Ultimate power lay with the towns and in order to mobilize it the convention resolved to meet again, urging every town in the county to participate in its proceedings. It closed its first meeting by ordering its proceedings printed as handbills and distributed with a covering letter to all the towns and districts in Worcester.

When the convention met again at the end of August, more than 130 town delegates and members of local committees of correspondence attended, nearly three times the number present at the first meeting

---

7. *Ibid.*, 630–631. The town of Worcester did draft a covenant on Aug. 22, 1774, and this was known as the "Worcester Covenant" described in Albert Mathews, "The Solemn League and Covenant, 1774," Publications of the Colonial Society of Massachusetts, *Transactions*, XVIII (1915–1916), 103–122. This covenant is found in William Lincoln, *History of Worcester* (Worcester, 1837), 92–93.

and a gathering equal in size to a meeting of the Massachusetts House. Their most immediate problem was to prevent submission to the newly organized "unconstitutional" courts of common pleas and general sessions. Their method was to block the scheduled sessions. The convention resolved that this was the "indispensable duty" of Worcester inhabitants, so it urged every individual in the county to personally come to Worcester on September 6 when the courts were to meet. It intended that the people assembled would convince the justices not to sit and the jurors and litigants to boycott the courts.[8]

At the same time the convention recognized that the "gloomy aspect of our public affairs has thrown this province into great convulsions, and the minds of the people are greatly agitated" by the prospect of slavery. Therefore, "to regulate the movements of each town, and prevent any disorder which might otherwise happen," the convention recommended that town officers be chosen and charged with this special responsibility. Townspeople were cautioned to "adhere strictly to the orders and directions of such officers." The convention itself, in terms similar to those of the Berkshire covenant, recommended to all and pledged its members "to use the utmost influence in suppressing all riotous and disorderly proceedings in our respective towns." In addition everyone was advised to pay his just debts and to avoid all disputes and litigation. By these resolutions the convention began the process of transforming the local committees of correspondence into omnibus committees responsible for the general political behavior of each town.[9]

To facilitate local activities and to avoid submission to the "unconstitutional" government acts, the towns were advised to hold their meetings as they had always done and, in effect, to ignore both the "reform" acts and the governor's proclamations. Moreover, so that courts and government could be properly restored, the convention urged towns to send delegates to the Provincial Congress which would be held at Concord in October. This "general convention" was expected to devise a way "to resume our original mode of government, whereby the most dignified servants were, as they ever ought to be, dependent on the people for their existence as such." Until such a government was formed, towns were advised to withhold their taxes from the province treasury. The hope of the convention and the towns was that the current "state of nature" created by Parliament's dissolution of the charter

8. Lincoln, ed., *Journals of Each Provincial Congress*, 632.
9. *Ibid.*, 632–633.

could be quickly replaced by a properly constituted government which would assure both liberty and order.[10]

Owing to a report that the governor was planning to send troops to secure the court sessions, the convention went on to recommend a plan for defense, voting that if an "invasion" threatened, the committees of correspondence should warn each other, and every town "properly armed and accoutred" should come to the defense of the invaded town.[11] The convention simply assumed its competence to make such recommendations, never bothering to justify its transactions, even though the royal administration and all of England would regard their activities as the purest sedition. In Massachusetts people believed they were not acting contrary to "lawful authority" because in the absence of a constitutional government all authority rested in the people organized in towns.

The people of Worcester County dramatized these beliefs in a public demonstration on September 6 when, with the leadership of the convention, they closed the courts. They had arrived in the town of Worcester 6,000 strong, organized in town militia companies. Following the instructions of the convention, each of the companies elected a representative to meet the judges to tell them the courts must be closed. This done, all were to assemble on the Worcester Common, grouped by town. There, late in the afternoon, the people of Worcester performed a pageant of popular sovereignty — requiring the court officials to tread a path through the ranks of the people while continuously reading aloud their pledge to ignore the government acts and suspend the courts. Here the governing assumptions of contemporary politics were explicitly acted out. Before the day ended and the people went home, the convention extended the nullification of English authority to include all militia officers, resolving that they should resign their commissions since they came from the governor. Instead the towns themselves should elect their militia officers.[12] The assumption, and it was accurate, was that the same men who resigned from the governor's service would normally be elected to the same position by their towns. As a result the shift in the base of militia authority rarely affected local leadership.

The following day the convention asked for recantations from those justices of the peace who had sent an address to the governor pledging

10. *Ibid.*, 633–634.
11. *Ibid.*
12. *Ibid.*, 635–638.

REVOLUTIONARY POLITICS IN MASSACHUSETTS

support and criticizing the actions of the people. Eleven of the fourteen justices complied, so the convention resolved that all of the justices of the peace who had held office as of June 30, excepting only Timothy Ruggles, John Murray, and James Putnam who continued to support Gage, should be obeyed until the Provincial Congress made other provisions. The convention recommended "to the people of this county, that they consider and treat them as being in their said offices, and support and defend them in the execution thereof, according to the laws of the province."[13] Here the popular sanction which lay behind legal authority was made explicit without the least hesitation, and with full confidence that the inhabitants would find it reasonable and submit.

The convention's last meeting before the Provincial Congress convened was held on September 21 and 22. No new efforts were undertaken; rather, directions already begun were elaborated. A county committee of correspondence was chosen.[14] In internal government the convention recommended that all disputes and litigation that could not be settled amicably should be submitted to arbitration; and if either party refused, "they ought to be considered as co-operating with the enemies of the country." Moreover in order to enforce the restraints on imports, the convention urged committees of correspondence or selectmen in the port towns to inspect all imports and publish information on imports and importers of contraband goods so that the boycott could be more effective.[15] Here the convention's recommendation tended once more to broaden the role of local committees of correspondence, altering them in the manner which the Continental Congress would reinforce and finally establish.

By this time the convention believed it had substantially passed through the critical challenge to order, and it devoted considerable attention to military preparation. At earlier meetings in the preceding weeks it had already recommended that the towns follow the Norfolk plan of training their militia, and that they do their best to acquire and master field artillery. Now they suggested a reform in the organization of regiments in the county, including an elective system for selecting all officers.[16] The same assumptions regarding the source of authority which ruled other aspects of political organization ruled the military.

13. Lincoln, ed., *Journals of Each Provincial Congress*, 639.
14. *Ibid.*, 642.
15. *Ibid.*, 643.
16. *Ibid.*, 639, 636, 643.

Even the militia was to be organized according to the practices of town meetings and the principle of electing officials on a representative basis.

The Worcester convention, although it continued to meet fairly regularly well into 1775, like the other county conventions ceded its position of leadership to the Provincial Congress when it met in October 1774.[17] Yet, during a brief but critical period when the fear of anarchy and tumult was widespread, conventions like those of Berkshire and Worcester had exercised substantial leadership in the province. Their power, entirely dependent on public approval and the support of the towns, had been sufficient to provide for a relative uniformity of measures with virtually no conflict among towns and a minimum of division within them. This "government," entirely based on representation and consent, with enforcement a matter of town volition, was not the anarchic confusion that any contemporary theorist would have predicted, because there were no substantial conflicts of interest to test the arrangement, and because it conformed entirely with public assumptions about the nature of government and authority. The old political and social leaders normally continued to rule because, excepting the few who sided with the royal government, the basis for their political strength, the agreement and respect of their neighbors, remained secure. The "federal" structure of town, county, and provincial government was satisfactory because at every level, from the town to the Provincial Congress, power was exercised by representative officials operating entirely with consent.

The role of the Boston committee in these developments was peripheral. Boston, boxed in with its own critical problems, its committee of correspondence engaged in a variety of local as well as intercolonial activities, was in no position to provide the province with continuous leadership. Moreover the provincial unwillingness to join the Solemn League and Covenant had, while illustrating local independence, also unintentionally implied a repudiation of the Boston committee's leadership. The actions of the towns and the county conventions showed that the Boston committee's first priority, creating an impact on British politics, was not the first concern in the towns. Unity within towns, among them, and among the colonies, together with maintaining order, were more important than British politics from the local vantage point. As a consequence, effective leadership in Massachusetts passed to the county conventions. These representative assemblies, both by their exis-

17. At least nine counties held conventions in August and September 1774.

tence and by their mode of direction, demonstrated that popular support of the forms of laws and authority had become the entire basis for effective government in Massachusetts.

II

While these developments were eliminating the Boston committee's role as a leader of local activity, the crisis in Boston created by the Port Act made fresh demands on the committee and its members. As a result the committee concentrated its attention on Boston, seeking to connect Boston irrevocably to the towns and to the other colonies, and to maintain its morale in the meantime. To achieve this goal, civil order in Boston and throughout Massachusetts was vital. The committee, listening to the warnings of its correspondents in other colonies, believed that disorder or armed conflict would frighten many colonists away from resisting Britain, thereby permitting Massachusetts and the other colonies to be divided and subdued by the feints and thrusts of a devious and powerful ministry.

One of the primary circumstances that reshaped the committee's role was the closing of the port of Boston. Interrupting nearly every branch of commerce, it threatened merchants, and much more immediately the hundreds of mechanics and laborers whose daily earnings were entirely dependent on shipping activity. The latter, lacking substantial reserves of savings or capital, rapidly faced distress if not starvation. The town, recognizing this danger as soon as the Port Act became known, quickly sought means to provide for their livelihood, and almost immediately the Boston committee became involved.

At the town meeting of May 13, a committee of eleven, including five of the most active members of the Boston committee, was chosen to prepare a report on what should be done to maintain Boston's economic and political vigor. This "Committee on Ways and Means," gradually became recognized as a standing town committee which, together with the Overseers of the Poor, was responsible for those who were unemployed as a result of the Port Act.[18] But after six weeks of efforts under this arrangement, at the end of July, the Overseers of the Poor became dissatisfied and asked to be relieved. They preferred to restrict themselves to their regular duty of caring for Boston's poor,

18. *Boston Town Records, 1770–1777,* Boston Record Commissioners, *Report,* XVIII (Boston, 1887), 173, 175.

rather than undertaking the larger and more complicated task of seeking to employ and maintain the hundreds who were now out of work. As a result the town meeting reorganized the "Ways and Means" committee, adding fifteen members and making it a committee of "Donations." This new committee of twenty-six, six of whom were also members of the committee of correspondence, was made responsible for receiving and disbursing the donations sent to Boston for the employment and relief of people affected by the Port Act.[19]

Technically, as a matter of formal organization, the committee of donations and its administration of poor relief had nothing to do with the Boston committee. Yet because of the dual membership of Adams, Warren, Quincy, Molineux, Appleton, and Mackay in both committees, the two worked closely together, so closely that in performing one important task, letterwriting, they were indistinguishable. Moreover, since Boston's unemployed became a central concern of members of the Boston committee some examination of the donations committee is necessary in order to understand the new role of the committee of correspondence and the intensity of its concern for Boston rather than Massachusetts as a whole.

The donations committee, which met regularly five days a week, approached its task systematically. It began by making an inventory of "all classes of people" who were "suffering by the Port Bill," requesting inhabitants to come to Faneuil Hall and explain their individual circumstances. Ten afternoons were spent in this inquiry, since "a great number appeared, of all classes of mechanics and laborers." The laborers were the most numerous and most distressed, so the donations committee with the consent of the selectmen quickly decided to set them to work repairing the streets. Thus "a great number of our most indigent inhabitants [were] enabled to earn their bread." The cost was divided between the donations committee and the selectmen. But "mending the pavements" was regarded as only a temporary expedient, since the investment of labor and materials provided no return for future use.[20]

To meet this need for continuing revenue, and to furnish a greater

19. *Boston Town Records, 1770–1777*, pp. 184–185. After the disastrous Boston fire of 1760 Boston had met the calamity in part by successfully seeking outside contributions. See Gerard Bryce Warden, "Boston Politics, 1692–1765," Ph.D. diss., Yale University, 1966, p. 234.

20. William Cooper to ?, Sept. 12, 1774, Massachusetts Historical Society, *Collections*, 4th Ser., IV (Boston, 1858), 68–69n.

variety of jobs, the donations committee, with the consent of the town meeting, rapidly began several more complicated projects. First, a brick factory was set up. By September it was employing more than eighty men a day. The committee hoped to sell the bricks at cost. In addition the committee was having a house constructed partly out of donated materials. This too would be sold. When the few ships under construction were finished, several more would be built to provide employment for the shipbuilding trades. So that work would "be as universal as possible, the Committee have purchased a stock of wool, flax and cotton, to be distributed to all the spinners." Further, they had looms erected for weaving the homespun thread into textiles. Shoemakers were sold leather which they paid for in finished shoes. The committee planned to furnish ropemakers with hemp, and blacksmiths with nail-rods so that they could turn out rope and nails, two staples, throughout the winter. These various projects, requiring a substantial quantity of planning and administration, kept members of the Boston Committee of Correspondence occupied. Its clerk, William Cooper, also clerk of the donations committee, was so busy that he temporarily relinquished his part in the committee of correspondence and John Sweetser, a member, became acting clerk.[21]

An additional responsibility which the donations committee carried was sending letters of thanks to the scores of towns that sent donations. In June the Massachusetts House and the Connecticut assembly had urged their constituents to send donations to Boston, and in September the Continental Congress made a similar recommendation to every colony. As a result, over a period of months hundreds of donations were received in Boston, often accompanied by requests for information on the local state of affairs. The replies of the donations committee, usually written by members of the Boston Committee of Correspondence — Warren, Appleton, Adams — were not merely polite notes of thanks. They carried a political appeal, extending the Boston committee's message to many towns that had experienced no previous contact with Boston.

This message in the summer and fall of 1774 was relatively simple. The cause of Boston, the letters urged, was the cause of America, and the cause of America was liberty. Boston, the committee warned, was

21. *Ibid.*; Boston Committee of Correspondence, minutes, Aug. 18, 1774, Minute Book, IX, 780, New York Public Library, photostats at Massachusetts Historical Society.

merely "the stage on which our tyrants choose to act at present, but how soon they will choose to figure in some spot where they have greater possibility of success." [22] At the moment, they assured their correspondents, Boston's morale remained high in spite of its suffering. Dramatizing Boston's situation, the letters sought to identify other towns in other colonies with it. Nathaniel Appleton wrote to a Connecticut town that "whenever a revenue-chest, a board of commissioners, and a band of pensioners, civil, military and ecclesiastical, shall be stationed in your happy land, you will then realize the public calamity and danger of this oppressed people." [23] Using the same technique of reinforcement which the Boston committee had used with the Massachusetts towns, the donations committee quoted back to the authors remarks included in the letter received in Boston with hearty approval: "your sentiments are perfectly just, that, 'If Boston is subjugated, all British America must fall.' This sentiment cannot be spread too far and wide." [24] Moreover, the significance of the final outcome was greater than the well-being of any town, province, or even all the colonies, since "America is designed by Heaven for an asylum for oppressed and injured virtue, rather than to be a theatre of sport for usurping despots." [25] These sentiments, frequently repeated with variations in the donations committee replies, were identical to the ideas which were being stressed in the letters sent by the committee of correspondence to the other colonies.

At the same time that the Boston committee was seeking to tie Boston to the rest of the continent, hoping to demonstrate conspicuously that Boston would not be isolated or defenseless, the committee continued to urge the rapid establishment of a boycott. Even though Boston's inhabitants were still purchasing British goods, the committee encouraged other colonial ports to enter boycott agreements. This suggestion, strongly urged, even appeared in letters of thanks sent by the donations committee.[26] Though it was clear to everyone that the colonies would not mount a boycott that could have an immediate impact in England, the Boston committee hoped that the threat would at least worry English manufacturers and merchants into supporting colonial relief. To accompany a boycott, the committee planned "a consilatory Address to the

22. Joseph Warren to East Haddam, Conn., Sept. 1, 1774, Mass. Hist. Soc., *Collections*, 4th Ser., IV, 58.
23. Nathaniel Appleton to Brooklyn, Conn., Aug. 22, 1774, *ibid.*, 52.
24. *Ibid.*, 53.
25. Joseph Warren to East Haddam, Conn., Sept. 1, 1774, *ibid.*, 58.
26. Joseph Warren to Norwich, Conn., Aug. 27, 1774, *ibid.*, 47.

Manufacturers of Great Britain."[27] But no address was ever drawn. For although the committee's strategy of a boycott joined with friendly overtures coincided with the plans of leaders in other colonies, it had to await the meeting of the Continental Congress for fruition as colonial policy.

Similarly, the Boston Committee of Correspondence continuously promoted colonial unity, a goal which was being urged everywhere. However the committee possessed neither the recognition nor the constituency necessary for intercolonial leadership, and it tended to outpace the tempo of colonial action. In August, for example, it again anticipated the Continental Congress by inviting Halifax, Quebec, and Montreal to join in the colonial cause. [28] But this early attempt, like the Congress's later Canadian overtures, was rejected.

III

While the Boston committee was actively seeking to bind Boston and Massachusetts in a union with the other colonies, New York, Philadelphia, and Charleston hesitated over strategy. They supported Boston in principle, but in each of these ports leading inhabitants were divided or uncertain. Some were suspicious of both Boston and Massachusetts, others were merely cautious and anxious to deliberate before making any commitments. The committee's contacts in these ports assured Boston that their cities would join in "proper" measures, but that time was needed to bring them to act. Boston, they urged, must be discreet; it must do nothing to confirm hostile suspicions.[29] Boston and Massachusetts should appear as paragons of firmness, order, and restraint. Tumults or riots, it was thought, would compromise Boston's posture, and might even lead to armed conflict. Such events, the committee was informed, would alienate and confuse potential friends of the colonial cause and probably frustrate the movement for union. For these reasons the committee believed Massachusetts must act with restraint. Moreover, since the committee was convinced that the ministry's express design was to isolate Massachusetts by bribing the other colonies in

27. Boston Committee of Correspondence, minutes, July 7, 1774, Minute Book, IX, 771.
28. *Ibid.*, Aug. 12, 1774, Minute Book, 776–777.
29. Miles Brewton to Josiah Quincy, July 12, 1774, *Memoir of Josiah Quincy junior*, ed. Elizabeth S. Quincy (Boston, 1874), 151–153; Josiah Quincy to John Dickinson, Aug. 20, 1774, *ibid.*, 149–151.

one way or another, it was particularly anxious to prevent outbursts of popular anger.

In its official capacity the committee had no responsibility for public order. But because of their special concern, its members worked individually to insure peace and order in Boston. The peace was threatened from several quarters. The troops occupying the town were at least as provocative in the summer of 1774 as they had been in the months preceding the Boston Massacre, and fistfights were equally likely to generate full scale battles. Moreover those who were unemployed by the Port Act and "the poor" tended to be "very difficult" to keep in order.[30] With the troops and warships, the instruments of English "oppression" immediately at hand, restraint was a difficult task for the selectmen and constables. Members of the committee, respected as "patriots," were often able to discourage disorderly behavior even when its purpose might be considered patriotic. Therefore in an informal way local order became another of the committee's responsibilities.

Outside Boston the problem of maintaining order was less acute, but the potential of disorder was equally dangerous. All reports, Tory and Whig, agreed that the height of public ardor in the countryside was unprecedented. This spirit was most frequently expressed by military drilling. Many towns had offered to come to Boston's assistance with force if necessary. As a result every excursion of the troops outside Boston, or any tumults within the town, raised the possibility that dozens of town militia companies would, as several threatened to do, march on Boston and directly engage the regular troops.

Boston and its committee of correspondence could not, of course, do much to regulate or restrain the towns, especially since the capital had come to rely on the country militia for its defense should a crisis occur. Nevertheless a circular which Boston directed the committee to send in late July, did seek to restrain the towns while encouraging them to maintain a firm, uncompromising stand. This circular, prepared for the town meeting by Josiah Quincy, Joseph Greenleaf of the committee, and selectman William Phillips, was primarily intended to inform the towns of the impending arrival of the two Massachusetts Government Acts.[31] But at the same time, it made several other points. First, Boston's

30. Josiah Quincy to Samuel Adams, Aug. 20, 1774, Samuel Adams Papers, New York Public Library.
31. *Boston Town Records, 1770–1777*, p. 186. Samuel Adams was on the letter committee, but he was excused from duty.

misfortunes, the letter stressed again, were being suffered "in a COM-MON CAUSE." Second, in an oblique request for donations, the letter reported that it was the towns that had so far provided *"that countenance and aid,* which have strengthened our hands, *and that bounty which hath* occasioned *smiles on the face of distress."* The question of order was raised indirectly by Boston's assurance that for its own part it would do nothing "unworthy the fame of our ancestors, or inconsistent with our former professions and conduct," and that furthermore Boston looked to the towns for "wisdom, advice and EXAMPLE." These expressions, carrying a double message, called upon towns to remain firm in opposition, but at the same time to be sure that their opposition was rational and not tumultuous.[32] Boston, and the Boston committee, were relying on full continental support, indeed they were expecting it; so peace must be preserved. Moreover, though it was seldom mentioned, it appears to have been generally believed that if any major conflict occurred, Boston, already suffering, would be physically ruined. Therefore restraint was the policy of the Boston town meeting, selectmen, and committee of correspondence.

This policy was severely tested on September 2, the day after the royal government confiscated the province's gunpowder stored at Mystic. For after this incident a report spread that the inhabitants of Boston had been disarmed by the governor's orders. In the retelling the story became exaggerated, and by the time it reached the Connecticut River in the west, and the towns of eastern Connecticut to the south, events had grown into a full scale attack on Boston, including fighting in the streets and a naval bombardment of the town.[33] Town militia companies, anticipating the worst, rapidly formed and began to march on Boston prepared to fight. Excitement had been so high that a rumor provoked the very crisis which the Boston committee had feared.

By eight o'clock on the morning of September 2, three thousand armed men under their regular leaders had collected on Cambridge common. Ten thousand more were reported to be on the road in Middlesex within twenty miles of Boston. Expresses arrived in Boston telling that more "are continually coming down from the country back: that their determination is to collect about forty or fifty thousand by night (which they are sure of accomplishing) when they intend to fling in

32. All from circular on July 26, 1774, *Boston Town Records, 1770–1777,* pp. 186–187.

33. Letter from five hundred men under arms at Pomfret, Conn., Sept. 4, 1774, Boston Committee of Correspondence, Minute Book, X, 826–828.

about fifteen thousand by way of the Neck, and as many more over the ferry: when once got possession, to come in like locusts and rid the town of every soldier." These reports were so dangerous, "so big with mischief and calamity," that the selectmen and committee of correspondence of Charlestown, and the Boston committee, and later the Boston selectmen set out to meet the militia men, hoping to avert the battle.[34]

Joseph Warren, chairman of the Boston committee while Adams was absent at the Continental Congress, described events in a letter to Adams. He had, he said, been informed shortly after six in the morning that "incredible numbers were in arms, and lined the roads from Sudbury to Cambridge." Immediately he summoned the members of the committee, but to avoid spreading the alarm he "judged it best not to inform the person who warned the committee of the business they were to meet upon." As a result they did not hurry to appear, and so "after waiting some time, I took as many of the members as came in my way to Charlestown, fearing that something amiss might take place." At Charlestown the local committee of correspondence urged them to go on with them to Cambridge.[35] When they arrived the immediate crisis had already passed: "Judge Danforth was addressing, perhaps four thousand people in the open air; and such was the order of that great assembly that not a whisper interrupted the low voice of that feeble old man from being heard by the whole body." The rumor of Boston's bombardment had already been overturned, and the gathering was being transformed into a political meeting demanding that officials pledge noncompliance with the Massachusetts Government Acts. The Boston committee's presence was superfluous.[36]

As a result, the Boston committee was merely a spectator to the whole incident. The committee, confined in Boston and thoroughly involved in the solution of local problems, was in no position to exercise decisive influence over the country towns. Although the towns had less appreciation of the need to avoid incidents, and of the need to quietly hold the line while the Congress settled on political strategy, their own self-restraint had proved effective. For if in their excitement townspeople had been hasty in accepting a violent report, they had also maintained

34. John Andrews to William Barrell, Sept. 2, 1774, Massachusetts Historical Society, *Proceedings*, VIII (Boston, 1864-1865), 351-352.

35. Joseph Warren to Samuel Adams, Sept. 4?, 1774, in Richard Frothingham, *Life and Times of Joseph Warren* (Boston, 1865), 355-357.

36. Thomas Young to Samuel Adams, Sept. 4, 1774, Samuel Adams Papers.

sufficient order so that they could reverse their steps and march peacefully home when they were properly informed. None of this was the Boston committee's doing; and for that reason the committee found the whole affair profoundly reassuring.

IV

The rising of September 2, 1774, was more than encouraging to the Boston committee, it was exhilarating. It had tested the popular mood and the structure of provincial responses; and the reactions to a mere rumor fulfilled the committee's long-held aspirations. At Cambridge they had witnessed the proof of the "patience, temperance, and fortitude" of the country people. During the afternoon the people had listened to speeches and "kept their particular stations for three hours in the scorching sun of the hottest day we have had this summer." Their *"patient endurance"* in a posture of determined opposition was ideal. Reports of what had happened in the western counties gave "the most exalted idea of the resolution and intrepidity of the inhabitants." Warren told Adams that "the people from Hampshire County crowded the county of Worcester with armed men; and both counties received the accounts of the quiet dispersion of the people of Middlesex with apparent regret, grudging them the glory of having done something important for their country without their assistance. Had the troops marched only five miles out of Boston, I doubt whether a man would have been saved of their whole number." [37] At Worcester "it was merrily said that had not Worcester men been absent themselves the town would not have held the volunteers. The smallest computation was twenty thousand." Thomas Young, who with Adams had been among the original planners of committees of correspondence, congratulated Adams with the assurance that "the temper of your countrymen [is] in the condition your every wish, your every sigh for years past panted to find it." People in Massachusetts were "thoroughly aroused and unanimously in earnest." [38]

The committee was further encouraged by the activities of the county

37. Joseph Warren to Samuel Adams, Sept. 4?, 1774, in Frothingham, *Warren*, 355–357; Thomas Young to Samuel Adams, Sept. 4, 1774, Samuel Adams Papers.
38. Thomas Young to Samuel Adams, Sept. 4, 1774, Samuel Adams Papers. Later word arrived that in Pomfret, Conn., alone five hundred militia men had gathered to march to Boston's aid. Boston Committee of Correspondence, Minute Book, X, 826–828.

conventions. Though it had itself been a primary leader in Massachusetts for a year and a half, the committee was pleased to yield initiative to the towns which were organizing the conventions. In Suffolk the invitation for a convention had come from Roxbury, Dorchester, Brookline, and Milton—Thomas Hutchinson's old residence. The Boston town meeting, already aware that "some Towns in the Country were about applying for a Meeting of Deputies," had directed the committee of correspondence and the selectmen to appoint a committee of five to attend the county meeting if it should take place. Four of the delegates chosen, Warren, Church, Wendell, and Pitts, were themselves members of the Boston committee.[39] The convention was held at Dedham on August 17.

But though there were sixty delegates present, the Suffolk convention postponed taking any action. Like the first meeting in Worcester County, it was discovered that a number of towns and districts had not been notified of the meeting. Moreover many of the town committees present were "not Specially Authoriz'd to negociate the affairs of a County Congress." As a result the gathering decided that all the towns and districts "should have Special Meetings, (Town or Precinct) to Chuse Delegates." The delegates were particularly anxious "to show our Contempt of the Act of Parliament touching Town Meetings," and they considered their decision to hold special meetings as an especially appropriate way to express their opposition to the act. The convention was said to be "Perfectly Unanimous." The next meeting, now properly constituted, was scheduled for September 6.[40]

But before Suffolk convened again the Boston committee received a request from the Worcester committee calling for a joint meeting of the committees of correspondence from several counties. Worcester had asked to meet with Suffolk and Middlesex committees; but the Boston committee decided to include the port towns of Salem and Marblehead, so that four counties were represented in all.[41] On August 26 and 27 they all met at the Boston committee's regular meeting place, and their proceedings were recorded in the Boston committee's minute book.

Colonel Jeremiah Lee of Salem was chosen to serve as chairman, but

39. Aug. 9, 1774, *Boston Town Records, 1770–1777*, p. 188; Boston Committee of Correspondence, minutes, Aug. 12, 1774, Minute Book, IX, 776–777.

40. All from Benjamin Kent to Samuel Adams, Aug. 20, 1774, Samuel Adams Papers. Thomas Young was disappointed at the lateness of the adjournment. Thomas Young to Samuel Adams, Aug. 19, 1774, *ibid*.

41. Thomas Young to Samuel Adams, Aug. 19, 1774, *ibid*.; Boston Committee of Correspondence, minutes, Aug. 17, 18, 1774, Minute Book, IX, 779–780.

when he declined, Joseph Warren was chosen instead. Then, following discussion the joint committee formally voted that every official affected by the government acts had been "rendered unconstitutional." Therefore, in order to plan appropriate measures to be taken by the province in the "novel and unconstitutional" situation of the courts, a subcommittee was appointed to prepare a report. The subcommittee, including Elbridge Gerry of Marblehead, Timothy Bigelow of Worcester, Captain Thomas Gardner of Cambridge, and two members of the Boston committee, Young and Joseph Greenleaf, was to report the next morning.[42]

Their report was adopted. It called for a provincial congress, which was "necessary for concerting and executing an effectual Plan for counteracting the System of Despotism mentioned, as well as for Substituting Referee Committees during the unconstitutionality of the Courts of Justice."[43] Everyone recognized that the committees of correspondence or even the county conventions could not manage unified measures for defense. It advised that no one was to comply with the government acts and in addition any officials or private persons who attempted to enforce the acts were to be regarded as traitors and should be personally boycotted. To preserve Massachusetts liberties the joint committee recommended that the people of the province ought to study "the Military Art according to the Norfolk Plan."[44] The purpose of these recommendations was to provide a united form of resistance to the government acts and uniform emergency measures for the entire province.

The recommendations of the joint committee were, it subsequently appeared, generally acceptable to the people of Massachusetts. For each of the nine county conventions recommended more or less similar measures, though only four counties had been at the joint meeting. Every convention called for a provincial congress, which had come to be generally regarded as an absolute necessity. They all expressed the same principles, the same desire for a rigorous opposition to the government acts, and they all called for the prevention of "any routs, riots, or licentious attacks upon the property of any persons whatsoever, as being subversive of all order and government."[45]

42. Boston Committee of Correspondence, minutes, Aug. 26, 1774, Minute Book, IX, 780–782.
43. *Ibid.*, Aug. 27, 1774, Minute Book, IX, 782–785.
44. *Ibid.*, 783–785.
45. Lincoln, ed. *Journals of Each Provincial Congress*, 605. For the whole Suffolk proceedings see pages 601–609.

From the Boston committee's viewpoint the resolves of the county conventions and the universal attitude of resistance was ideal. The committee saw no need to make further efforts in that direction. On the contrary the committee's main concern continued to be restraining, moderating the political as well as military ardor of Boston and the province. For as the weeks went by, people all over Massachusetts became more and more impatient with what they regarded as the slow deliberations of the Continental Congress. They were firmly committed to following its directions and they had great faith in its proceedings, but at the same time they were restless.

"The Country is very uneasy," Church warned Adams, "long they cannot be restrained they urge us & threaten to compel us to desert the Town, they swear the Troops shall not continue unmolested . . . ; the utmost extent of their forbearance is limitted to the rising of the Congress." The news that the Continental Congress had adopted the militant resolves of the Suffolk County convention "brightened & invigorated," but the anxiety continued. The countryside was so restless that they were "continually sending Committees down upon one errand or another — which has caus'd the Governor to say, that he can do very well with the Boston Selectmen, but the damn'd country committees plague his soul out, as they are very obstinate and hard to be satisfied." [46] Again and again members of the Boston committee remarked that it had now become their task to restrain the country from over-reacting to offensive incidents. They argued that strategy demanded restraint; that Massachusetts would remain an injured innocent in the minds of colonists and informed Englishmen only so long as it continued on the defensive.

The province recognized this view, accepted it, and stayed quiet. But it was not at all content. Uncertainty over the form of provincial government excited impatience and anxiety. Warren explained the state of opinion to Adams:

Many among us, and almost all in the western counties, are for taking up the old form of government, according to the first charter. It is exceedingly disagreeable to them to think of being obliged to contend with their rulers, and quarrel for their rights every year or two. They think this must always be the case in a government of so heterogeneous a kind as that under

46. Benjamin Church to Samuel Adams, Sept. 29, 1774, Samuel Adams Papers; William Tudor to John Adams, Sept. 26, 1774, John Adams Papers, Mass. Hist. Soc.; John Andrews to William Barrell, Oct. 5, 1774, Mass. Hist. Soc., *Proceedings*, VIII, 373.

which they have lived. They say, too, that no security can be given them that they shall enjoy their estates without molestation, even if the late charter should be again restored in all its parts, since the possession of their lands may be rendered precarious by any alterations in the charter which the parliament shall think fit to make.

Other persons, more especially in the eastern counties, think that it will be trifling to resume the old charter. They say that the connection between the king and the people is dissolved by his breaking the compact made between them; and they have now a right to form what government they please, and make such proposals of a certain limited subjection to the king, as they shall judge convenient, which he may accept or reject as he pleases.[47]

Thomas Young reported that even "the cautious Major Hawley is strongly convinced of the necessity of resuming the Old Charter." In addition Young described the thoughts of the people in the western counties with considerably more detail than Warren. The detail revealed a significant degree of dissatisfaction with the traditional politics of the province:

They say we can never be easy in the condition we have been in for years past — that our privileges are just enough to tempt a British Minister to attack us; and that tho' we should now come to a temporary compromise, a creature of the Minister having all posts of honor and profit in his disposal will still have it in his power to draw many aside from their duty to their Country — that when they have finished a war with a foreign enemy they ought to enjoy some leisure to improve the arts of civil life and not be held in one eternal political jangle; rankling their minds and destroying their greatest bliss of society, a union of sentiment and endeavor to render our public and private interests one and the same thing. They observe further that being the natural butt of ministerial jealousy and resentment we ought to be in the best condition to frustrate their machinations against us — this they say is impossible while a party is so easily made of the most powerful men in every County and even town against the common People.[48]

The charter which had recently ruled the province, it was agreed, had inherent defects. They could only be remedied by a return to the old charter in which the governor was elected; or, since Massachusetts had been set adrift in the state of nature, a new government could be formed. In any case something should be done. Massachusetts found the state of nature disquieting.[49]

47. Joseph Warren to Samuel Adams, Sept. 12, 1774 [should be dated Sept. 14, 1774], in Frothingham, *Warren*, 375–376.
48. Thomas Young to Samuel Adams, Sept. 4, 1774, Samuel Adams Papers.
49. See William Tudor to John Adams, Sept. 3, 1774, John Adams Papers; Joseph Warren to Samuel Adams, Sept. 4?, 1774, in Frothingham, *Warren*, 355–357;

Yet in spite of the pressure to form a new government, or at least resume the old charter, the members of the Boston committee continued to exercise their powers of restraint. Adams had advised them that any formal change in the government initiated by the people would alarm the Continental Congress and suggest that Massachusetts was not merely on the defensive. Firm, defensive opposition was the Congress' tacit demand. Moreover, Adams, pointing to the differences which had already emerged over what form to adopt, warned that the effort to form a government might destroy the unity which was so vital to defense. Adams urged that they proceed according to the recent charter insofar as they were able. As a result when the Provincial Congress took up business, the Boston representatives, three of whom belonged to the Boston committee, were said to be "by far the most moderate men." [50]

V

As soon as the Provincial Congress met in early October it extinguished whatever remaining need existed for Boston committee leadership. Enjoying the unanimous confidence and support of Massachusetts, it was fully capable and anxious to exert whatever direction the province needed. Partly for this reason the activities of the Boston committee became even more locally oriented. As it had been doing since midsummer, the committee continued to work to maintain the peace in Boston.

This task had become primarily the prevention of serious attacks on the persons and property of those sympathetic to the royal government. A "Hillsborough treat," the "desecration" of a building with buckets of waste, was permissible as a token of contempt, and also impossible to prevent. But the selectmen and the committee drew the line there, prohibiting physical reprisals on persons and property. When a merchant sold the troops a quantity of cannon and stores it created a small

Benjamin Kent to Robert Treat Paine, Sept. 15, 1774, Robert Treat Paine Papers, Massachusetts Historical Society; John Pitts to Samuel Adams, Oct. 16, 1774, Samuel Adams Papers.

50. Samuel Adams to Joseph Warren, Philadelphia, Sept. 24, 1774, *Warren-Adams Letters, Being Chiefly a Correspondence among John Adams, Samuel Adams, and James Warren*, Massachusetts Historical Society, *Collections*, LXXII–LXXIII (Boston, 1917–1925), III, 156–157; John Adams to William Tudor, Philadelphia, Sept. 29, 1774, William Tudor Papers, Massachusetts Historical Society; *Boston Town Records, 1770–1777*, p. 191, Cushing and Samuel Adams were absent at Philadelphia; John Pitts to Samuel Adams, Oct. 16, 1774, Samuel Adams Papers.

crisis, and the committee together with others had been hard pressed to prevent bloodshed. But in spite of the "many private insults we receive," and though Boston felt it was being treated as an enemy, the leaders of the capital succeeded in preventing serious conflicts.[51]

The committee of correspondence also worked with the selectmen in seeking a more generous administration of Boston's blockade from Governor Gage. When the governor refused to permit easy passage of supplies into Boston, the committee called a joint meeting with the committees of a dozen other towns. To retaliate they decided that the colonists, especially the residents of neighboring towns, should refuse to supply the troops with "labour, lumber, joice, spars, pickets, straw, bricks," or anything else which might be used to "annoy" the inhabitants.[52] This withholding of labor and supplies was intended to halt the erection of barracks. For a number of weeks it succeeded, until Gage imported labor and supplies from New York.

This "supply boycott," designed to force Governor Gage to relieve Boston's material wants, was carried out by means of a circular letter. It was sent out by the Boston committee acting for the joint committee as it had earlier done. The circular specifically advised that in the joint committee's opinion, "committees of observation and prevention should be appointed by each town." Specific recommendations were given to eight neighboring towns represented in the joint committee that they make particular efforts to see that the boycott was "faithfully executed."[53] The committees of correspondence, flexible in their duties, were turning toward the administration of resistance measures.

This labor and materials boycott, initiated before the Provincial Congress met, was the Boston committee's final circular letter. Its concern with the practical distresses being suffered in Boston was characteristic of the Boston committee's immediate local involvement during the autumn of 1774. It quickly relinquished a wider role since its larger concerns and activities had been taken up by large representative assemblies.

In December news arrived that the Continental Congress had adopted

51. John Andrews to William Barrell, Sept. 27, 1774, Mass. Hist. Soc., *Proceedings*, VIII, 368-369; Joseph Warren to Samuel Adams, Sept. 29, 1774, in Frothingham, *Warren*, 381-382; Joseph Greenleaf to Robert Treat Paine, Sept. 27, 1774, Robert Treat Paine Papers.
52. Joint committee circular broadside of Sept. 27, 1774, "At a Meeting of the several Committees of the Towns of Boston, Roxbury, Dorchester, Watertown, Charlestown, Cambridge, Mistick, Dedham, Milton, Malden, Braintree, Woburn, and Stow . . . ," Massachusetts Historical Society.
53. *Ibid.*

a Continental Association for a total boycott of British goods. In Massachusetts the Provincial Congress immediately voted supporting measures and distributed broadsides of its resolves to the towns for their direction. They were all to elect "Committees of Inspection" if they did not already have them, to see that the association was properly enforced.[54] For most Massachusetts towns this direction meant that their committees of correspondence were enlarged and assigned the additional duties of inspection to enforce the boycott. In Boston a separate committee of inspection composed of seventy-four members was formed, including eleven members of the committee of correspondence. As a result the original identity of the Boston committee, already vague, disappeared.

On December 7, 1774, the Boston town meeting voted unanimously "that the Committee of Correspondence now subsists & that they continue their good services, till the farther Order of the Town." The spirit of this "vote of confidence," declaring that the committee did still exist, contrasted sharply with the warm praise the committee had received six months earlier when its members had been asked to "persevere with their usual Activity & Firmness, continuing stedfast in the Way of well Doing."[55] For though the town officially recognized that the Boston committee still managed to "subsist," in its original form it had ceased to exist. Circumstances had first altered, then eliminated the committee's role in provincial politics. The original members, the men who had conceived and led the committee, were now engaged in other activities. Adams spent his energy on the Continental Congress or the Provincial Congress, where he was joined by Warren, Church, and Appleton. Otis, the original chairman, was in retirement owing to his mental illness. Quincy had gone to England on a diplomatic mission for the colonies. Young had moved to Providence, and Joseph Greenleaf had left Boston to settle temporarily in Taunton. Molineux had died in October, Thus, although the town retained a committee of correspondence until 1778, when it was reorganized as a committee of correspondence and inspection, its life as an initiator of political activity in Massachusetts had ended. Possessing no independent identity, the committee had become just another town body performing administrative tasks for the Boston town meeting during the Revolution.

54. Provincial Congress broadside of Dec. 5, 1774, "In Provincial Congress, Cambridge, December 5, 1774. Resolved, That the Proceedings of the American Continental Congress, held at Philadelphia on the Fifth of September last . . . ," Massachusetts Historical Society.
55. *Boston Town Records, 1770–1777*, pp. 205, 178.

By the end of 1774, barely two years after it had first been created, the Boston Committee of Correspondence had become obsolete. The Revolutionary movement in Massachusetts possessed a life of its own, and it had now passed beyond the early stages of expressing opposition and arousing resistance. With the province in open rebellion against parliamentary authority, the reordering of the structures of politics and government had begun. In this crisis, the activity at the local level proved decisive.

The towns, after all, possessed both a stable structure and uninterrupted authority. During the summer they had constituted the sole effective government in the province. Now, as their delegates flocked to the Provincial Congress, the political conceptions that had ruled Massachusetts in the summer became embodied in the Congress, an omnicompetent assembly which reflected the experience of the defunct General Court, but which ruled through the power of local consent. In this reconstitution of government conditions were fluid, and the province possessed no thoroughly rationalized plan. That would come later. The revolution, however, had swept past a critical, perhaps irreversible point. All power now derived directly and immediately from the people. At the level of day-to-day behavior, a republic had been established in Massachusetts.[56]

56. This interpretation coincides with that presented by Harry A. Cushing, *History of the Transition from Provincial to Commonwealth Government in Massachusetts*, Columbia University Studies in History, Economics and Public Law, VII, no. 1 (New York, 1896), 74–75, and Oscar and Mary F. Handlin, *Commonwealth: Massachusetts, 1774–1861* (New York, 1947), 1–3.

10

Epilogue: Provincial Congress to Constitutional Republic

When the Provincial Congress first convened in October 1774, circumstances were profoundly unsettled. Massachusetts was without a fixed government or a written constitution, its capital was occupied and under blockade, and the political deadlock with Britain promised a lengthy battle. Whether it would be a bloodless commercial struggle or a violent civil war, no one was certain. In any case the Massachusetts polity would be severely tested. Massachusetts, many believed, had returned to the "state of nature," to the primitive condition where society was potential, not actual, its future character contingent on the will of the people.

Six years later Massachusetts inaugurated Governor John Hancock as its first chief executive under a new constitution. Hancock, the outlaw of 1774, became successor to the royal governors by the nearly unanimous vote of his fellow citizens. After six years of quasi-legal interim arrangements, the people had created the Commonwealth of Massachusetts, a carefully rationalized structure for republican government. Under wartime conditions, and in spite of severe economic problems, the inhabitants of Massachusetts had systematically analyzed questions of representative government, and after rejecting one constitution, they had settled on a structure which was to prove both stable and durable.

At the time, of course, no one knew whether the new structure would survive and flourish, or whether it would ultimately lead to division and disorder. But in spite of the war that dragged on, in spite of recurrent financial crises, the inhabitants of Massachusetts were optimistic. For the past six years they had effectively employed the principles of popular sovereignty and government by consent under conditions of extreme pressure. They had maintained a working unity throughout the state, while at the same time local participation in provincial affairs was intense and all-pervasive. Herein lay a structure of attitudes and behavior that would secure the foundations of the new government. For although the new constitution was an artificial device, it grew out of the broad political awareness which had for years been developing; it was organically related to Massachusetts political experience.

I

Strictly speaking, the constitutional crisis lasted from the fall of 1774 until June 1780, when the new constitution was formally proclaimed. In the interim Massachusetts was governed by the towns, first in conjunction with the Provincial Congress, and then after August 1775, with the General Court. Under the latter arrangement, the charter of 1692, minus its royal elements, became the frame of government, with the Council exercising executive power in place of a governor. This structure, although never wholly satisfactory, did give Massachusetts a quasi-constitutional republic in which the powers and functions of government operated according to familiar definitions. Moreover it encouraged the elaboration and development of patterns of local activism and consent which had emerged in 1773 and 1774.

During this period central government possessed few sanctions, so it necessarily relied on consent. This reality was dramatically illustrated by the Provincial Congress in March 1775, when it was forced to cope with tax delinquents by merely "recommending" and "urging" that towns pay their taxes. The Congress could not threaten since it wielded no penalties. If towns failed to comply they would be asked for an explanation of their action, that was all.[1] The power to tax, the most critical element of authority, rested with each individual town.

Several months later, when the General Court assembled under the truncated charter, the power of central government was substantially restored, but more in theory than in practice. Local consent remained

---

1. William Lincoln, ed., *The Journals of Each Provincial Congress of Massachusetts in 1774 and 1775* . . . (Boston, 1838), 113–114.

crucial, as the General Court recognized by immediately extending the right of representation to every community that had been represented in the Provincial Congress.[2] Thereafter, at every stage leading to the formation of the Constitution of 1780 the General Court employed plebiscitary methods in which individual towns and voters exercised constituent power.

Moreover this pattern emanated largely from the towns rather than the General Court. The legislature did originate the idea of town plebiscites when it requested local decisions on the large question of American independence in May 1776, but it was only in response to local pressures, coming particularly from western towns, that the Court decided to ask towns if they wanted a new constitution drawn up and if they wanted the Court to prepare it. Furthermore, if left to itself, the General Court would not have submitted this constitution to the towns for ratification. But the majority of towns insisted on exercising the right to pass judgment on any proposed constitution. As a result, instead of routinely becoming established as the fundamental law of Massachusetts, the constitution that was prepared in 1777–1778 was submitted to the people, and they rejected it by the overwhelming margin of five to one.[3] Here the vitality of individual consent was effectively expressed by the plebiscitary method.

The reasons why the Constitution of 1778 was rejected were diverse, varying considerably from town to town. Many objected to the absence of a bill of rights; while some were reluctant to accept a document which provided no means for its own amendment. Others complained that because representation in the General Court was inequitable, the constitution it had prepared was unfair. Indeed a few towns believed that the entire structure was so misshapen and so seriously flawed as to be extremely dangerous.[4] People in Massachusetts wanted a new consti-

2. Act of August 23, 1775, in Oscar and Mary F. Handlin, eds., *The Popular Sources of Political Authority: Documents on the Massachusetts Constitution of 1780* (Cambridge, Mass., 1966), 59–60.

3. Harry A. Cushing, *History of the Transition from Provincial to Commonwealth Government in Massachusetts*, Studies in History, Economics and Public Law, Columbia University, VII, no. 1 (New York, 1896), 182; Handlins, eds., *Popular Sources*, 88–168; Samuel E. Morison, "The Vote of Massachusetts on Summoning a Constitutional Convention, 1776–1916," Massachusetts Historical Society, *Proceedings*, L (1916–1917), 244.

4. This view is based on a reading of the returns printed in Handlins, eds., *Popular Sources*, 202–365. It coincides generally with the Handlins' judgment (*Popular Sources*, 22), and that of Harry A. Cushing (*History of the Transition*, 216–226).

tution, but they remained discriminating and they were prepared to reject the work of the General Court and start again.

One question that was raised both before and after the General Court drafted this constitution was whether it could ever be an appropriate body to prepare the anterior, fundamental law of the commonwealth. In the autumn of 1776 a number of towns had specifically rejected the General Court's proposal to write a constitution on these very grounds. Several believed that constitutional proposals should originate in the towns, and that a single draft should be prepared by means of special county conventions followed by a statewide convention.[5] Some kind of special convention, created for the single purpose of constitution-making was a live possibility as early as 1776, and after towns had reviewed the handiwork of the General Court the idea gained increasing support. A constitutional convention, it was believed, could more faithfully represent the wishes of Massachusetts and could deliberate free of the pressures of running the state. Consequently when the effort to write a constitution was renewed in 1779, it was generally agreed that a special convention would be created, instead of merely empowering the representatives to do the job.

This second attempt began almost immediately after the towns rejected the Constitution of 1778. In February 1779 the House of Representatives resolved that town meetings be called to consider two questions: whether the people presently wanted to have a new form of government created; and if they did, whether they would empower their representatives to call "a State Convention, for the sole Purpose of forming a new Constitution."[6] Although the General Court did not move in the direction of town-prepared drafts or county conventions, the concept of active local participation was an integral part of the entire project. Thereafter, throughout the proceedings of the constitutional convention, delegates made a persistent effort to reconcile the abstract principles of constitutional theory with the varied and sometimes divisive proposals which came from towns and even a few county conventions.

The interlocking issues of consent and local participation were not, however, easily settled. During the entire period from 1775 to 1780, the constitutional questions that aroused the most passionate and divisive

5. Handlins, eds., *Popular Sources*, e.g., Stoughton (p. 106), Norton (pp. 124–125), Attleborough (pp. 143–144), Bellingham (pp. 160–162); see also Cushing, *History of the Transition*, 192–193.
6. Resolve of February 20, 1779, in Handlins, eds., *Popular Sources*, 383–384.

controversy were not the classic issues of the separation of powers or their distribution between the executive and legislative branches, but rather representation and centralization. Representation and centralization, the problem of reconciling the principles and practice of consent and local participation with unified state government, was the most difficult problem the constitutional convention faced. The issue of representation was particularly complex because three potentially antagonistic theories circulated, one saying that persons alone should be represented, another arguing that persons and property must be represented, and a third view that persons organized as communities — towns — should be the constituent elements in the legislature. Since each of these ideas promised practical benefits for different kinds of towns, debates over representation tended to assume a sectional character. The same tendency existed in the controversy over centralization, because centralization was often seen as favoring eastern towns at the expense of towns in the west.

The resolution of these conflicts was not to be found in any convenient state-wide consensus, but the convention did find solutions. Its ability to respond to local variations and create a consensus where none had existed is best illustrated in its formula for legislative apportionment, a formula that compromised by blending in a single legislature the three contradictory theories of constituent power. The convention could not, of course, resolve all of Massachusetts' political conflicts, and its success in achieving consensus even on the constitution was limited. But it was sufficient. When the Constitution of 1780 was submitted to the populace it was approved.[7]

The ratification of the constitution by the towns was, in a sense, the culmination of the process the Boston committee had begun in 1772 when it sought to engage the towns actively in provincial affairs. But in 1773 and 1774 the towns had merely been publicly stating their positions; now they were determining policy in a direct fashion. Over the years the breadth and intensity of local involvement had developed so that, by 1780, the vast majority of towns took an active part. The abstract ideal which Whigs of 1772 cherished had now become practical politics in Massachusetts.

The voluminous returns from the towns (about 180 have survived)

7. Handlins, eds., *Popular Sources*, 25–26; Samuel E. Morison, "The Struggle Over the Adoption of the Constitution of Massachusetts, of 1780," *Massachusetts Historical Society, Proceedings*, L (1916–1917), 399–401.

also illustrate another central element in Massachusetts revolutionary politics, the ability to contain diverse opinions within a general consensus. For although the returns exhibited sharp differences on some constitutional questions, especially the terms of the religious establishment, they also displayed broad areas of agreement on the shape of the new government with its bicameral legislature. The assumptions which lay behind the idea of a controlling written constitution, like the assumptions underlying the provision for annual elections, were fundamental to Massachusetts experience as well as ideology, and they provided the basis for agreement on the character of republican government.

Yet traditional elements in Massachusetts politics were not immediately extinguished. Old ideas and patterns of behavior were passing out of existence, but they sometimes lingered. In election sermons, for example, clergymen would still occasionally refer to magistrates as "fathers," even though public officials were much more commonly described as "servants" of the people and the public good.[8] The old vocabulary of politics was not simply erased from people's minds, but the old conception of a stable polity was shattered, and with it the idea that the people or the towns should play a passive role, merely offering their tacit consent to government decisions.[9] Though there was no cataclysm, a new ideal had been established, a new direction set toward the realization of a government that operated continuously by means of the actual consent of participating citizens.

At the level of practical politics the pattern was much the same. Town participation in the General Court did not undergo any radical transformation. Prior to 1773 a bare majority of towns had, on the average, sent representatives to the legislature; between 1773 and 1780 the percentage rose, but only to 60 percent. Even in 1776, the peak year of local participation in the General Court, just a little more than 70 percent of the towns sent representatives, and in 1778 and 1779 the percentage dipped to the pre-Revolutionary level. Partly this may be explained by objective conditions: some towns in Maine were under British control, and the wartime demands on local leadership and resources were so extreme as to make representation a substantial burden.

8. Samuel West, *A Sermon Preached before the Honorable Council . . . May 29th, 1776* (Boston, 1776), 68; Samuel Stillman, *A Sermon Preached before the Honorable Council . . . May 26, 1779* (Boston, 1779), 20.

9. Samuel Webster, *A Sermon Preached before the Honorable Council . . . May 28, 1777* (Boston, 1777), 23–24; Simeon Howard, *A Sermon Preached before the Honourable Council . . . May 31, 1780* (Boston, 1780), 39; Jonas Clarke, *A Sermon Preached before His Excellency . . . May 30, 1781* (Boston, 1781), 29.

At the same time it is clear that involvement in state politics was slackening, and that the self-absorption which was traditional in local politics was reappearing. In Middlesex County, where the percentage of towns represented in the legislature dropped from 92 percent in 1776 down to 52 percent in 1778 and 1779, this phenomenon is especially apparent.[10] Hardship may have played some role in this precipitate decline, but the fact that the immediate crisis had passed and the first ardor cooled was far more important. Sending a delegate cost money, and in some small towns it was still seen as an expense which was justified only under special circumstances. Participation in state government, in extralocal affairs generally, had not yet become an accepted, routine matter. Clearly, the vigorous controversy over legislative apportionment did not mean that now, suddenly, every town would actively exercise its right to participate in state government.

However in the western counties of Worcester, Hampshire, and Berkshire, the Revolution did produce a significant rise in the level of engagement in Massachusetts affairs. Throughout the debates surrounding the constitution the west exercised an influential role, and western participation in the General Court rose substantially.[11] In Berkshire the rise was particularly dramatic: whereas prior to 1773 an average of 22 percent of Berkshire towns sent delegates to the General Court, this percentage nearly doubled to 42 percent between 1773 and 1780, and it climbed to 57 percent in 1776. Berkshire still lagged behind eastern counties, but it had gained ground. If participation in the General Court was any yardstick, Berkshire was being integrated into the new structure of Massachusetts politics, painfully perhaps, but nonetheless integrated. Berkshire represents an extreme case, and yet its experience was characteristic of the kind of revolutionary change that was occurring in Massachusetts. In Berkshire, as elsewhere, the change was incomplete even by 1780, but the realities of the new situation and the new ideal of active participation in a government that actually ruled by consent were shaping a new pattern of behavior.

10. These percentages were compiled from the lists of representatives which appear in *The Acts and Resolves, Public and Private of the Province of the Massachusetts Bay* . . . , XIX, XX, and XXI (Boston, 1918-1922), in conjunction with the lists of towns on the tax lists in the same series, IV and V (Boston, 1886-1890). In referring to the average for the years prior to 1773 the period 1765-1772 (inclusive) is used.

11. This view has been argued by Robert J. Taylor, *Western Massachusetts in the Revolution* (Providence, 1954). The percentages referred to below are, as above, compiled from the *Acts and Resolves*, and 1765-1772 is the period prior to 1773.

II

The Boston Committee of Correspondence, obviously, was only one factor in this large and complicated revolutionary process. Yet its brief life, its swift rise and its equally swift disappearance, do raise important questions about the character of politics in Revolutionary Massachusetts. Was the Boston committee the vehicle of the opposition party as Hutchinson and Oliver believed, losing its purpose when the Boston Whigs came to power? Was it, as George Bancroft believed, the instrument that first revealed the breadth and depth of popular ideas of liberty? Or was it, as some have argued, a propaganda machine, discarded when its propagandizing goals had been realized? Conceivably, the Boston committee was in some measure all of these, but it was also something more. It was an integrating force in Massachusetts politics, acting to raise the level of local awareness and participation in general concerns.

Governor Hutchinson's estimate that the Boston committee was hostile to his politics and that its leaders stood consistently in opposition to him cannot be disputed. The committee was indeed a vehicle that the Boston Whigs used to oppose the administration he headed. But its purposes were broader than merely resisting the Hutchinson administration. The committee continually promoted a coherent political message based on a particular concept of constitutional liberty and public virtue. This message, originally derived from the writings of Radical Whigs in England and reinforced by provincial experience, was generally accepted in the province. Hutchinson was not, as he thought, the ultimate target of the Boston committee; he was merely a willful if superficial obstacle to the realization of the committee's cherished political ideal.

Certainly the committee acted as a propaganda machine. Its purpose was never to merely inform, but to provide information which encouraged the province to join in its conclusions. Every message it ever sent may be described as propaganda. Yet the committee was evangelizing rather than manipulating popular opinion. The evidence leaves little doubt that the members of the committee, whether Adams, Warren, Young, Joseph Greenleaf, or any of the others, themselves believed the propaganda they preached. As they saw it, the Boston committee was no self-conscious propaganda machine — it was an engine of political truth. From their standpoint the governor's speeches, the speeches of the judges to the grand juries, and the other administration efforts to promote its own opinions were propaganda. Engaged in a competition for popular support, the committee's propagandizing activities are most accurately described as persuasion rather than manipulation.

Moreover the nature of the Massachusetts response to the committee's appeals strongly suggests that people already believed its essential message. The committee of correspondence does not appear to have converted Massachusetts to its own views, but rather to have stimulated townspeople to express their own similar beliefs. Before this process began, no one could be sure what the people believed. Both the governor and the opposition were confident that most people shared their own basic assumptions concerning provincial government. After the responses to the Boston pamphlet came in, doubts vanished; it was clear that the Boston Committee of Correspondence did not merely reflect the views of a faction of opposition politicians. It reflected the general beliefs of Massachusetts inhabitants. George Bancroft, himself an inheritor of the tradition of a republic grounded on popular virtue, interpreted this process as the revelation of a general spirit of liberty.

The role of the Boston Committee of Correspondence in these complicated events should not be exaggerated. As an institution it was certainly far less powerful or influential than either the General Court or the Provincial Congress. Its leaders were active in both the assembly and the congress; for them the Boston committee seems to have been no more than a temporary device which lost its *raison d'être* once the towns of Massachusetts had openly assumed the responsibility of defending the constitution. Nevertheless during a brief time the committee had exercised an important role in the process whereby local communities recognized and asserted their own political power.

This process of developing local involvement in the larger concerns of provincial and continental politics did not, of course, start fresh in 1772 nor was it complete in 1774 or even 1780. The integration of local politics with extralocal affairs was a gradual, uneven process connected to the cycle of community growth and maturation and stretching far into the nineteenth century. The experience of the Boston committee itself demonstrated that by the early 1770's the process had already reached an advanced stage in many towns, though it is equally clear that the activities of the committee frequently quickened local involvement. The experience of the committee also illustrates that Britain played the decisive role in creating widespread awareness and concern for issues of broader significance than the location of meetinghouses and roads.

245

For it was the Crown and Parliament which from the 1760's onward generated issues arousing widespread local interest and participation. In Massachusetts, it seems, this local involvement reached a peak between late 1774 and early 1776. Then virtually every town acted in relation to the crisis — sending deputies to the Provincial Congress and the General Court, enforcing the continental boycott association, preparing its militia. Subsequently there was a falling off, but still the majority of towns remained active. The formation and ratification of the Constitution of 1780 were to establish and regularize the new pattern of local involvement, bringing political practice into line with political theory.

In this context one can hardly assess the lasting impact of the Boston Committee of Correspondence with any precision. In 1773 the committee clearly exercised a decisive role in arousing local activity, but later its influence on the pattern of behavior declined. From a historian's viewpoint the direct impact of the committee is perhaps less important than what its experience revealed about the existing conditions of political culture in Massachusetts — that in the crisis of constitutional authority the mechanisms, the capacity, and the outlook necessary for general political participation all existed and could be readily called into play.

Until the emergence of the Boston committee, however, these circumstances were not generally recognized by contemporaries. The activity of the committee stimulated an increased awareness of these characteristics as well as a shift in contemporary attitudes regarding political roles — a democratization — in which everyone was believed to have an active part in politics, every town and every individual. After six generations Massachusetts was turning away from the traditional ideal of active leaders with passive followers toward the radical goal of an alert, actively engaged populace.

Implied in this shift was a movement away from the old conception of a balance between the rulers and the people. Instead the tendency which emerged visibly in 1773 and 1774 and which was established by 1780 was to destroy the balance, placing the people over their rulers, who came to be regarded as instruments of popular will much more than leaders of it. Certainly the Boston Committee of Correspondence was not responsible for these changes; indeed it appears that the entire Revolution was only one episode in a long-term movement which began in the seventeenth century and continued well into the nineteenth century. But the Revolution was a critical episode, decisively shifting the balance in favor of popular representative government. In Massachusetts the Boston committee's primary function had been to call forth at the local level an articulation and rationalization of this process which would not otherwise have occurred.[12] As Samuel Adams later remarked, the committee had "raised the Spirits of the People, drawn off their attention from *picking up pins*, and directed their Views to great objects."[13] Indeed this was the central importance of the Boston Committee of Correspondence. It was a primary agent in a general process of self-revelation in the months culminating in overt rebellion. It led townspeople everywhere to realize at virtually the same moment that they all shared the same fundamental political beliefs, in which sovereignty lay with the people in the most concrete, immediate sense. This realization was the essence of the Revolution in Massachusetts and from it flowed the creation of republican government.

12. This judgment is based on a comparison of Massachusetts local proceedings in 1774 with those of Connecticut towns. In Connecticut the legislature called the towns to consider action, and while they generally acted in a manner similar to Massachusetts towns, they did not elaborate their political beliefs, but simply repeated the conventional phrase or two taken from the assembly resolve calling on them to act.

13. Samuel Adams to James Warren, Philadelphia, May 12, 1776, *Warren-Adams Letters, Being Chiefly a Correspondence among John Adams, Samuel Adams, and James Warren,* Massachusetts Historical Society, *Collections,* LXXII–LXXIII (1917–1925), I, 244–245.

Appendix

Bibliography

Index

Massachusetts Towns and Districts, 1772

(Italicized towns are part of the sample referred to in Chapter 5.)

BARNSTABLE

Barnstable
Chatham
Eastham
Falmouth
Harwich
Sandwich
Truro
Wellfleet
Yarmouth

BERKSHIRE

Alford
Becket
East Hoosuck
Egremont
Gageborough
Great Barrington
Jerico
Lanesborough
Lenox
New Marlborough
Partridgefield
Pittsfield
Plantation Hartwood
Plantation No. 5

Plantation No. 7
Richmond
Sandisfield
Sheffield
Stockbridge
Tyringham
Tyringham Equivalent
Williamstown

BRISTOL

Attleborough
Berkley
Dartmouth
Dighton
Easton
Freetown
Mansfield
Norton
Raynham
Rehoboth
Swanzey with Shawamet
Taunton

CUMBERLAND

Brunswick
Cape Elizabeth

Falmouth
Gorham
Harpswell
New Boston
New Gloucester
North Yarmouth
Piersontown
Scarborough
Windham

DUKES

Chilmark
Edgartown
Tisbury

ESSEX

Almsbury
Andover
Beverly
Boxford
Bradford
Danvers
Gloucester
Haverhill
Ipswich
Lynn

251

Marblehead
Methuen
Middleton
Manchester
Newbury
Newburyport
Rowley
Salem
Salisbury
Topsfield
Wenham

HAMPSHIRE

Amherst
Ashfield
Belchertown
Bernardston
Blanford
Brimfield
Charlemont
Chesterfield
Colrain
Conway
Deerfield
Granby
Granville
Greenfield
Greenwich
Hadley
Hatfield
Monson
Montague
Murrayfield
New Salem
Northampton
Northfield
Palmer
Pelham
Shelburne
Shutesbury
South Brimfield
South Hadley
Southampton
Southwick
Springfield

Sunderland
Ware
Warwick
Westfield
Whatley
Willbraham
Williamsburgh
Worthington

LINCOLN

Bowdoinham
Boothbay
Bristol
Broadbay
Gardinerstown
Georgetown
Hallowell
Medumcook
Newcastle
Pownallborough
St. George
Topsham
Vassallborough
Winslow
Winthrop
Woolwich

MIDDLESEX

Acton
Ashby
Bedford
Billerica
Cambridge
Charlestown
Chelmsford
Concord
Dracut
Dunstable
Framingham
Groton
Holliston
Hopkinston
Lexington
Lincoln

Littleton
Malden
Marlborough
Medford
Natick
Newton
Pepperell
Reading
Sherburne
Shirley
Stoneham
Stow
Sudbury
Tewksbury
Townshend
Waltham
Watertown
Westford
Weston
Wilmington
Woburn

NANTUCKET

Sherburne

PLYMOUTH

Abington
Bridgwater
Duxbury
Halifax
Hanover
Kingston
Marshfield
Middleborough
Pembroke
Plymouth
Plymton
Rochester
Scituate
Warham

SUFFOLK

Bellingham
Boston

APPENDIX

Braintree
Brookline
Chelsea
Cohasset
Dedham
Dorchester
Hingham
Hull
Medfield
Medway
Milton
Needham
Roxbury
Stoughton
Stoughtonham District
Walpole
Weymouth
Wrentham

WORCESTER

Ashburnham
Athol
Bolton
Brookfield

Charlton
Douglas
Dudley
Fitchburgh
Grafton
Hardwick
Harvard
Holden
Hubbardstown
Lancaster
Leicester
Leominster
Lunenburgh
Mendon
New Braintree
Northborough
Oakham
Oxford
Paxton
Petersham
Princeton
Royalston
Rutland
Rutland District
Shrewsbury

Southborough
Spencer
Sturbridge
Sutton
Templeton
Upton
Uxbridge
Westborough
Western
Westminster
Winchendon
Worcester

YORK

Arundel
Berwick
Biddeford
Buxton
Kittery
Lebanon
Pepperrellborough
Sanford
Wells
York

Source: *The Acts and Resolves, Public and Private, of the Province of the Massachusetts Bay*, V (Boston, 1886), 307–317.

Bibliography

The central sources for this study are the records of the Boston Committee of Correspondence and the town meeting records of just over one hundred towns. The Boston committee records include both its formal minutes and its correspondence. These documents comprise nearly 2,000 folio pages and are located in the George Bancroft Collection at the New York Public Library. The Massachusetts Historical Society possesses the numbered photostatic copies from which I worked. The committee's minutes are arranged chronologically, and the letters and town proceedings the committee received are grouped alphabetically by town of origin. The town meeting records are in most cases located in the town or city clerk's office of the respective locality, although for the period that I examined, 1765–1775, the records of fourteen towns are also published.

Next in importance have been the letters of various members of the committee, especially Samuel Adams, Joseph Warren, and Thomas Young. Most of the surviving Adams letters have been collected and published by Harry A. Cushing, although a few others exist among the Adams Papers at the New York Public Library and among the Adams-Warren Papers at the Massachusetts Historical Society (published in the *Adams-Warren Letters* cited below). Other Adams letters are scattered. Most of Joseph Warren's letters, also at the New York Public Library, have been published by Richard Frothingham in his *Life and Times of Joseph Warren*. The few letters by Thomas Young which survive are divided among the John Lamb Papers at the New-York Historical Society, the Samuel Adams Papers at the New York Public Library, and the miscellaneous collection of bound documents at the Massachusetts Historical Society. The letters of both Warren and Young are often exceptionally detailed and candid.

For an understanding of the royal government's reaction to the committees of correspondence, Thomas Hutchinson's extensive papers are indispensable. His letter books fill three volumes at the Massachusetts Archives; the Massachusetts Historical Society has typescript copies. These letters furnish much information about events as well as Governor Hutchinson's reactions to them.

Newspapers, generally speaking, contain little information about either the Boston committee or the town committees of correspondence. They were useful for background material, and in several instances Richard Draper's *Boston Weekly News-Letter* provided information not available elsewhere concerning opposition to committees of correspondence. The broadsides relating to the committee's efforts were consulted at the Massachusetts Historical Society.

The list of secondary works is not exhaustive. It includes only those titles which I actually used in some positive way, not every work I consulted.

I. PRIMARY SOURCES

A. MANUSCRIPTS

Boston Public Library, Boston, Massachusetts
American Revolution manuscripts.
William Brattle's notes of Cambridge town meeting, Dec. 14, 1772, in "Letters and Documents relating to Harvard College and Cambridge."

Harvard University, Houghton Library, Cambridge, Massachusetts
Francis Bernard Letter Books, 1765–1772, in Jared Sparks Manuscripts, part IV, vols. III–VIII.
Palfrey Family Papers, Correspondence of Palfrey Family, part II, a, b.
Sparks Manuscripts, New England Papers, II, III, IV.

Massachusetts Archives, State House, Boston
Boston Tax Return, 1771, CXXXII, 92–147.
Thomas Hutchinson Letter Books, XXV, XXVI, XXVII; typescript transcriptions at the Massachusetts Historical Society.

Massachusetts Historical Society, Boston
John Adams Papers
Broadside Collection; see list below under I. Primary Sources, B. Printed Works.
Elbridge Gerry Papers
Miscellaneous Bound Documents, 1765–1775
Miscellaneous Photostats

Robert Treat Paine Papers
William Tudor Papers
Israel Williams Papers

New-York Historical Society, New York City
John Lamb Papers

New York Public Library, New York City
Samuel Adams Papers, George Bancroft Collection.
Joseph Hawley Papers; on microfilm at the Massachusetts Historical Society.
Letters and Proceedings received by the Boston Committee of Correspondence, George Bancroft Collection; photostatic copies at the Massachusetts Historical Society.
Boston Committee of Correspondence, Minute Book, November 1772–December 1774, George Bancroft Collection; photostatic copies at the Massachusetts Historical Society.

B. PRINTED WORKS

Adams, John. *Diary and Autobiography of John Adams.* Edited by Lyman H. Butterfield and others. 4 vols. Cambridge, Mass.: Harvard University Press, 1961.

———— *The Works of John Adams, Second President of the United States.* Edited by Charles Francis Adams. 10 vols. Boston, 1850–1856.

Adams, Samuel. *The Writings of Samuel Adams.* Edited by Harry Alonzo Cushing. 4 vols. New York: G. P. Putnam's Sons, 1904–1908.

[Allen, John]. *The American Alarm, or the Bostonian Plea, For the RIGHTS, and LIBERTIES, of the People.* Boston, 1773.

———— *An Oration, Upon the Beauties of Liberty, or the Essential Rights of the Americans.* Boston, 1773.

Andrews, John. "Letters of John Andrews of Boston, 1772–1776." Massachusetts Historical Society, *Proceedings*, VIII (1864–1865), 316–412.

Appleton, Nathaniel. *Considerations on Slavery.* Boston, 1767.

Boston. *Boston Town Records, 1770–1777.* Boston Record Commissioners, *Report*, XVIII. Boston, 1887.

———— "Correspondence in 1774 and 1775 between a Committee of the Town of Boston and Contributors of Donations for the Relief of Sufferers by the Boston Port Bill." Massachusetts Historical Society, *Collections*, 4th Ser., IV (1858), 1–278.

———— *Selectmen's Minutes, 1769–1775.* Boston Record Commissioners, *Report*, XXIII. Boston, 1893.

———— *Votes and Proceedings of the Freeholders and other Inhabitants*

of the Town of Boston. In Town Meeting Assembled. Boston, 1772.
Boston Gazette, 1765–1775.
Boston Weekly News-Letter, 1772–1774.
[Bowdoin, James, Joseph Warren, Samuel Pemberton]. *A Short Narrative of the Horrid Massacre in Boston.* Boston, 1770.
Bradford, Alden, ed. *Speeches of the Governors of Massachusetts, 1765–1775.* Boston, 1818.
Braintree. *Records of the Town of Braintree, 1640–1793.* Edited by Samuel A. Bates. Randolph, Mass. 1886.
Broadside. "At a Meeting of the several committees of the Towns of Boston, Roxbury, Dorchester, Watertown, Charlestown, Cambridge, Mistick, Dedham, Milton, Malden, Braintree, Woburn, and Stow . . ." Boston, September 27, 1774.
Broadside. "Boston, June 10, 1774. Gentlemen, Whereas several of our brethren members of the committees of correspondence in the neighbouring towns, have since our letter of the 8th instant applied to us . . ." Boston, June 10, 1774.
Broadside. "By Direction of the Committee of Correspondence for the Town of Boston, I now transmit to you an attested Copy of the Proceedings of said Town on the 8th Instant . . ." Boston, March 30, 1773.
Broadside. "Gentlemen, By the last advices from London we Learn that an Act has been passed by the British Parliament for blocking up the Harbour of Boston . . ." Boston, May 12, 1774.
Broadside. "Gentlemen, the evils which we have long foreseen are now come upon this town and province . . ." Boston, June 8, 1774.
Broadside. "Gentlemen, The State of Public Affairs undoubtedly still demands the greatest Wisdom, Vigilance and Fortitude . . ." Boston, September 21, 1773.
Broadside. "In consequence of a conference with the committees of correspondence for the towns in the vicinity of Boston . . ." Boston, November 23, 1773.
Broadside. "In Provincial Congress, Cambridge, December 5, 1774. Resolved, That the Proceedings of the American Continental Congress . . ." n.p., 1774.
Broadside. "Sir, the Committee of Correspondence of the Town of *Boston,* conformable to that Duty which they have hitherto endeavoured to discharge with Fidelity, again address you with a very fortunate important Discovery . . ." Boston, June 22, 1773.
Broadside. "Sir, The efforts made by the legislative of this province in their last sessions to free themselves from slavery, gave us, who are in that deplorable state, a high degree of satisfaction . . ." Signed by the committee of slaves headed by Peter Bestes. Boston, April 20, 1773. [At M.H.S., not in Evans.]

Broadside. "The Committee of Correspondence of this Town have received the following Intelligence . . ." Boston, April 9, 1773.

Cooper, Samuel. "Letters of Samuel Cooper to Thomas Pownall, 1769–1777." *American Historical Review*, VIII (1902–1903), 301–330.

Cushing, Thomas. "Letters of Thomas Cushing, from 1767 to 1775." Massachusetts Historical Society, *Collections*, 4th Ser., IV (1858), 347–366.

Dorr, Harbottle. Harbottle Dorr Collection of Annotated Massachusetts Newspapers, I (1765–1767). Massachusetts Historical Society.

Eliot, Andrew. "Letters from Andrew Eliot to Thomas Hollis." Massachusetts Historical Society, *Collections*, 4th Ser., IV (1858), 398–461.

Essex Gazette. November 1772–February 1773, nos. 224–238.

Franklin, Benjamin. *The Works of Benjamin Franklin*. Edited by John Bigelow. Federal ed. 10 vols. New York: G. P. Putnam's Sons, 1904.

Gordon, William. *History of the Rise, Progress, and Establishment, of the Independence of the United States of America*. 4 vols. London, 1788.

Handlin, Oscar and Mary F., eds. *The Popular Sources of Political Authority: Documents on the Massachusetts Constitution of 1780*. Cambridge, Mass.: Harvard University Press, 1966.

[Holly, Israel]. *God Brings about His Holy and Wise Purpose or Decree . . . a Sermon . . . after . . . the People at Boston had Destroyed a Large Quantity of Tea . . .* Hartford, 1774.

Hulton, Ann. *Letters of a Loyalist Lady, 1767–1776*. Cambridge, Mass.: Harvard University Press, 1927.

Hutchinson, Thomas. *Additions to Thomas Hutchinson's "History of Massachusetts-Bay."* Edited by Catherine B. Mayo. Worcester, Mass.: American Antiquarian Society, 1949.

——— *Copy of Letters Sent to Great-Britain, by his Excellency Thomas Hutchinson, the Hon. Andrew Oliver, and several other Persons, Born and Educated Among Us . . .* Boston, 1773.

——— *The History of the Colony and Province of Massachusetts-Bay*. Edited by Lawrence Shaw Mayo. 3 vols. Cambridge, Mass.: Harvard University Press, 1936.

——— *The Speeches of his Excellency Governor Hutchinson, to the General Assembly of the Massachusetts-Bay. At a session begun and held on the 6th of January, 1773. With the answers of his Majesty's Council and the House of Representatives respectively*. Boston, 1773.

Lincoln, William, ed. *The Journals of Each Provincial Congress of Massachusetts in 1774 and 1775*. Boston, 1838.

Massachusetts. *The Acts and Resolves, Public and Private of the Province of the Massachusetts Bay* . . . Vols. V, XIX, XX, XXI. Boston: Commonwealth of Massachusetts, 1886–1922.

Massachusetts Committee of Correspondence. "Journal." Massachusetts Historical Society, *Proceedings*, 2d Ser., IV (1887–1889), 82–90.

Massachusetts Gazette and Boston Post-Boy, 1772.

Massachusetts Spy. Boston, 1772–1774.

Mauduit, Jasper. *Jasper Mauduit: Agent in London for the Province of the Massachusetts-Bay, 1762–1765.* Massachusetts Historical Society, *Collections,* LXXIV (1918).

Mayhew, Jonathan. *A Discourse Concerning Unlimited Submission to the Higher Powers.* Boston, 1750.

New York Gazette and Weekly Mercury. July 24, 1769.

Orations Delivered at the Request of the Inhabitants of the Town of Boston to Commemorate the Evening of the Fifth of March, 1770. Boston, 1785.

Pickering, Danby, ed. *The Statutes at Large from Magna Charta to the End of the Thirteenth Parliament of Great Britain, Anno 1773.* Cambridge, Eng., 1773.

Quincy, Josiah. *Memoir of Josiah Quincy junior.* Edited by Elizabeth S. Quincy. Boston, 1874.

Rowe, John. *Letters and Diary of John Rowe, Boston Merchant, 1759–1762, 1764–1779.* Edited by Annie Rowe Cunningham. Boston: W. B. Clarke Co., 1903.

Upton, L. F. S. "Proceedings of Ye Body Respecting the Tea." *William and Mary Quarterly,* 3d Ser., XXII (1965), 287–300.

Warren-Adams Letters, Being Chiefly a Correspondence among John Adams, Samuel Adams, and James Warren. Massachusetts Historical Society, *Collections,* LXXII–LXXIII (1917–1925).

C. MASSACHUSETTS ELECTION SERMONS, 1740–1784.

For reasons of space, full titles of sermons are omitted. All were delivered in the presence of the governor, the Council, and the House of Representatives on the occasion of the election of the new Council at the opening of the new session of the General Court in the month of May. All were published at Boston in the same year. Fuller titles are given in the footnotes and complete bibliographic information is available in Charles Evans, *American Bibliography.* Sermons by the following persons were consulted: Zabdiel Adams (1782), James Allen (1744), Nathaniel Appleton (1742), William Balch (1749), Edward Barnard (1766), John Barnard (1746), Thomas Bernard (1763), Ebenezer Bridge (1767), Charles Chauncy (1747), Samuel Checkley (1755), Jonas Clarke (1781), Samuel Cooke (1770), Samuel Cooper (1756), William Cooper (1740), John Cotton (1753), Henry Cumings (1783), Samuel Dunbar (1760), Nathaniel Eells (1743), Andrew Eliot (1765), Thomas Frink (1758), Ebenezer Gay (1745), Jason Haven (1769), Moses Hemmenway (1784), Gad Hitchcock (1774), Simeon Howard (1780), Daniel Lewis (1748), Jonathan Mayhew (1754),

Joseph Parsons (1759), Moses Parsons (1772), Phillips Payson (1778), Ebenezer Pemberton (1757), Samuel Phillips (1750), Daniel Shute (1768), Benjamin Stevens (1761), Samuel Stillman (1779), John Tucker (1771), Charles Turner (1773), Samuel Webster (1777), William Welsteed (1751), Samuel West (1776), Abraham Williams (1762), William Williams (1741).

D. *MASSACHUSETTS TOWN RECORDS*

Those town records which have not been printed are located in the clerk's office of the city or town to which they pertain. Where changes in political jurisdictions have occurred, the current location is cited. The titles of the volumes are listed as they actually appear on the first leaf of the book or its spine.

Amherst. John Franklin Jameson, ed. *Records of the Town of Amherst, from 1735 to 1788.* Amherst, 1884.

Andover. Town Records of Town Meeting, 1709–1808.

Attleborough. Town Records, 1757–1778.

Barnstable. Town Records, vol. 3. Transcript.

Barnstable. "Barnstable Town Records," in *Library of Cape Cod History and Genealogy,* no. 105. Yarmouthport, 1910. These records are incomplete.

Becket. Town Records, vol. 2.

Bedford. Town Records, 1729–1780, vols. A, D.

Belchertown. Town Records, 1774–1801.

Berwick. Town Records, 1751–1788. Transcript.

Bradford. Town Records. Now in Haverhill city clerk's office.

Braintree. Samuel A. Bates, ed. *Records of the Town of Braintree, 1640 to 1793.* Randolph, Mass., 1886.

Bridgewater. Town Records. Copy of Bridgewater Records, vol. 3, 1739–1784.

Brimfield. Town Records, no. 1.

Bristol (Lincoln Co.). Town Records, vol. 1.

Brookline. *Muddy River and Brookline Records, 1634–1838.* n.p., 1875.

Brunswick. Town Records, vol. 1.

Cambridge. Town and Selectmen's Records, B–1, 1704–1788. Transcript.

Charlestown. Town Records, vol. 7, 1761–1779. Now in Boston city clerk's office.

Charlton. Town Records, 1755–1785.

Chatham. Town Records, vol. 2, 1749–1787.

Chesterfield. Town Records, vol. 1. Microfilm at Forbes Library, Northampton.

Concord. Town Records, vol. 4, 1746–1777.

Cummington. Proprietor's Book of Plantation No. 5, 1762.

Dorchester. Town Records, vol. 3, 1740–1779. Now in Boston city clerk's office.

Dracut. Town Records, vol. 2, 1750–1780.

Dudley. *Town Records of Dudley, Massachusetts, 1732–1794.* 2 vols. Pawtucket, R.I., 1894.

Duxbury. *Copy of the Old Records of the Town of Duxbury, Mass., From 1642 to 1770.* Plymouth, Mass., 1893.

Eastham. Town Records, vol. 2, 1745–1797. Transcript.

Falmouth (Cumberland Co.). Town Records, book 2, 1728–1773. Typescript.

Fitchburg. Walter A. Davis, comp. *The Old Records of the Town of Fitchburgh, Massachusetts, 1764–1789.* Vol. 1. Fitchburg, Mass.: Sentinel Printing Co., 1898–1913.

Gloucester. Town Records, book 3, 1753–1800.

Granville. Town Records, vol. 2.

Groton. Town Meeting Records.

Hadley. Records, 1719–1805.

Hallowell. Town Records, vol. 1, 1771–1782.

Hanover. Town Records, 1727–1799.

Harvard. Town Records, vols. 1, 2.

Harwich. Town Records, vol. 2.

Haverhill. Town Meeting Records, 1724–1769.

Holden. Town Records, vol. 1 (1741–1773), vol. 2 (1774–1793).

Holliston. Town Records, 1724–1790.

Ipswich. Town Records, no. 4, 1738–1779.

Kittery. Town Records, 1710–1799.

Lancaster. Town Records, vols. 1, 2.

Lanesborough. Records of Proceedings, 1765–1816.

Leicester. General Records, 1745–1787.

Lenox. Town Records, vol. 1. Transcript.

Lenox. "Lenox Covenant, July 14, 1774," Lenox Public Library. Printed in Lenox, Mass., *Bicentennial, 1767–1967, Historical Souvenir and Official Program,* n.p., n.d., 41–42.

Leominster. Town Records, vol. 1, 1740–1779.

Lexington. Records of Town Meeting and Selectmen, 1755–1778.

Lunenburg. Town Records, 1763–1793.

Lynn. Town Records, 1765–1775. Transcript at Lynn Historical Society.

Manchester. *Town Records of Manchester.* Salem, 1889.

Marblehead. Town Records, vol. 4. Transcript.

Marlborough. Town Records, Town Meetings, 1742–1790.

Marshfield. Town Records, vol. 1. Transcript.

Medford. Town Records, vol. 3, 1735–1781.

Methuen. Town Record, no. 2, 1768–1831.

Middleborough. Town Records, 1746–1772, 1772–1788.

Montague. Town Records, vol. 1. Now at town clerk's office, Turners Falls, Mass.

Needham. Town Records, vol. 2, 1731–1769; vol. 3, 1770–1799.

Newton. Town Meeting Records, vol. 2, 1759–1795.

Northampton. Town Records, vol. 2.

Northborough. Town Records, vol. 1.

North Yarmouth. Town Records, vol. 1. Transcript.

Oakham. Town Records, vol. 1.

Pembroke. Town Records, 1735–1791.

Petersham. Town Records, 1757–1793.

Plymouth. *Records of the Town of Plymouth.* Vol. III (1743–1783). Plymouth, Mass.: Memorial Press, 1903.

Pownallborough. Records of the Town of Wiscasset, vols. 1–2.

Princeton. Town Records, vol. 1.

Raynham. Town Records, 1731–1810.

Reading. Record of Town Meetings, 1644 to 1773, transcript. Record of Town Meetings, 1774–1827, original.

Rehoboth. Town Records, vol. 3, Town Meetings, 1740–1778.

Roxbury. Town Records, vol. 2, 1730–1790. Now at Boston city clerk's office.

Sandwich. Town Records, vol. 2, 1692–1767; vol. 3, 1768–1796.

Scarborough. Town Records, vol. 1. Transcript.

Sheffield. Town Records, vol. 1.

Shrewsbury. Town Records, vol. 2, 1760–1785.

Springfield. Town Book, no. 5, 1736–1799.

Stockbridge. Town Book, 1760–1835.

Stoneham. Town Records, 1725–1777.

Stoughton. Town Records, 1715–1798. Transcript.

Stoughtonham. Sharon Town Records, vols. 1, 2.

Stow. Town Records, 1747–1790.

Sunderland. Town Records.

Swansea. Town Records, 1667–1793.

Tisbury. *Records of the Town of Tisbury, Mass.* (1669–1864). Arranged and copied by Wm. S. Swift . . . and Jennie W. Cleveland. Boston: Wright & Potter Printing Co., 1903.

Topsfield. *Town Records of Topsfield, Massachusetts.* Vol. 2 (1739–1778). Topsfield, Mass.: Topsfield Historical Society, 1920.

Topsham. Town Records, vol. 1.

Tyringham. General Records, 1762–1782.

Upton. Town Records, nos. 1, 2. Transcript.

Waltham. Town Records, 1750–1768, 1769–1787. Transcript.

Watertown. *Watertown Records*. 8 vols. Watertown and Boston, Mass.: Watertown Historical Society, 1894–1939.

Wellfleet. Town and District Records, 1763–1787.

Wells. Town Book, vol. 1. Microfilm.

Wenham. *Wenham Town Records, 1730–1775*. Wenham, Mass.: Wenham Historical Society, 1940.

Weston. *Records of the First Precinct, 1746–1754 and of the Town, 1754–1803*. Boston, 1893.

Weymouth. Town Records, vols. 1, 2.

Wilmington. Town Meetings, 1730–1807.

Winchendon. Town Records, 1764–1786. Transcript.

Woburn. Town Records, vol. 8, 1748–1766, vol. 9, 1766–1779.

Worcester. Franklin P. Rice, ed., *Worcester Town Records From 1765 to 1774*. Worcester Society of Antiquity, *Collections*, IV (1881–1882).

Wrentham. Selectmen & Freeholders Records, 1760–1781, vol. 4.

York. Town Records, vol. 2, 1724–1802.

E. CONNECTICUT TOWN RECORDS

In 1895 the legislature of Connecticut required all towns to copy out of their records from 1774–1784 materials on the Revolution. These extracts are collected together in bound volumes at the Connecticut State Library in Hartford. For the year 1774 the recorded extracts of the following towns were consulted: Ashford, Bolton, Branford, Canaan, Canterbury, Chatham, Colchester, Coventry, Derby, East Haddam, East Windsor, Enfield, Fairfield, Farmington, Goshen, Groton, Guilford, Hartford, Hartland, Hebron, Kent, Killingly, Killingworth, Lebanon, Litchfield, Lyme, Mansfield, Middletown, Milford, New Hartford, New Haven, New London, New Milford, Norwalk, Norwich, Plainfield, Preston, Ridgefield, Salisbury, Simsbury, Stafford, Stamford, Stonington, Stratford, Suffield, Wallingford, Waterbury, Wethersfield, Windham, Woodbury, and Woodstock.

II. SECONDARY WORKS

Abbot, Abiel. *History of Andover*. Andover, Mass., 1829.

Allan, Herbert S. *John Hancock, Patriot in Purple*. New York: Macmillan, 1948.

Andrews, Charles M. "The Boston Merchants and Non-Importation." Publications of the Colonial Society of Massachusetts, *Transactions*, XIX (1917), 159–259.

Archer, Cathaline A., and Mitchell G. Mulholland. *Bicentenniel History of Becket*. Compiled by Esther T. Moulthrop. Pittsfield, Mass.: Becket Historical Society, 1964.

Austin, James. *The Life of Elbridge Gerry.* 2 vols. Boston, 1828–1829.

Babson, John J. *History of the Town of Gloucester.* Gloucester, Mass., 1860.

Bailey, Sarah Loring. *Historical Sketches of Andover.* Boston, 1880.

Bailyn, Bernard. *The Ideological Origins of the American Revolution.* Cambridge, Mass.: Harvard University Press, 1967.

——— *Pamphlets of the American Revolution.* Cambridge, Mass.: Harvard University Press, 1965———.

Baldwin, Alice M. *The New England Clergy and the American Revolution.* Durham, N.C.: Duke University Press, 1928.

Bancroft, George. *History of the United States.* Centenary ed. 6 vols. Boston, 1876.

Banks, Charles Edward. *History of York, Maine.* 3 vols. Boston: Calkins Press, 1931.

Barry, John S. *A Historical Sketch of the Town of Hanover, Massachusetts.* Boston, 1853.

Baxter, William T. *The House of Hancock: Business in Boston, 1724–1775.* Cambridge, Mass.: Harvard University Press, 1945.

Beard, Charles A. *An Economic Interpretation of the Constitution of the United States.* New York: Macmillan, 1959.

——— *The Economic Basis of Politics.* New York: Knopf, 1924.

Benedict, William A., and Hiram A. Tracy. *History of the Town of Sutton, Mass., 1704–1876.* Worcester, Mass., 1878.

Billias, George A., ed. *Law and Authority in Colonial America.* Barre, Mass.: Barre Publishers, 1965.

——— *The Massachusetts Land Bankers of 1740.* University of Maine Studies, 2d Ser., no. 74. Orono, Me.: University of Maine, 1959.

Bining, Arthur C. *British Regulation of the Colonial Iron Industry.* Philadelphia: University of Pennsylvania Press, 1933.

Blake, Francis E. *History of the Town of Princeton.* 2 vols. Princeton, Mass.: Published by the town, 1915.

Bolton. *History of Bolton, 1738–1938.* Bolton, Mass.: C. E. and P. V. Bacon, 1938.

Bourne, Edward Emerson. *History of Wells and Kennebunk.* Portland, Me., 1875.

Bouvé, Walter L. "Military History." In *History of the Town of Hingham,* I, pt. I, 209–374. Hingham, Mass., 1893.

Bowles, Francis T. "The Loyalty of Barnstable During the Revolution." Publications of the Colonial Society of Massachusetts, *Transactions,* XXV (1922–1924), 265–345.

Boyer, Paul S. "Borrowed Rhetoric: The Massachusetts Excise Controversy of 1754." *William and Mary Quarterly,* 3d Ser., XXI (1964), 328–351.

Bradford, Alden. *History of Massachusetts for Two Hundred Years: From the Year 1620 to 1820.* Boston, 1835.

———— *History of Massachusetts*. 3 vols. Boston, 1822–1829.

Bridenbaugh, Carl. *Mitre and Sceptre: Transatlantic Faiths, Ideas, Personalities, and Politics, 1689–1775*. New York: Oxford University Press, 1962.

Brinton, Crane. *Anatomy of Revolution*. Vintage ed. New York: Knopf, 1956.

Brooks, Charles. *History of the Town of Medford*. Boston, 1855.

Brown, Ernest Francis. *Joseph Hawley, Colonial Radical*. New York: Columbia University Press, 1931.

Brown, Richard D. "The Massachusetts Convention of Towns, 1768." *William and Mary Quarterly*, 3d Ser., XXVI (1969), 94–104.

Brown, Robert E. *Middle-Class Democracy and the Revolution in Massachusetts, 1691–1780*. Ithaca: Cornell University Press, 1955.

Buel, Richard, Jr. "Democracy and the American Revolution: A Frame of Reference." *William and Mary Quarterly*, 3d Ser., XXI (1964), 165–190.

Bumsted, John M., and Charles E. Clark. "New England's Tom Paine: John Allen and the Spirit of Liberty." *William and Mary Quarterly*, 3d Ser., XXI (1964), 561–570.

Bushman, Richard L. *From Puritan to Yankee: Character and the Social Order in Connecticut, 1690–1765*. Cambridge, Mass.: Harvard University Press, 1967.

Butler, Caleb. *History of the Town of Groton, Including Pepperell and Shirley*. Boston, 1848.

Cary, John. *Joseph Warren: Physician, Politician, Patriot*. Urbana, Ill.: University of Illinois Press, 1961.

Chase, Fannie S. *Wiscasset in Pownalborough*. Portland, Me.: Southworth-Anthoensen Press, 1941.

Chase, George W. *History of Haverhill*. Haverhill, Mass., 1861.

Colegrove, Kenneth. "New England Town Mandates: Instructions to the Deputies in Colonial Legislatures." Publications of the Colonial Society of Massachusetts, *Transactions*, XXI (1919), 411–449.

Collins, Edward D. "Committees of Correspondence." American Historical Association, *Annual Report for the Year 1901*, I, 243–271.

Currie, Harold W. "Massachusetts Politics and the Colonial Agency, 1762–1770." Ph.D. dissertation, University of Michigan, 1960.

Cushing, Harry A. *History of the Transition from Provincial to Commonwealth Government in Massachusetts*. Columbia University Studies in History, Economics and Public Law, VII, no. 1. New York, 1896.

Cushing, John D. "The Judiciary and Public Opinion in Revolutionary Massachusetts." In *Law and Authority in Colonial America*, edited by George A. Billias, pp. 168–186. Barre, Mass.: Barre Publishers, 1965.

Daggett, John. *A Sketch of the History of Attleborough*. Boston, 1894.

266

Damon, Samuel C. *History of Holden, Mass., 1667–1841.* n.p., 1841.

Davidson, Philip G. *Propaganda and the American Revolution, 1763–1783.* Chapel Hill, N.C.: University of North Carolina Press, 1941.

Dawley, Alan. "The Political Theory of Church Government: Ministerial Dismissions of the 1770's." Seminar paper, Harvard University, 1966.

Dow, George F. *History of Topsfield, Massachusetts.* Topsfield, Mass.: Topsfield Historical Society, 1940.

Edes, Henry H. "Memoir of Dr. Thomas Young, 1731–1777." Publications of the Colonial Society of Massachusetts, *Transactions,* XI (1906–1907), 2–54.

Felt, Joseph B. "Statistics of Population in Massachusetts." American Statistical Association, *Collections,* I, pt. ii, 121–215. Boston, 1845.

Ford, Worthington C. *Broadsides, Ballads, etc. printed in Massachusetts, 1639–1800.* Massachusetts Historical Society, *Collections,* LXXV (1922).

Freiberg, Malcolm. "Thomas Hutchinson and the Province Currency." *New England Quarterly,* XXX (1957), 190–208.

——— "Thomas Hutchinson: The First Fifty Years (1711–1761)." *William and Mary Quarterly,* 3d Ser., XV (1958), 35–55.

Frothingham, Richard. *The History of Charlestown, Massachusetts.* Boston, 1845–1849.

——— *Life and Times of Joseph Warren.* Boston, 1865.

Fuess, Claude M. *Andover: Symbol of New England.* Andover, Mass.: Andover Historical Society, 1959.

Gipson, Lawrence H. *The British Empire Before the American Revolution.* 13 vols. New York: Knopf, 1936–1967.

Goss, Elbridge H. *The Life of Colonel Paul Revere.* 2 vols. Boston, 1891.

Grant, Charles S. *Democracy in the Connecticut Frontier Town of Kent.* New York: Columbia University Press, 1961.

Green, Mason A. *Springfield 1636–1886.* n.p., 1888.

Green, Samuel A. *Groton Historical Series.* Vol. II. Groton, Mass., 1890.

Grigg, Susan L. "The Office of Representative in Eighteenth-Century Massachusetts." Seminar paper, Oberlin College, 1968.

Handlin, Oscar and Mary F. *Commonwealth: Massachusetts, 1774–1861.* New York: New York University Press, 1947.

Henretta, James A. "Economic Development and Social Structure in Colonial Boston." *William and Mary Quarterly,* 3d Ser., XXII (1965), 75–92.

Hobart, Benjamin. *History of the Town of Abington.* Boston, 1866.

Howe, Joseph S. *Historical Sketch of the Town of Methuen.* Methuen, Mass., 1876.

Hunt, Agnes. *Provincial Committees of Safety of the American Revolution.* Cleveland: Press of Winn and Judson, 1904.

Jameson, John Franklin. *The American Revolution Considered as a Social*

Movement. Introduction by Arthur M. Schlesinger. Boston: Beacon Press, 1956.

———"Origin of the Standing Committee System in American Legislative Bodies." *Political Science Quarterly,* IX (1894), 246–267.

Johnson, Donald E. "Worcester in the War for Independence." Ph.D. dissertation, Clark University, 1953.

Labaree, Benjamin W. *Boston Tea Party.* New York: Oxford University Press, 1964.

———*Patriots and Partisans: The Merchants of Newburyport, 1764–1815.* Cambridge, Mass.: Harvard University Press, 1962.

Labaree, Leonard Woods. *Royal Government in America: A Study of the British Colonial System Before 1783.* New Haven: Yale University Press, 1930.

Lemisch, Jesse. "Jack Tar in the Streets: Merchant Seamen in the Politics of Revolutionary America." *William and Mary Quarterly,* 3d Ser., XXV (1968), 371–407.

Lewis, Alonzo, and James R. Newhall. *History of Lynn.* 2 vols. Boston, 1865.

Lincoln, William E. *History of Worcester.* Worcester, Mass., 1837.

Lockridge, Kenneth A. "Land, Population and the Evolution of New England Society, 1630–1790." *Past & Present,* no. 39 (April 1968), 62–80.

———and Alan Kreider. "The Evolution of Massachusetts Town Government, 1640 to 1740." *William and Mary Quarterly,* 3d Ser., XXIII (1966), 549–574.

Lockwood, John H. *Westfield and Its Historic Influences, 1669–1919.* 2 vols. Springfield, Mass.: Springfield Printing and Binding Company, 1922.

Lord, Donald C., and Robert M. Calhoon. "The Removal of the Massachusetts General Court from Boston, 1769–1772." *Journal of American History,* LV (1969), 735–755.

Maier, Pauline R. "From Resistance to Revolution: American Radicals and the Development of Intercolonial Opposition to Britain, 1765–1776." Ph.D. dissertation, Harvard University, 1968.

———"Popular Uprisings and Civil Authority in Eighteenth-Century America." *William and Mary Quarterly,* 3d Ser., XXVII (1970), 3–35.

Marshfield. *The Autobiography of a Pilgrim Town.* Marshfield, Mass.: Town of Marshfield, 1940.

Mathews, Albert. "The Solemn League and Covenant, 1774." *Publications of the Colonial Society of Massachusetts, Transactions,* XVIII (1915–1916), 103–122.

Miller, John C. "The Massachusetts Convention of 1768." *New England Quarterly,* VII (1934), 445–474.

———*Origins of the American Revolution.* Palo Alto, Calif.: Stanford University Press, 1962.

────── *Sam Adams: Pioneer in Propaganda.* Boston: Little, Brown, 1936.

Miner, Ward L. *William Goddard, Newspaperman.* Durham, N.C.: Duke University Press, 1962.

Morgan, Edmund S. "The Puritan Ethic and the American Revolution." *William and Mary Quarterly,* 3d Ser., XXIV (1967), 3–43.

────── "Thomas Hutchinson and the Stamp Act." *New England Quarterly,* XXI (1948), 459–492.

────── and Helen M. *The Stamp Act Crisis: Prologue to Revolution.* Rev. ed. New York: Collier Books, 1963.

Morison, Samuel E. "Elbridge Gerry, Gentleman-Democrat," *New England Quarterly,* II (1929), 6–33.

────── "The Struggle Over the Adoption of the Constitution of Massachusetts, of 1780." Massachusetts Historical Society, *Proceedings,* L (1916–1917), 353–411.

────── "The Vote of Massachusetts on Summoning a Constitutional Convention, 1776–1916," Massachusetts Historical Society, *Proceedings,* L (1916–1917), 241–249.

Morse, Jedidiah. *Annals of the American Revolution.* Hartford, 1824.

Nash, Gilbert. *Historical Sketch of the Town of Weymouth, Massachusetts, 1622–1884.* Boston, 1885.

Newcomer, Lee N. *The Embattled Farmers: A Massachusetts Countryside in the Revolution.* New York: Columbia University Press, 1953.

Newfield, Lillian E. "Worcester on the Eve of the Revolution." Master's thesis, Clark University, 1941.

Paige, Lucius R. *History of Cambridge, Mass., 1630–1877.* Boston, 1877.

Paine, Josiah. *A History of Harwich, Barnstable County, Massachusetts, 1620–1800.* Rutland, Vt.: Tuttle Publishing Co., 1937.

Patterson, Stephen. "A History of the Political Parties in Revolutionary Massachusetts, 1770–1780." Ph.D. dissertation, University of Wisconsin, 1968.

Plumb, John Harold. *The Origins of Political Stability in England, 1675–1725.* Boston: Houghton Mifflin, 1967.

Pole, Jack R. "Historians and the Problem of Early American Democracy." *American Historical Review,* LXVII (1962), 626–646.

────── *Political Representation in England and the Origins of the American Republic.* New York: St. Martin's Press, 1966.

Pratt, Enoch. *Comprehensive History, Ecclesiastical and Civil, of Eastham, Wellfleet and Orleans, 1644–1844.* Yarmouth, Mass., 1844.

Richards, Lysander S. *History of Marshfield.* 2 vols. Plymouth, Mass.: Memorial Press, 1901–1905.

Roads, Samuel, Jr. *History and Traditions of Marblehead.* Boston, 1880.

Schlesinger, Arthur M. *The Colonial Merchants and the American Revolution, 1763–1776.* New York: Ungar, 1957.

————*Prelude to Independence: The Newspaper War on Britain, 1764–1776.* New York: Knopf, 1958.

Schutz, John A. *William Shirley, King's Governor of Massachusetts.* Chapel Hill, N.C.: Published for the Institute of Early American History and Culture by the University of North Carolina Press, 1961.

Sedgwick, Sarah C., and Christina S. Marquand. *Stockbridge, 1739–1939,* Great Barrington, Mass.: Berkshire Courier, 1939.

Shipton, Clifford K. "The Locus of Authority in Colonial Massachusetts." In *Law and Authority in Colonial America,* edited by George A. Billias. Barre, Mass.: Barre Publishers, 1965.

————*Sibley's Harvard Graduates.* Boston: Massachusetts Historical Society, 1873——.

Sly, John F. *Town Government in Massachusetts, 1620–1930.* Cambridge, Mass.: Harvard University Press, 1930.

Smith, John M. *History of the Town of Sunderland.* Greenfield, Mass., 1899.

Smith, Page. *As a City Upon a Hill: The Town in American History.* New York: Knopf, 1966.

Stackpole, Everett S. *Old Kittery and Her Families.* Lewiston, Me.: Press of Lewiston Journal Co., 1903.

Sutherland, Stella H. *Population Distribution in Colonial America.* New York: Columbia University Press, 1936.

Swift, Charles F. *History of Old Yarmouth.* Yarmouthport, Mass., 1884.

Taylor, Charles J. *History of Great Barrington.* Great Barrington, Mass., 1882.

Taylor, Robert J. *Western Massachusetts in the Revolution.* Providence: Brown University Press, 1954.

Thomas, Leslie J. "Partisan Politics in Massachusetts during Governor Bernard's Administration, 1760–1770." Ph.D. dissertation, University of Wisconsin, 1960.

Trumbull, James Russell. *History of Northampton, Mass.* 2 vols. Northampton, Mass.: Press of Gazette Printing Co., 1898–1902.

Ubbelohde, Carl. *The Vice-Admiralty Courts and the American Revolution.* Chapel Hill, N.C.: Published for the Institute of Early American History and Culture by the University of North Carolina Press, 1960.

Walett, Francis G. "The Massachusetts Council, 1766–1774: The Transformation of a Conservative Institution." *William and Mary Quarterly,* 3d Ser., VI (1949), 604–627.

Warden, Gerard Bryce. "Boston Politics, 1692–1765." Ph.D. dissertation, Yale University, 1966.

———— "The Caucus and Democracy in Colonial Boston," *New England Quarterly,* XLIII (1970), 19–45.

Washburn, Emory. *Topographical and Historical Sketches of the Town of*

Leicester. Worcester, Mass., 1826.

Waters, John J., Jr. *The Otis Family in Provincial and Revolutionary Massachusetts*. Chapel Hill, N.C.: Published for the Institute of Early American History and Culture by the University of North Carolina Press, 1968.

———and John A. Schutz. "Patterns of Colonial Politics: The Writs of Assistance and the Rivalry between the Otis and Hutchinson Families." *William and Mary Quarterly*, 3d Ser., XXIV (1967), 543–567.

Waters, Thomas Franklin. *Ipswich in the Massachusetts-Bay Colony*. 2 vols. Ipswich, Mass.: Ipswich Historical Society, 1905–1917.

Wells, William V. *The Life and Public Services of Samuel Adams*. 3 vols. Boston, 1865.

Weston, Thomas. *History of the Town of Middleboro, Massachusetts*. Boston and New York: Houghton, Mifflin & Co., 1906.

Weymouth Historical Society. *History of Weymouth, Massachusetts*. 4 vols. Boston: Weymouth Historical Society, 1923.

Zemsky, Robert M. "The Massachusetts Assembly, 1730–1755." Ph.D. dissertation, Yale University, 1967.

———"Power, Influence, and Status: Leadership Patterns in the Massachusetts Assembly, 1740–1755." *William and Mary Quarterly*, 3d Ser., XXVI (1969), 502–520.

Zuckerman, Michael W. "The Massachusetts Town in the Eighteenth Century." Ph.D. dissertation, Harvard University, 1967.

———*Peaceable Kingdoms: New England Towns in the Eighteenth Century*. New York: Knopf, 1970.

———"The Social Context of Democracy in Massachusetts." *William and Mary Quarterly*, 3d Ser., XXV (1968), 523–544.

Index

Dockyards Act, 76, 114
Dorchester, 131n, 132n, 234n; on participation, 106–107; on vigilance, 106–107; joint-committee (Tea Act), 159; joint-committee (Port Act), 186; initiates Suffolk convention, 229
Draper, Richard, 91
Dukes County, response to BCC in, 97n
Dummer, Jeremiah, 2
Dutch Republic, 40, 41, 88, 129

East Hoosuck, 173n
East India Company, 149, 154, 155, 158, 159; and Port Act, 185
Edes and Gill, 69, 90, 91
Egalitarianism, 5, 6; decried, 9–10
Elections, 27
Election sermons, 8–14, 20, 242
Eliot, Samuel, attacks BCC, 197
England: pre-Norman, 40; Tudor, 56; Stuart, 50, 56, 170, 202; Hanoverian, 20, 40, 41, 117; importance of harmony with, 92
English: church, 42, 45, 71, 76–77, 191; commerce, 187, 188, 191, 193, 223; common-law courts, 76; constitution, 21, 22, 25, 26, 52, 84, 102, 109, 173; king, 51, 77, 87, 101, 109, 111, 117, 144, 215; manufacturers, 223–224; merchants, 69, 223; people, 73, 76, 87–88, 175; politics, 69, 91, 153–155, 159–160, 189, 193. See also British Empire; British government; Crown; Ministry
Erving, John, 196
Essex County: response to BCC in, 97n; convention, 211
Excise controversy, 16

Falmouth (Barnstable Co.), 110n
Falmouth (Cumberland Co.), 29n, 110n
Faneuil Hall, 196; BCC meeting-place, 62, 125; joint-committee meets at, 159; Meeting of the People, 161; unemployment hearings, 221; view of by Paul Revere, following 96
Farmers, 160, 190
Farmer's Letters, 68
Fasting and prayer, 111, 214–215
Fire companies, 60
Framingham, 126n, 170n, 172n
France, 88, 116, 129, 171
Franklin, Benjamin: agent, 141; sends Hutchinson and Oliver letters, 143; post office, 183n; political advice, 189
Freetown, 168n

Gage, Governor Thomas, 203, 204, 215, 217, 231, 234; merchants greet, 189; proclamation, 204–205; burned in effigy, 205; supporters in Worcester County, 218
Gardinerstown, 127n
Gardner, Thomas, 159, 230
Gaspee incident, 126, 129–130
General Court, 23, 35, 36, 46, 55, 56, 78, 245, 246; authority, 3, 4, 75, 110, 173, 175; participation in, 6–7, 14–15, 30, 242–243; forum for public discussion, 21, 43, 86–90, 141; Stamp Act, 26; "purge" of 1766, 26, 27, 28; Hutchinson addresses, 86–90; replies to Hutchinson, 98, 102; role changing, 148; seeks removal of Hutchinson, 151; defunct, 236; re-established, 238–239; constitution-making, 239–240. See also Governor's Council; House of Representatives
Gerry, Elbridge, 65, 80–81, 82, 84–85, 203–204, 230
Glorious Revolution, 20, 115, 172
Gloucester, 111n, 119 n.87, n.89 and n.91, 131n, 200n
Glover, John, 203
Goddard, William, post office, 181–184
Goldthwait, Ezekiel, attacks BCC, 197
Gordon, Thomas, 20
Gordon, Reverend William: on Boston town meeting politics, 54n; Petersham resolves, 108n
Gorham, 116n, 200n; asserts colonial rights, 104–105; resolves (Jan. 1773), 118–119; BCC replies to, 128; active, 138 n.48 and n.50; antislavery, 174
Government by consent, asserted by towns, 105. See also Ideology, social compact; Republicanism
Governor, 49, 101; authority, 1, 2, 3, 8, 29, 190; salary, 1, 50–52, 75–76
Governors' committee of correspondence, 35
Governor's Council, 31, 33, 67, 101; authority, 3; election, 9, 10–11, 15, 26; replies to Hutchinson, 90; altered by Massachusetts Government Act, 190; assumes executive power, 238
Grafton, boycott, 168
Grand juries, 21, 152; charges to, 84–85; Suffolk, 151
Granville, boycott, 202
Gray, Harrison, attacks BCC, 197
Gray, Thomas, attacks BCC, 197

Topsfield, 29n; boycott, 169
Tories, 60, 85, 206–208; called desperate, 196
Town meetings, competence, 56–57. *See also* Local government; and specific towns
Towns. *See* Local government; Public opinion; and specific towns
Townshend, 111n
Townshend Acts, 28, 32, 35, 42, 59, 63, 149, 154
Trenchard, John, 20
Trowbridge, Edmund, 151
Turkey, 53

Upton, 29n

Vice-Admiralty courts, 25, 32, 76
Virginia, 129, 140–141, 153
Virginia assembly: founder of committees of correspondence, viii; resolves on comm. of corres., 140–141, 143, 147, 148
Virginia Committee of Correspondence, 123–124, 130, 140–141
Votes and Proceedings of the Town of Boston, 67, 68–80, 84, 86, 91, 92; local response to, ch. 5 *passim*; statistics, 95–99; opposed, 112–113

Wanton, Governor Joseph, letter from Lord Dartmouth, 126, 129–130
Warren, James, 199; leader of opposition, 19, 80–81, 82, 204–205; drafts Massachusetts CC circular, 155
Warren, Joseph, 41, 59n, 188, 228; creation of BCC, 55; role in BCC, 63–64, 65, 74, 124–126 *passim*, 142, 152, 158, 159, 165, 185, 186, 194, 227; prepares vindication, 139; North End Caucus, 156–157; Ways and Means comm., 187, 194–195; Boston town meeting, 197; Donations comm., 221, 222; Suffolk convention, 229; joint-committee, 230; views public opinion, 231–232; Provincial Congress, 235;

believes propaganda, 244; portrait, following 96
Watertown, 29n, 168n, 234n
Wellfleet, tea at, 184
Wendell, Oliver, 59, 187, 188; Suffolk convention, 229
Westborough, 106n, 107 n.38 and n.41, 111 n.57 and n.59; BCC replies to, 127
Westford, 108n; follows Boston, 112; BCC replies to, 127
Weymouth, BCC replies to, 130
Whigs, 20, 38–44, 49, 61, 62; assessment of Coercive Acts, 178–179. *See also* Opposition; Boston, Whigs
Willbraham, 137
William III, 75, 109
Williams, Israel, 34, 50, 208n. *See also* Hutchinson, Thomas, friends
Williams, Jonathan, 196–197, 198
Wilmington, 106n
Winchendon, 131n
Winslow, Edward ("Ned"), 205
Woburn, 234n
Woolwich, 134n, 138n
Worcester, 24, 216, 217, 228, 230; comm. of corres., 152, 229; boycott covenant, 201, 206, 215n; revolution in local politics, 205–207
Worcester County, 34; response to BCC in, 97n; towns propose foreign intervention, 110; convention, 211, 213, 215–219; readiness, 228; participation in General Court, 243
Wrentham, 100n
Wyllis, George, 181

York County, 211; response to BCC in, 97
Young, Thomas, 59n, 228, 230, 235; creation of BCC, 46–48, 54; role in BCC, 63–64, 68, 74, 124, 130n, 158, 165; prepares vindication, 139; North End Caucus, 156–157; post office, 182; reports on Boston politics, 196; Boston town meeting, 197; reports on public opinion, 232; believes propaganda, 244